EUROCOMMUNISM
Its roots and future in Italy and elsewhere

Edited by G.R. Urban

EURO-COMMUNISM

Its roots and future in Italy and elsewhere

Maurice Temple Smith

This symposium (with the exception of the
chapter by Manuel Azcárate) consists of
interviews broadcast in 1977 and 1978 by the
Radio Free Europe Division of RFE/RL Inc.,
with whose kind cooperation it is here published.

First published in Great Britain 1978
by Maurice Temple Smith Ltd
37 Great Russell Street, London WC1

© 1978 RFE/RL Inc.

ISBN 0 85117 154 0

Printed in Great Britain by
Billing & Sons Limited
Guildford, Worcester & London

Contents

GEORGE URBAN
Introduction   7

1   MANUEL AZCÁRATE
What is Eurocommunism?   13

2   LUCIO LOMBARDO RADICE
Communism with an Italian Face   32

3   FABIO MUSSI
A Communist view of Fascism   58

4   JEAN ELLEINSTEIN
'The Skein of History Unrolled Backwards'   73

5   RENZO DE FELICE
Varieties of Fascism   97

6   ROSARIO ROMEO
The Uses of Anti-Fascism   116

7   DOMENICO SETTEMBRINI
Mussolini and Lenin   146

8   ALTIERO SPINELLI
How European are the Italian Eurocommunists?   179

9   LUIGI BARZINI
The Italians and the Communist Party   211

10   ANDREI AMALRIK
Russia and the Perplexing Prospects of Liberty   236

11   BARTOLOMEO SORGE, S. J.
Will Eurocommunists and Eurocatholics Converge?   255

Notes on Contributors   279

Index   281

Introduction

Trendy simplifications lie at the bottom of much historical mis-understanding. Is the Soviet system more Russian than Communist, or more Communist than Russian? Does the Soviet Union behave more like a cause than a country? Such tidy presentations of an untidy reality come easily to the minds of headline writers. We have tried in this symposium not to follow so simple a questioning, but rather to probe into 'Eurocommunism' precisely at those critical junctures where ideological commitment and the demands of practical politics mutually condition and react upon one another.

Inevitably, the result is disturbing, not because we are left thinking that Eurocommunism is the work of Soviet disinformation, nor because we have reason to suspect that it is a latin-European device to deceive national electorates, but rather because Eurocommunism amounts to no doctrine, has created no centre, has (as yet) produced no generally accepted model—but has nevertheless earned the censure of the Soviet Union as though it had done all these things.

The shared 'model', such as it is, certainly rejects the Soviet type of socialism on grounds of irrelevance, but beyond that every Eurocommunist is the keeper of his own conscience and the maker of his own doctrine. Only in Spain has one variant been institutionalised, and even there the voices opposing it are powerful. In all other cases the Eurocommunists display a spectacular eclecticism, choosing and rejecting whatever bits of party history or ideological furniture fit their case or have ceased to support it. Whether so much sectarianism is more dangerous to the papacy in Moscow than it is to the future of Eurocommunism itself is a moot point. The 'movement' is in its infancy, and the iconoclasts

7

are savouring the heady excitement of challenging the past, including their own.

Such are our immediate impressions of the state of Eurocommunism in the late 1970s. Taking a larger view, however, a question-mark hangs over the tenability of Eurocommunism as a *Communist* movement. Marxism on any interpretation means the dictatorship of the proletariat, and dictatorship (despite Marx's protestations to the contrary) requires a party. But no party can effectively impose dictatorship unless it is subject to rigorous discipline, which in turn invites the dictatorship of a ruling group and eventually of one man. The progression from Marxism to Leninism, and from there to Stalinism inheres in Marxism itself. It stems from Marx's statement in the *Communist Manifesto*: 'The Communists ... openly declare that their ends can be attained only by the forcible overthrow of all existing conditions. Let the ruling classes tremble at a communistic revolution.'

The Eurocommunists are attempting to unbutton the Marxist-Leninist-Stalinist straitjacket in reverse order. Under the impact of Khruschev's report to the 20th Soviet Party Congress, they first read Stalinism out of the movement without (to this day) agreeing on the doctrinally crucial point of whether Stalinism had been an accretion or a systemic disorder. Next, some of the more outspoken Eurocommunists such as Jean Elleinstein, and before him the intellectual leaders of the Czechoslovak reform movement, and earlier still Djilas, proceeded to repudiate (though not always explicitly) certain aspects and then whole chunks of Leninism as a distortion peculiar to Russia's backward conditions. More recently the lure of electoral victory moved the French Communist Party, and is apparently also leading the Italian CP, officially to repudiate the dictatorship of the proletariat—unofficially it has been gradually abandoned since 1947—and with it (although this is as yet not admitted) Marxism itself.

Whether or not these moves have been merely tactical, their political implications are significant, They reveal a geological fault running through the base of the Eurocommunist initiative—the logic of de-Stalinization leading to de-Leninization and that inevitably to the repudiation of Marx. If so, Eurocommunism, to the extent that it really exists (and we have it on Giorgio Amendola's authority that it does not), is a freak which must either end in Social Democracy or revert back to some form of Leninism. In the first case it will cease to be Communist, in the second it will no longer be Euro.

Is this posing the dilemma too categorically? Recent West European elections suggest that the Communist vote is, and seems destined to remain, a protest vote rather than a vote for government. The abandonment of the myths of the Communist past and the Europeanization of Communist ground-rules would, therefore, seem to be doubtful assets. The protest vote is attracted precisely because Communists are thought to stand for everything for which Social Democrats do not—a seamless world-view; uncompromising hostility to the existing order; authoritarian decision-making; firm guidelines and the will to enforce them.

But can such hopes be satisfied by a party which has cast doubt on the myth of 'Great October'; irreparably damaged the image of an all-just, all-successful and all-powerful Soviet society; and undermined the hope that somewhere, out there, dedicated and unyielding men have created a superior dispensation which, though no Frenchman or Italian would want to see it realised in his own backyard, can nevertheless be admired from a distance and, above all, held out as a threat to his rulers? The secret of the appeal of the Communist Party is its extremism, not its moderation. Take that away, and the Party faces the sobering prospect of being overtaken on its Left.

Georges Marchais's insistence in his April 1978 Report to the Party Central Committee that both Eurocommunism and a return to orthodoxy 'would lead the Party into liquidation' fails to recognise this point. Eurocommunism would—Leninism would not, as it certainly did not in the past.

Where radicalism has a constituency, the Communist Party is strong because, rightly or wrongly, it is identified with Leninism. Where it has not and a viable Social Democratic Party exists to offer an alternative, the Social Democrats prosper. But there seems to be little room for a watered-down version of Communism.

None of this is admitted by Eurocommunists. Their drift towards Social Democracy is denied; so, of course, is any suggestion that self-preservation if nothing else may put them back on the Leninist road. Indeed, the Soviet variant of Leninism is derided as the 'anti-model of socialism'. No one has yet defined with certainty what socialism is, as Jean Elleinstein has argued in *Le Monde* (13 April 1978) but we know from the Soviet example what it is not—a far cry from the days when Elleinstein wept (as he tells us) on hearing the news of Stalin's death.

The Eurocommunist suspicion of Social Democracy is repaid, though not uniformly so, by Socialist suspicions of Eurocommunism. The West European Social Democrats are extremely conscious that the evolution of Eurocommunists propels them in the direction of Social Democracy, and they abhor the prospect on grounds of history as well as of electoral politics. ' "Eurocommunism" is becoming respectable,' Dr David Owen, the British Foreign Secretary, said in a lecture (18 November 1977).

> It is a term which socialists should eschew. We should give it no currency. . . . I reject the term because I do not wish to give communism anywhere, particularly in Europe, a coherent entity. I reject the term because it can easily mean lowering the guard of democratic socialists. It will not be long before we will be asked to link the British Communist Party with Eurocommunism. . . . The danger is that the Labour Party will be slowly turned away from its present outright opposition and traditional hostility to the Communist Party in Britain. We will be asked first to tolerate, then to associate and then to combine with the Communists under the broad banner of the left and embraced within the heady froths of Eurocommunism. We must resist, for it could spell electoral death for the Labour Party.

The Soviet rejection of Eurocommunism is less clearly worded but no less clear. It expresses the fear that the Soviet Party's remaining authority in its struggle with China and other 'splitters' of the world Communist movement will be further eroded, with incalculable consequences for the uncertain stability of Eastern Europe, especially if the Eurocommunists remain in opposition, retaining their freedom to criticise the Soviet system without the inhibitions of office. The Soviet leaders are shrewd enough to realise that where Socialism with a human face is made possible, Socialism with a Russian face can have singularly few attractions. Their formula for putting the Eurocommunist heresy under anathema is to insist that Leninism, and especially the experiences bequeathed by the Bolshevik revolution, are 'laws' of international validity on which national parties may embroider, but which they cannot structurally change or ignore.

This is a feeble claim—indeed it is mendacious. Communism of the Western confession draws at least implied sanction from Lenin's own observation: ' . . . after the victory of the proletarian revolution in at least one of the advanced countries things will in all probability take a sharp turn—Russia will soon cease to be a model country and once again become a backward country (in the 'Soviet' and the socialist sense) . . .' (*'Left-Wing' Communism—an Infantile Disorder*). The Eurocommunists contend that it is precisely the backwardness of the Russian example that has barred the proletarian revolution from victory in Western Europe and will continue to do so until Marxism is reclaimed from Slavic corruption and returned to its Western moorings. That the Soviet Union does not relish the prospect of being relegated to the status of a 'backward country'—even if this is done in Lenin's name—need not surprise us. Hence the counter-accusations that Eurocommunism is an 'imperialist plot'; that the Eurocommunists are conducting a 'crusade' against the Soviet Union and attempting to put the Communist movement 'under the control of the bourgeoisie'.

I have not gone into some of those immediate issues which Eurocommunism raises in respect of the future of parliamentary democracy, NATO, the East-West relationship and what remains of détente, because these have been amply dealt with in the pages that follow. A few points nevertheless need summarising.

No Italian or French Eurocommunist claims that he would, in office or out of office, unconditionally honour his country's obligations to NATO in an East-West confrontation—indeed, the Spanish Communists (Spain is, in 1978, not a member of NATO) are directly opposed to NATO.

The West European Communist Parties' links with Moscow have been weakened—not cut. Although most Eurocommunists insist that they and their parties (and it is uncertain to what extent Eurocommunists can speak for their parties) will attend no further international Communist gatherings of the East Berlin type, there is no institutional guarantee that they will not.

The Eurocommunist commitment to parliamentary democracy is ambiguous. The freedom of political parties, from far Left to far Right, to function outside the framework of 'socialism', more particularly to seek office with a mandate to *replace* 'socialism', is not clearly stated. Nor have Eurocommunists told us how exactly the application of Gramsci's 'hegemony' of the working class would differ from the dictatorship of the proletariat—whether 'hegemony' would be exercised under one-party rule or the aegis of a 'front' of some description, all in a genuinely multi-party system.

The internal organisation of the West European Communist Parties—'democratic centralism'—has not been liberalised. 'The Stalinist tradition survives in the Party apparatus,' Louis Althusser (no Eurocommunist) wrote of the French CP in April 1978. One consequence is that the balance of forces in the Party leaderships between Eurocommunists and conservatives cannot be reliably estimated. It is, from what we know, nevertheless clear enough that even in Italy and Spain Eurocommunism has an uncertain constituency. Among the establishment it is unevenly supported; among the rank and file it is barely understood, and to the extent that it is understood, it is opposed. In France, the

process of de-Stalinization, spectacularly set in train at the 22nd
Party Congress in 1976, has made so little impact that Eurocommunist (and other) critics of Communist defeat at the 1978 general
elections were not permitted to publicise their views in *L'Humanité* and were ostracized when they published them elsewhere.

Finally, the history of the Communist movement is a standing
warning to us that the Communist reflex reaction in critical situations is to revert to dogmatism and strong-arm solutions. Lenin's
call to 'use barbaric methods to fight barbarism'—barbarism
being whatever stood in the way of the advance of Bolshevism—
has sunk deep roots in the Communist psyche.

What are we to make of all this? Eurocommunism is the latest
and for Moscow perhaps the most dangerous split in a once
centrally controlled ideological and power-political movement. It
is not a fraud even though its claims may turn out to be fraudulent
if the Eurocommunists succeed in persuading Western electorates to support policies which the Eurocommunists themselves
may eventually prove unable to control. Its leading proponents,
though still hemmed in by the legacy of their Marxist-Leninist,
and frequently Stalinist, antecedents, appear to be as genuinely
convinced of the need to combine 'socialism' with liberty as were
their ill-fated forerunners in Prague in 1968. And they have as
hard a row to hoe, though of course with a better chance of
success because, paradoxically, the prospects of renewing Communism in a bourgeois/capitalist environment are infinitely
brighter than they are in the world of Soviet 'socialism'.

One lesson which I believe emerges from this symposium with
reasonable clarity is that the obstacle to Communism is
Communism—Soviet style. The spectre haunting Eurocommunism (we may well say, *pace* Marx) is the spectre of Communism.
Indeed, it is under capitalism alone that Communism can change
and prosper.

                                                        G. R. Urban

Manuel Azcárate

1 What is Eurocommunism?

The emergence of Eurocommunism coincides with two major phenomena in the political and economic life of Europe: the disappearance of the Fascist dictatorships in Greece, Portugal and Spain; and an economic crisis of almost unprecedented dimensions. Indeed, the economic crisis is a political, moral and ideological crisis as well, calling in question those political and ideological structures which have provided the framework for life in Western Europe since the Second World War. It is clear that in the disappearance of the Fascist dictatorships a crucial part was played by internal factors, but it is no less clear that other factors of a more general and more international character also played a part. One of these was the weakening of North American imperialism and its inability to preserve its hegemony and control over Europe. It is common knowledge that the government of the United States, the American military-industrial complex, used the Greek, Spanish and Portuguese Fascist dictatorships as convenient tools for preserving their hegemony. I am not suggesting that these dictatorships were mere instruments; but I do believe that North American imperialism played an important part in prolonging their lives. This was certainly indisputable in the case of Spain, and few Spaniards would deny it.

It was the defeat of US imperialism in the Vietnam war that opened the way to certain changes in the international balance of forces, more particularly in Europe. It was this defeat which directly contributed to the replacement of the Fascist dictatorships by regimes based on universal suffrage and a respect for human liberty.

As for the economic crisis, we are not experiencing a mere repetition of the 1929–1930 depression; we are not experiencing a simple crisis of capitalism. The present crisis shows the capitalist

13

system to be incapable of coping with the problems of modern life—economic and social problems in the first place, but also the problem of extending democracy to all levels of the masses so that they may fully participate in national life, and that of finding a new relationship between mass civilisation and the environment.

This crisis of European society shows no signs of crystallising into the sort of desperation which led in the thirties to the rise of Fascism and the upsurge of the extreme Right in European politics. There are, of course, worrying symptoms, such as terrorism, behind which, in certain cases, we may discern the dark visage of those who would like to see Fascism restored. Nor can it be denied that here and there forces of the Right are increasing their electoral representation. But nevertheless the general tendency is to seek a progressive, left-wing solution of European problems. If the crisis is to be solved, there can be no simple return to the past.

At the root of the crisis lies, among other factors, the emergence of the ex-colonial world—countries which are rich in primary raw materials, not only oil (although this is of cardinal importance), thanks to which they can exercise an unprecedented influence on the world's economy. The world crisis requires a new model of society. This is precisely what Eurocommunism offers, and if asked for a brief definition of Eurocommunism, I should say: Eurocommunism is a cluster of new theories, new political and strategic ideas which have arisen among a number of Communist parties, and which seek to give a new answer to the problems thrown up in the crisis of our time. It seeks to find ways of achieving the Socialist transformation of society by means of democratic methods, and of advancing towards a new Socialist society based on full respect for human liberties, on pluralism and on a better social deal for all. In brief, it seeks to end man's exploitation by man. To put it another way, Eurocommunism aims at establishing a new relationship between democracy and the Socialist transformation of society.

Eurocommunism believes that in the industrially advanced society of Western Europe democracy is the only way in which capitalist society, dominated as it is today by the great monopolies and multinational companies, may be overcome. It believes that a Socialist system capable of replacing the present system must be a Socialism in which democracy shall find its most complete expression.

But is what the Eurocommunists say true? Are they sincere when they talk about 'a new face of Communism'? Or is Eurocommunism a trick? Is it (as the British Foreign Secretary, David Owen, said recently) no more than 'a Trojan horse'?

The odd thing about this argument is that it is used by two quite ⱽ different opponents of Eurocommunism who have nothing in common. Let me explain. Soviet attacks (and under 'Soviet' I include also press campaigns in Czechoslovakia and other East European countries) make much of the suggestion that Eurocommunism is a sort of infernal machine invented and promoted by the imperialists in order to wreck the Communist movement. Yet at the same time, in official and semi-official statements reaching us from North America and other Western sources, Eurocommunism is depicted as a Machiavellian manoeuvre designed to let the wolf in sheep's clothing penetrate the political bastions of capitalist democracy.

For an argument to be employed by two such contrasting parties at one and the same time is a rare and not unwelcome coincidence. What it means is that Eurocommunism, since it cannot be a manoeuvre in both these senses, is not a manoeuvre at all: it is something authentic, something new, something arising from the realities of Europe. It seeks to answer the crisis of Western society.

What are we Eurocommunists to say to those who accuse us of carrying out nothing more than a tactical manoeuvre? I believe that the best answer is to tell the simple truth, and the truth, which any *bona fide* student of history can check for himself, is that the Eurocommunist position is the outcome of a long process, a process of carefully thought-out political action, which has gradually taken shape along a complex and difficult path.

It seems to me therefore appropriate at this point to set out my opinion on the origins of Eurocommunism. I shall distinguish here between the more remote origins and those more immediate influences which have actually shaped current Eurocommunist thinking.

To begin with the more distant background, we must briefly remind ourselves of our points of departure. They arose, as is well known, at the end of the First World War, in the wake of the collapse of the Socialist International, which had up to then embraced and unified the various workers' parties of Marxist ideology. During the First World War, the Socialist parties ranged themselves on the side of their respective governments and the international links were broken. The very idea of international solidarity between workers was blotted out.

Incipient Communist parties started to take shape in small groups at various conferences held in Switzerland and attended by Lenin, and their aim was to re-establish international links among the Socialist forces once the war was over. At these conferences Lenin called for the transformation of the imperialist war into a civil war. He was hoping to bring about the Socialist revolution in countries where the capitalist system was weakest.

Lenin's dream became reality in Russia in 1917, where the routed Tsarist army turned into a revolutionary factor which contributed to the victory of the Bolsheviks. The Russian exemplar, the attack on the Winter Palace, Lenin's theories, the Soviets, have provided the Communist parties with their ideological inspiration since their foundation to this day. Thus the Russian Revolution has acquired the status of a powerful myth which stimulates the revolutionary struggle and feeds the hopes of workers and of the exploited all over the world.

The achievements of the Russian Revolution were thrown into even sharper relief by the part played by Social Democracy, principally in Germany, in crushing the revolutionary movements which sought to transform German society after the fall of the Kaiser. The comparison between the triumphant revolution in Russia, and the prompt nipping of the revolutionary bud in Germany by the same Socialist leaders who headed the young Weimar Republic, contributed very largely to ensuring that the 'Soviet model' should be seen by the incipient Communist parties, and for a long period of their history, as the one and only viable model whereby capitalist society could be overthrown. It goes without saying that there was—perhaps from the very beginning—a certain contradiction between the objective conditions with which workers' movements in western countries had to contend, and the adoption of the 'Russian model' as a doctrinal and political base for Communist parties.

If we examine the history of a number of Communist parties, we shall find, right at their very inception, interesting attempts which diverge from the 'Russian model' and the directives of the Communist International.

This is not the place to go into the matter in detail. I would simply underline the enormous theoretical value of the work of Antonio Gramsci who, in spite of his long years of imprisonment and the attendant difficulty of keeping in touch with the outside world, elaborated a number of new concepts which enabled Marxist analysis to accommodate itself far more successfully to the conditions obtaining in western society than could be hoped from the dictates of the Communist International.

Stalinism of course destroyed the Communist parties' unorthodox initiatives, using repressive and often brutal methods. Certain phenomena of the Stalinist period have to be examined more closely, since they are not susceptible of simplistic or unilateral explanations. The Popular Front tactics, for example, clearly served the interests of the Soviet Union in getting as large a grouping of forces as possible to confront the threat which Hitlerism was beginning to represent for the Soviet régime itself. But there was something else besides. The practical application of Popular Front policies in France and, above all, in Spain, where for the first time in history it was found possible to have governments comprising men drawn from the Liberal, Nationalist, Socialist and Communist parties, provided original experience of a new type of co-operation which did not follow Soviet rules, but which seemed nevertheless appropriate to supersede capitalist society.

The experience gained by the Popular Front still influences us today; albeit remotely, it enshrines lessons which may be usefully studied by Eurocommunists. And if we are asked why the Communist Party of Spain has gone further than others in working out Eurocommunist attitudes, one possible answer will point to the fact that it was precisely the Communist Party of Spain which was the first to take part (on Republican territory during the Civil War) in governments with other parties, on a pluralist basis, in an atmosphere of free political debate. I am saying all this without forgetting the more negative facts such as the repression of the Trotskyites as the result of the transfer to Spain of Stalinism from the Soviet Union.

Another period which repays study is the period of coalitions after the Second World War—in France, Italy, Belgium and other countries—in which Communists co-operated in government with Socialists, Christian Democrats, Liberals and other anti-Nazi forces. Some parties at this stage even began to envisage the possibility of a democratic transition to Socialism. The process was cut short by the creation of the Cominform and the imposition of Stalinist totalitarianism, laying it down that there was one way and one way only to revolution—the Russian way.

I have quoted examples because I believe they reveal something profound and objective, namely, that the Communist movement in western Europe generated its own pressures for a type of political practice and strategy which is different from that dictated by the Third International under the impact of the Soviet model. It is important to recognise this if we are to see the phenomenon of Eurocommunism in its true perspective.

The eventual rupture with the Soviet model was greatly hastened by the 20th Soviet Party Congress. There Khruschev disclosed that Stalinism had been guilty, not only of criminal repression, but also of far-reaching deformations of Marxist theory which the Soviet system had tolerated. From 1956 onwards, the umbilical cord which had bound the Communist parties to the Soviet Union as their sole source of nourishment, was broken. Each party now began to work out its own approach to Communist theory and practice, until, after many ups and downs, successes and reverses, true independence was attained by a number of Communist parties in western Europe.

When did Eurocommunism actually take off? It did so in 1968 and for two reasons. Firstly, the explosion in Paris in May 1968 put an end to the illusion that post-war neo-capitalism was well and thriving. West European ideology from the end of the Second World War to 1968 was based on the belief that capitalism had found a solution for its contradictions: that the Labour movement was being 'integrated' into capitalist society; that the economic boom had ruled out the Socialist revolution. But 1968 demonstrated, not only that the labour movement, far from being integrated, was still a militant force against capitalist exploitation, but that it was bringing to the surface fresh social forces equally opposed to the domination of monopoly-capitalism— technicians, scientists, intellectuals, professional men—that is, those sectors of society whose number and influence show a steady growth as a result of the scientific-technical revolution.

Secondly, in Czechoslovakia, where the Prague Spring had shown itself to be a considered attempt to give Socialism a democratic basis, the Soviet invasion made the Western Communist parties realise with unprecedented force and urgency that they had to separate themselves off from the Soviets by rejecting the 'Soviet model'. They recognised that they had to declare unequivocally for a Socialism which would be different from the Soviet system, because the latter had now shown itself to be ready, not only to suppress fundamental liberties, but also to take actions inimical to national independence, and contrary to the interests of the progressive movement and world revolution.

The Czechoslovak events made it imperative to examine far more critically than had been done before all that the Soviet model stood for and the reasons for its prestige in the Communist movement. It was necessary to analyse the whole character of Soviet society, to put an end to its myth, and to carry out a genuinely Marxist critique of the East European societies as well.

What has emerged as Eurocommunism is therefore a Marxist response, firstly, to the new realities in the capitalist countries of western Europe; and, secondly, to the Marxist critique of Soviet society and especially its negative aspects—its incapacity to be a model for the advance of Socialism in the world.

The process leading to Eurocommunism takes independent and autonomous forms and national characteristics of many kinds, particularly in the Communist parties of Italy, Spain and France, and to a certain extent in those of Japan, England, Belgium and Switzerland. Driven by the necessity to respond to concrete situations, these parties are forced to affirm their independence of the Communist Party of the Soviet Union and to think for themselves. This in turn encourages the development of attitudes which have eventually crystallised into what we may call the fundamental concepts of Eurocommunism.

That this process has been diverse accounts for the fact that Eurocommunism cannot be considered to be a body of doctrines, still less an organisation. There is no Eurocommunist centre. There is no Eurocommunist organisation nor a Eurocommunist discipline. Hence some people leap to the conclusion that there is no such thing as Eurocommunism; that at most there are national phenomena, attitudes and postures proper to Italian, Spanish or French Communists. This way of looking at things misses the fundamental point: namely, that through a series of unrelated processes, Marxist thinking in a number of Communist parties has nevertheless converged towards positions which in many respects coincide. They coincide, above all, in the realisation that Socialism in Western societies is attainable *only* through the democratic process; and that the Socialism to which the workers and intellectuals in our countries aspire is a Socialism of liberty—a democratic Socialism. The great diversity of the ways which have severally converged on this central point reinforces the validity of my conclusion. It shows that we are not dealing with something fortuitous but with a natural upshot of our age.

Is Eurocommunism a deception to confuse our opponents? That at one time or another tactical considerations have played a part in the elaboration of Communist policies is clear. But the fact that a group of Communist parties—precisely those most deeply rooted in the masses of western Europe—should have arrived at closely coincident conclusions, and are now engaged in persuading their rank and file members and their sympathisers that the only way to Socialism is the democratic way—this *cannot* be a tactical move. It is a qualitatively new departure. It represents a new stage in Marxist thinking, a new phase in the development of the Communist movement, one that breaks with the myth of the Soviet model, with Stalinist totalitarianism and its consequences. It is a way of finding answers to the crisis of capitalism in an age of scientific-technical revolution which has posed problems unimaginable when the classics of Marxism were written.

Today the Communist movement is pluralistic. This pluralism does not derive from any sort of schism, with orthodoxy on one side and heresy on the other. It derives, above all, from the variety of objective conditions in which the revolutionary movement has lately evolved, and from the continuing inability of Marxism to answer the internal problems of those societies which have destroyed capitalism but have not been able to progress beyond 'primitive Socialism'. It derives from the contradictions posed by the survival of the State—not to say the *increasing* part played by the State—in such countries as China and the USSR, even after the disappearance of capitalist property relations.

In this diversified Communist movement, Eurocommunism is beyond doubt one of the main currents. It represents needs felt by a large part of both manual and intellectual workers in the world's largest concentration of industrial, technological and scientific manpower.

Some commentators treat Eurocommunism as a return of sorts to Social Democracy. This approach falls into the serious error of drawing comparisons without taking into account differing historical contexts. It is clear that Eurocommunism centres its present strategy on respect for the rules of democracy; it expresses the conviction that it is through universal suffrage that historical change must be brought about. Taking this as our starting point it is tempting to make a comparison with the Second International's trust in the power of the ballot box ('electoralism'), which had the consequence that in none of the countries where parties belonging to the Socialist International formed governments was capitalism destroyed, because the revolutionary drive for Socialism fizzled out in office. Eurocommunism's aim is exactly the opposite: it is to supersede capitalism, albeit by democratic means, in order to end the exploitation of man by man, and to create a Socialist society as a basis for the rapid advance to Communism.

Today the objective conditions for a democratic advance towards Socialism are completely different from what they were in the first decades of this century. Eurocommunism duly reflects the conditions created in our society by the scientific-technological revolution, and the extraordinary growth of social forces which have an interest in ending capitalist exploitation. It is not only the working classes, exploited as they are by capitalism, that are interested in building Socialism; they are joined in this by broad strata of scientists and technicians, members of the professions and intellectuals—in a word, those sections of society which the Spanish Communists call the 'forces of culture'. These people have come into conflict with capitalist domination, not only because more and more of them are, in fact, wage-earners, but because there is a contradiction between the mentality demanded by their scientific and cultural creativity, and the fact that they have to submit to decisions taken by capitalists, whose only law is the maximisation of profits. This is a new factor with enormous potential for the democratic advance towards the Socialist transformation of society.

The case of the small and medium businessmen is similar. This stratum has undeniable ideological links with bourgeois society and is traditionally conservative and conformist in its attitudes. And yet members of this class often find themselves in deep conflict with the interests of monopoly-capital. Many small businessmen, managers and industrialists are in fact salaried staff whose 'salaries' are the bank-credits extended to them. Such openings as they have for 'private enterprise' are decreasing. For them, the prospect of a gradual advance towards Socialism under conditions of coexistence between a public sector directed by the democratic organs of society, and a private enterprise sector, appears much more promising than a continuation of the present state of affairs in which they find themselves more and more subjugated by an oppressive oligarchy. Thus, in this sector too, a growing number of people support the democratic way to Socialism. I want to emphasise here that our attitude to the middle classes, to the small and medium sized businesses, is not a tactical manoeuvre. We are persuaded that services and the provision of certain goods must rely at present—as they have done in the past—on private enterprise. A Socialism which did not take this into account would impose on the public a drop in its standard of living, since only private enterprise can satisfy a whole string of mass necessities. It would be a Socialism with precious little room in it for public acceptance.

But our concept of Socialism is not exhausted by the proposition that it must end capitalist exploitation. It tries to provide answers to a whole series of problems which have arisen in the wake of the scientific-technical revolution, and others which have acquired unprecedented urgency and cannot be solved in a society guided by the principle of capitalist profit-making.

Take the problem of women's liberation. This is not a new one, but it is surely evident that thanks to recent scientific discoveries, modern contraceptives, and so on, this problem appears to us in a different light from the way it appeared to our predecessors. Capitalist society *requires* woman to be inferior to man. This means that women not only serve as a reserve labour force, but also carry out their unpaid task of reproducing the labour force via the family. Ideologically, woman's reduction to an inferior status in the home is a necessary precondition of keeping alive that attitude of submission and conformity which is typical of the bourgeois family. The success of the fight for the liberation of women implies the transformation of society in a Socialist direction. That is not to say that the end of capitalism will in itself mean equality for women. The feminist struggle will have to continue in Socialist society too, since the roots of discrimination antedate the growth of class society, and will only be torn up by a far-reaching cultural revolution.

Let me now consider the problem of urbanisation, the despoliation of wide tracts of land in the advanced industrial countries, and the destruction of the ecological balance. If we are to solve these problems it is imperative that economic development be planned and controlled, not in order to maximise profits, but as an act of public morality. Furthermore, the new vistas of permanent or recurrent education presuppose an ethos different from that governing modern capitalist societies; an ethos of democracy and Socialism, which will ensure that the masses, the people, become the real beneficiaries of history.

If Engels could speak at the close of the nineteenth century of the revolution of majorities in different countries, Eurocommunism presents itself to us today as a way of achieving a policy of broad consensus on a world scale: a revolution of the majority of mankind which must lead humanity to a higher form of civilisation, based not on private profit, not on capital, not on the exploitation of man by man, but on a type of collective society in which the individual's self-realisation means at the same time his conscious participation in the historical process. It is in this sense that Eurocommunism postulates a revolution conceived in and brought forth by the masses—a full and authentic democracy which will extend to the economic sphere: it will guarantee, first, an advance towards Socialism, then the realisation of Socialism and, ultimately, Communism itself.

Another characteristic of Eurocommunism is the distance it has put between itself and the Soviet type of Socialism. This is not the place to recount the history of the reasons and processes whereby the first Socialist revolution in the history of the world turned into an authoritarian régime, a despotism in which power resides undemocratically in the hands of a small nucleus. The upshot is a contradiction between the letter of the Socialist principle that the workers are the masters of the State, and the actual Soviet practice which means that the labouring masses, if not exploited in the same way as they are in capitalist countries, nevertheless lack liberty and are alienated—in some ways even oppressed—so that the State in the Soviet Union retains many of the typical features of the capitalist State. This State is used by a minority, which has equipped itself with certain blatant privileges, to rule over the great mass of the people.

Two of the decisive causes of this strange process were Russia's low level of productive capacity at the time of the 1917 October Revolution and, immediately thereafter, the imperialist intervention which forced the infant Soviet power to have recourse to centralised management and force used as a means of centralised State policy. What is not in doubt is that the very nature of the national and international matrix in which the capitalist system was for the first time overthrown, made it inevitable that many of the features inseparable from a truly Socialist system existed in the Soviet Union only in its initial stages. After these initial stages the Soviet Communist Party, whose role was to lead the workers as their political spearhead in their struggle against what remained of the past and in the dialectical advance towards a superior form of society—this Communist Party was practically absorbed by the State and integrated into it; it became part of the State apparatus. Perhaps the most obvious characteristic of Stalinism in the theoretical domain, in its distortion of Marxism, is the decisive role it conferred upon the State. Stalinism is a policy which gives the State absolute power and makes the State the shaper of the new society. We all know what practical results this policy led to!

Even though Soviet repression is no longer as massive or as bloody as it was in Stalin's day, the theory and practices of the State are still imbued with a strong dose of Stalinism. For example, it is very hard to believe that in a world in which a powerful and widespread demand for democracy exists elections can be held in the Soviet Union with candidates polling over 99.9 per cent of the votes—elections, moreover, which by their very nature cannot serve to represent the opinion of the people and merely discredit those who persist in arranging them. As for the theoretical domain, it is clear that (apart from certain steps in this direction taken after the 20th and the 22nd Congresses between 1956 and 1960) no genuine historical investigation is permitted; indeed the very concept is proscribed. In the Soviet Union history, too, is an ideological and political instrument, subject to the interests and whims of a small number of leaders. The fact that in the country which originally proclaimed Marxism as its official ideology—that is to say, a materialist conception of history—contemporary history should be thus reduced to a mere matter of personal rule, to the status of an instrument to be used in the service of political ends, is a most serious indictment.

Thus, without denying the achievements of the Soviet Union in education, health-care and so on, starting as it did from the Asiatic backwardness of Tsarist Russia, we members of Communist parties who for many years presented the Soviet Union as the model of a more humane, more free and just society, find ourselves compelled to carry out a Marxist critique of the Soviet State—a State which is neither Socialist nor democratic, and which fails to meet our basic requirement—that Socialism shall represent a transitional stage towards Communism.

In Communism, the State as a political entity, as a coercive force, is destined to vanish. It is obvious that as long as there exist capitalist states in the world, it would be wishful thinking or plain suicide to think of dismantling the State in those parts of the world where capitalism has disappeared. The problem is not that the State has not disappeared in the Soviet Union. The problem is that the so-called Socialist State in the Soviet Union retains non-democratic features—authoritarianism, negation of liberties etc.—which often compare unfavourably with conditions existing in capitalist countries where the masses have been able to win for themselves an important degree of political democracy. (Incidentally, the problem of the withering away of the State is now being tackled via an interesting new concept of pluralism in Socialist Yugoslavia.)

For Eurocommunism the problem poses itself in completely different terms. The central issue thrown up by conditions in the industrially advanced capitalist countries is the ever-sharpening tendency on the part of monopoly-capitalism to reduce the scope and effectiveness of democracy, and to obstruct the will of the electorate vis-à-vis major political options. Even ignoring the occasional throw-back to the violence and terrorism of Fascism, it is obvious that the political structures of many western countries exhibit a tendency to reinforce the role of executive organs and of the top echelons of the bureaucracy to the detriment of Parliament, that is to say of the organ directly elected by the people. This shows a degeneration of some of the principles which triumphed in the period of what might be called the 'zenith' of liberal democracy of the British type. At the same time, on the managerial level, we can observe an increasing remoteness of managers and other decision-makers from the mass of those who do the work—not just from the working class, but also from a widening sector of brain workers, technicians, scientists and so forth.

The tendency of monopoly-capital to put decision-making into the hands of a small number of key people clashes with the need for democracy, freedom and creativity. The whole productive process shows a striking rise in the input of scientific and technological brainpower, and this implies a correlative need for free human creativity in the political sphere as well. The need for liberty and democracy has acquired a metapolitical dimension.

Thus Eurocommunism corresponds to, and is the political expression of, a phenomenon which has its roots in the advance of productive forces generated by the scientific-technological revolution.

Many of the problems which were, in their day, the direct cause of the break between Socialists and Communists, lie today on a different plane. In view of this, it is urgently necessary for the European Left as a whole to tackle these new problems in a spirit of free debate, without prejudice and untrammelled by past experience, in order to delimit as concretely as possible those sectors in which Communists and Socialists can join forces in common action, and those in which there remain substantial differences between them. The debate should be open towards the future; it should sketch out a pluralistic way forward along which Communists, Socialists, Social Democrats and all those of Christian and liberal inspiration who are agreed on the necessity for the structural transformation of society on Socialist lines can advance towards the creation of a new Europe.

We Eurocommunists are still searching our own consciences with regard to a series of deformations which affected us during one stage of our career. We are looking and working for a new model of society, a new and democratic way towards Socialism; a pluralist way; a vision of Socialism in a state of freedom.

At the same time, we hold it to be important that the Socialist and Social Democratic parties of Europe should search their own consciences. After all, in no country governed by Socialists or Social Democrats has the capitalist system been transformed. The realisation of this failure is stimulating a process of critical self-appraisal within the French and Italian Socialist parties, the Swiss Social Democrats, and also in some sectors of the British Labour Party and the German Social Democrats. It is a process which could have important consequences.

Western Europe is gripped by a crisis of unprecedented dimensions. Enormous technical and economic potential exists side by side with a disarray in labour relations and signs of an unmistakable political and moral degeneration. Western Europe sharply underlines the need to find a new democratic way towards a Europe of the peoples, a Europe of workers—a Socialist Europe. We Eurocommunists consider ourselves part of this process, a part, moreover, which can open up new horizons on the European plane, and perhaps even internationally.

There is, then, a Eurocommunist way of looking at things; and no doubt there are different shades within it—French, Italian, Spanish Communist ways of assessing the problems of inter-European relations and relations between the West European states.

We are, as Eurocommunists, favourably disposed towards the unity of Western Europe. We believe that Spain must become a member of the EEC. And the task we have set ourselves is to

combat the domination exercised on the European economy by
the big monopolies and the multinational companies. This we
propose to do, not on the fringes of the Common Market structures as problems arise and take shape, but at their very heart—
democratising them, increasing the representation and the
influence of the Trade Unions, and furthering the process of
Trade Union unity on a European scale. Similarly, we shall seek
new ways of uniting workers in the multinational companies,
ways which will promote vis-à-vis the power of the monopolies
the growth of worker organisations capable of leading to working-class action on the international level—the level on which
the multinational companies operate.

We regard the election of the European Parliament by universal
suffrage as an important step forwards. As Spain is unlikely to be
a full member of the EEC at the time of the European Parliamentary elections it seems to us indispensable that a special formula
should be worked out whereby the Spanish people can take part
in the election, and their elected representatives will be allowed
to sit, under whatever title, in the Parliament. It would be strange
if, at the moment when Spain has started out on her democratic
path after so many years when 'Liberty for Spain' was the banner
under which all the democratic forces in Europe marched—if at
that moment the first European Parliament were to be elected by
universal suffrage *leaving out Spaniards!* And doubly strange if we
consider that a great many Spaniards live and work in other
European countries. If anybody can be called European it is these
workers. They live in two countries—the one they work in and
their homeland to which they remain bound by family, political
and cultural ties. By what authority could these workers be deprived of the right to vote in the elections of the first European
Parliament?

Furthermore, we Spanish Communists consider it necessary
that the process towards the unity of Western Europe should
have a political dimension shaped by democratic considerations
which I have already mentioned. And this implies, although the
matter has not yet reached the stage where it could be given
concrete expression, joint European defence.

Coming now to the question of relations between Europe and
the rest of the world, Eurocommunism is against Eurocentrism.
We recognise the new and important role which the former
colonies are now playing in the world. We even tend to think that
a Western Europe in which the hegemony of the workers is
assured would be in a good position to initiate a new type of
relationship with the Third World, one which would be unbur-
dened by any residue from the colonial or neo-colonial past. We

have to put an end to the reactionary notion of 'aid'. We have to realise that economic growth in the Third World is today a condition favouring growth in our own industrially advanced countries. This new way of looking at things demands a corresponding political attitude. It must have nothing to do with the logic of capitalist profits.

As things are today it would, of course, be wishful thinking to imagine that anything of the sort could be initiated in the United States where the forces of the Left, indeed all progressive forces, are weak. Western Europe, on the other hand, has not only the economic, scientific and technical potential, but is also at an advanced stage of political thinking which makes it possible for West Europeans to envisage the hegemony of workers and intellectuals as a realistic possibility. It is therefore capable of developing new solutions for the world's problems. It is capable of finding a new approach for restructuring the relationships between North and South, between the developed and the undeveloped or insufficiently developed countries. And it is precisely because Eurocommunism represents in some ways the attitudes of the labouring masses of the South who want to play a bigger role in Europe as a whole, that we consider that the prospect of marking out a new relationship with the Third World very largely depends on the acceptance by western Europe of our democratic and pluralist programme towards Socialist solutions.

A question that seems to bother many commentators is: How is it possible that Eurocommunism can be the object of attacks and criticisms—often couched in very similar terms—by both North American imperialism and the Soviet Union? There is no simple answer; many factors play a part. But one of them—perhaps the most important—is that, in international relations, Eurocommunism offers a choice which lies outside the two great military blocs which divide Europe. One might even say that Eurocommunism is the only European option which lies outside the two blocs.

Our view is that a united Europe must be an independent Europe, independent as much of the United States as of the Soviet Union—a Europe with its own autonomous policies with regard to all international problems. The Europe we want will co-operate in a spirit of friendship with the Soviet Union as much as with the United States and with China. The Europe to which we aspire will be a basic factor, alongside the powerful and now fully grown movement of the non-aligned countries, in the struggle to overcome the present bipolarity of the world. This bipolarity is beginning to weaken. Of course, we do not deny that it is important for the human race as a whole that the two superpowers, who hold in their hands the means of wiping out the human race, should maintain relations with each other and ward off the threat of a nuclear holocaust by affirming the principle of peaceful coexistence. But bipolarity tends to inhibit the fruitful discussion of certain highly important questions, especially that of disarmament. The security of the world's peoples must not continue to depend on the 'balance of terror'. What we need is the democratisation of international relations in which the small and medium sized states will play an increasingly important rôle.

Eurocommunism's approach to a united Europe can be an important contribution to giving peaceful coexistence a much-needed shot in the arm, to breaking up the log-jam of international problems, to reinforcing the independence of all countries, and strengthening the growing tendencies all over the world for peoples to take their destinies into their own hands and decide for themselves in democratic fashion how they want to live and what sort of régime they want now and in the future.

Eurocommunism is paying a great deal of attention to formulating its theoretical infrastructure. The Communist Party of Spain has devoted a good deal of effort to this task. We are, of course, well aware that we have not been able to do more than scratch the surface, and that there exists today a rich terrain for Marxist investigation, both in respect of the analysis of the newly emerging characteristics of the capitalist economy, and in respect of the study of the problem of the State as it is found in the industrially advanced countries of the capitalist world—a State which differs in many of its characteristics from the State studied in his day by Marx or by Lenin in his. We are concerned with stimulating the free theoretical analysis of all these problems along Marxist lines.

In the field of the international ideological struggle, we note that an offensive has been launched against Marxism by people whose ambition appears to be to revive the principles of anarchism and irrationalism; in some cases we even see a wilful return to nihilist fanaticism which is used to justify acts of terrorism carried out for the most part by the blackest forces of reaction. It is for this reason that we believe that a Marxist theoretical counter-offensive would be in the interests of the labour and progressive movements. 'Offensive' does not mean repeating slogans and catchwords—exactly the opposite. What we need to do is to deepen our analytical method and perfect our thinking.

One most serious question confronts us: Marxism has suffered a substantial degeneration precisely in those countries where it has been made the official ideology. After the death of Lenin the word 'Leninism' was used as an instrument of legitimation and as a watchword by the various factions which sought to gain or retain control of the Communist Party of the Soviet Union. It was not long before Leninism was turned into 'Marxism-Leninism' by Stalin. During the thirties the official doctrine came to be called 'Marxism-Leninism-Stalinism'. This process of degeneration reduced Marxism to a congeries of dogmas, of 'absolute' truths, with a Holy Office appointed to watch over its enforcement. In reality, this Soviet Holy Office was one man; and ultimately the stage was reached when Stalin's writings could be presented as the last word on subjects as varied as linguistics and biology. These utterances not only purported to be absolute truths; they were supposed to be *the* absolute truth on every question. This sort of Marxism-Leninism claimed the prerogative of imposing a totalitarian philosophy on all fields of thought. This was the doctrine of monolithic Communism.

Unfortunately, relics of this monolithic Communism, this parody of Marxism as a collection of dogmas, still haunt 'Soviet Marxism' and certain theories which the Communist Party of the Soviet Union feels itself called upon officially to defend. The same goes for a group of other Communist parties which continue to regard as Holy Writ anything emanating from the Soviet Union.

The idea is fostered in the Soviet Union that there exists such a thing as a definitive corpus of Marxism-Leninism. This corpus is duly condensed in a Soviet publication entitled 'Manual of Marxism-Leninism', a text which is compulsory reading in the schools and universities of the Soviet Union and of certain other countries, and is treated with the force of a catechism. A recent series of Soviet attacks aimed at various theories espoused by the Communist Party of Spain goes to show that there are still people around who regard themselves as spokesmen of a Holy Office, and thereby empowered to pronounce sentence of excommunication on those whom they consider to be 'heretics'. Excommunication of this sort has very little effect beyond the confines of the text announcing it.

It is now many years since the Communist Party of Spain took important steps—especially after the 20th Congress and the denunciation of Stalinism—to expunge whatever remained of Stalinism in its thought processes and political actions. Eurocommunism reflects a break with Stalinism and its sequel, both in theory and practice.

It is clear from our daily policies and from the internal working and make-up of our Party that we impose no obligatory philosophy, we make no moral stipulations. For us, it is completely logical that diverse cultural currents should co-exist within the Communist Party.

As regards religious faith, there is today within the Communist Party of Spain no difference between a Communist who has religious faith and one who has not. The two attitudes involved are equally Communist. The leadership of the Spanish Communist Party—indeed the Central Committee itself—includes members who are well-known figures in the Catholic world.

This is no mere eclecticism—much less a return to revisionism *à la* Bernstein. It is an education of our thought processes up to the point at which they can adequately cope with current problems, and a retrieval of the most essential scientific and methodological and, by this very token, revolutionary truths of Marxism.

Marxism represents a great revolution in human thinking. It represents the discovery of a new method of tackling the problems of man's chequered history; it is the science of history and of historical change and, hence, the science of revolution.

Leninism represents the ideology and political practice which led Russia in 1917 to the world's first Socialist revolution. The historical importance of this revolution, the first to overthrow a capitalist régime and launch the process of transforming the world in a Socialist direction, cannot be belittled. It was in the fire of this experience that our Communist parties were born. Of course, the doctrinal corpus of Leninism is, as one would expect, conditioned by the historical epoch and environment in which Lenin worked. But it is our belief that Lenin's insights have a validity going beyond Russia. We believe that Leninist thought has valid implications for us today. When we Spanish Communists study Lenin's work we find in it a very rich fount of inspiration for the formulation of our own theories and policies. But we will not treat Lenin as a once-and-for-all Absolute. It is our contention that there are others who can take their due places beside Lenin—such as Rosa Luxemburg, Mao Tse-tung and above all Gramsci. They too can serve as sources of inspiration and experience so necessary to modern Marxist thought.

Therefore, at the 9th Congress of the Communist Party of Spain, we changed the wording we had hitherto used to define our Party: we renounced the formula describing ourselves as a 'Marxist-Leninist' Party or a 'Leninist' Party. We shall no longer identify Leninism as the fountainhead of our inspiration. We have defined the Communist Party of Spain as 'a revolutionary Marxist Party', a democratic Party, a Party whose methods draw their inspiration from Marxism and from whatever continues to be valid in the thought of Lenin and other revolutionaries.

The Communist Party of Spain considers the October Revolution to be part of its patrimony, and the same goes for the other Socialist revolutions which have liberated peoples. But at the same time we reject bureaucracy and Stalinism as developments alien to Marxism. Anti-democratic attitudes of this sort have been responsible for serious setbacks to the progress of revolutionary Marxism among workers in the advanced capitalist countries. We Spanish Communists have by our own critical efforts successfully surmounted the Stalinist stage and recovered the democratic and anti-bureaucratic essence of Marxism.

Thus we totally reject any and every dogmatic reading of Marxism. In the theses presented to the 9th Congress, the Communist Party of Spain affirmed unequivocally that 'Marxism is scientific in character, not dogmatic'. We Spanish Communists will spare no effort to enhance our ability to prove ourselves equal to social change, to the new world opened up by science, to the lessons of revolutionary practice. We want to assimilate in a spirit of constructive criticism every new development in the evolution of Marxism. It is my opinion that this new approach (new—though at the same time it respects the deepest truths of Marxism) to the problems raised *pari passu* with the development of our theory, reflects the depth and the authenticity of the phenomenon called Eurocommunism.

Lucio Lombardo Radice

2 Communism with an Italian Face?

Urban My admiration for the Italian Communist Party's rapid advance from orthodoxy to liberalism—to 'Eurocommunism'—is tempered by a nagging doubt whether such dramatic transformations can be genuine, and whether indeed they are possible in human affairs.

Let me put to you two ideas to illustrate my scepticism. The first might appeal to Lucio Lombardo Radice the scientist/mathematician. It is the commonplace observation: *natura nihil facit per saltum*, there are no leaps, no sudden changes in nature.

The second might appeal to you as a leading member of the Central Committee of the Italian Communist Party, and is well formulated by Marx: 'The tradition of the dead generations weighs like an incubus upon the brain of the living.' Whether we stress the first or the second—and the two really come down to the same thing—your Party's spectacular leap from Marxism-Leninism-Stalinism to its present position seems to call for an explanation.

Lombardo Radice I have been a member of the Party for forty years. My authentic knowledge, therefore, is confined to that period. Certainly at the time when I joined the Party in 1937, there was no 'Italian Communist Party'. I became a member of the 'Communist Party of Italy', which was a section of the Comintern, of the Third International. The change from that perspective to the Party as it is today is certainly considerable. But if you take that change in its historic context, not in terms of two isolated *termini*, but as an evolutionary process, then one can speak of no leap but much rather of continuity.

I became a Communist because I wanted to make a contribution to the struggle for liberty, and the best way of doing that in Mussolini's Italy was to join the Communist Party. My father was

32

a left-wing liberal (after he had been, in his youth, a member of the Socialist Party); but I didn't think the most effective manner of fighting for freedom in Italy was to continue in my father's foot-steps. Mine was, of course, no special case. Hundreds and thousands joined for similar reasons. Giorgio Amendola's father was a Liberal minister who perished at the hands of the Fascists. Amendola, too, became a Communist because, in the context of the 1930s, the Communist Party offered the best hope of defeat-ing Fascism and promoting democracy. The continuity between then and now is, really, rather convincing. The 'leap' is between the false image painted of the Italian Communist Party by anti-Communist propaganda, and the true history of the Party.

Urban I wasn't so much thinking of any leap in your personal attitude to what Communism stands for as of the entire profile—internal and external—of the Italian Communist Party. And here it would be difficult to deny that the change has been dramatic. From Togliatti's stewardship (under the pseudonym 'Ercoli') of the Central European Section of the Comintern at the time of the Great Terror, to Berlinguer's and Amendola's present show of reasonableness, Europeanism and compromise, there has cer-tainly been a leap of amazing proportions. I would say the most revolutionary thing about the history of the Italian Communist Party has been its retreat from revolution.

Lombardo Radice I disagree with you fundamentally on some of these points.

First, after 1935, Stalin and the Soviet Communist Party spoke with two voices. The 7th Congress of the International marked the beginning of a policy of Popular Front cooperation with other progressive forces to resist Nazism, Fascism and aggression. Stalin wore one face towards *Western Europe*, where the abuse of 'Social Fascism', that is, of the Social Democrats, was suddenly stopped and cooperation and popular unity encouraged, indeed demanded, and another face towards the *Soviet Union*, where repression and all the abuses of power continued. But you must remember that, once he realised the dangers of Nazism, it was Stalin who supported Dimitrov's and Togliatti's Popular Front policies and thereby, in the situation existing at the time, Stalin was, objectively speaking, supporting the struggle for freedom, democracy, and peace.

Second, Togliatti was, with Dimitrov, the originator of the Comintern's great turn in 1935, i.e. it was *he* who initiated the Communist Parties' democratic approach to Socialism in Western Europe. There is no contradiction, indeed there is a distinct continuity, between the Popular Front policies of the 1930s, on the one hand, and the idea of 'historic compromise' on the other—between Togliatti and Berlinguer. Berlinguer is in fact a disciple of Togliatti, and so are Amendola, Ingrao and the other leaders of the Italian Communist Party. None of this is my personal opinion; it is Party history.

Urban But all this happened after 1935. Before that Stalin pursued, as you say, somewhat different policies.

Lombardo Radice For our present purposes, I don't think it would be very profitable to examine what happened 50 or 60 years ago. Forty years give us an intelligible enough time-span. What is important is that the class struggle, the fight for the dictatorship of the proletariat, and the fratricidal war against the Social Democrats were superseded. Stalin supported that change. Its architects were, as I say, Dimitrov and Togliatti. Let me remind you that the newly-born Italian Communist Party—it came to life in 1921—was the only force in our country that fought Fascism with single-minded determination. Let me also remind you that a great many 'liberal' and 'democratic' leaders of the Italian bourgeoisie supported Fascism!

Urban Stalin discovered what everyone in the West had known for a long time, namely that Hitler was more dangerous to democracy and, what was for him much more important, to the survival of the Communist Parties, than were the Social Democrats?

Lombardo Radice I wonder if 'everyone' in the West recognised Hitler to be the major danger. The Munich agreement of September 1938 seems to prove the opposite. In any case, Stalin, in that particular situation, did a fundamentally new thing by adopting a policy, not modelled on Soviet experience but, in fact, running diametrically counter to Soviet domestic policies. From that moment on there was a split between the political posture adopted by the West European Communist parties on the one hand, and the political realities inside the Soviet Union, on the other. With one half of his psyche Stalin spoke of freedom and democracy, but with the other half he pursued and deepened the terror within the Soviet state.

Now the contradiction in our situation arose from the fact that while we, West European Communists, worked for freedom and democracy, we believed at the same time that Russia was a different case, and the Soviet leaders had to act differently. We justified both in our own minds and in our public policies the repression and the Purge trials, because we thought that the mother-country of Communism, threatened and surrounded as she was at the time, had to be defended, whatever the cost.

The psychology of this is wonderfully depicted by Ernst Fischer's book *Erinnerungen und Reflexionen*. Fischer was an

Austrian friend and comrade who probed more deeply than I can hope to do here into the mentality that induced us to justify the crimes of Stalin. Remember: the times were terrible. We, Italian, French and other Western Communists, had every logical and psychological inducement to suppress in our own minds the facts about Stalin's Russia because, for democracy and ourselves to stay alive, we had to support, and be supported by, the Soviet Union. I'm not offering this as self-justification but merely as comment on your assertion that there is a break in our policies. There isn't. Our concern with liberty has been continuous.

Urban Ernst Fischer argues that, despite this merciless confrontation with the lies he had written over a period of a great many years, he would, in comparable circumstances, act exactly as he did in the 1930s. Would you and your colleagues in the leadership of the Italian Communist Party do likewise today?

Lombardo Radice Of course we would. We might do it with a different consciousness and we might not do the same things in detail, but our general line would be the same, exactly the same. Remember, this wasn't an attitude thought up in a political vacuum. We were fighting Hitler, and the future of Socialism absolutely demanded that we choose sides. What the Russians were doing was wrong but impossible not to do and not to sanction. One couldn't fight Hitler with half-measures.

Urban The implication of what you say is rather interesting. Suppose there is, in 1978, or 1984, or whenever, a grave international crisis between the Soviet Union and the West. Suppose, further, that the Communist parties of Italy and France have by then come to power, or to share power, and would therefore have to make a quick decision whether to stay loyal to the Western Alliance, or not to stay loyal to it. What would you do?

Lombardo Radice It depends. If there is an imperialist aggression with the avowed objective of rolling back Socialism, we would feel entirely absolved of any obligation of 'loyalty' to the 'defensive' character of NATO and take the side of the Soviet Union. But we would, in such an extreme emergency, also do our utmost to restore peace.

We would stand for Socialism, real Socialism, in the awareness that there are two ways of supporting Socialism in Russia. The first, which is the wrong way, is to give everything that has been done in the Soviet Union our blanket approval. The second way is to say to the Russians: 'I don't approve of your policies in this or that matter; I even violently disagree with many of them, but I don't want to see the achievements of Socialism in your country destroyed. I am not interested in putting up a defence for Khrushchev or Brezhnev, but I *will* defend the historical results of the October Revolution.' You can criticise the Soviet Union from the Left and from the Right. We look at it from the Left— constructively.

The attitude of the Italian Communist Party to dissent in the Soviet Union and Eastern Europe rests on the same principle. We have been telling, and are still telling, the Russians that the suppression, harassment, and deportation even of people like Solzhenitsyn and Amalrik and Bukovsky are totally wrong. There must be complete freedom in Socialist society or else it cannot call itself Socialist.

Urban   Freedom for every kind of opinion?

Lombardo Radice   Every kind of opinion.

Urban   Freedom to write and to publish, for example, Social Democratic or Monarchist opinion?

Lombardo Radice   Yes, every kind of opinion as long as it does not amount to conspiracy. Nowhere is conspiracy permitted—East or West. But every kind of opinion—yes.

Urban   And you would also support everyone's right to fight for such opinions?

Lombardo Radice   Yes, in lawful ways—by the spoken and written word, etc.

Let me give you some examples. While Solzhenitsyn was still in Moscow, I was very much interested in him politically. I wrote a long essay about him in one of my recent books, *L'Accusati (The Accused)*; and I stood four-square behind him in his struggle for civil liberties. Today, I am politically no longer interested in Solzhenitsyn although I am, of course, interested in him intellectually. Why? Because, since his arrival in the West, Solzhenitsyn has abandoned his earlier position of criticising the Soviet régime from within, and has gone over to a frontal attack on Soviet Socialism with the avowed intent to destroy it. He is toying with Slavophile ideas, and perhaps even some version of Tsarism. Now, our Party's position is that we will fight for everyone's right to express himself freely; but, of course, that does not mean that we will abstain from fighting some of the views expressed. In a Socialist society Solzhenitsyn must have every right to say whatever he likes. The Party, on the other hand, has every right to disagree with him.

But there are, in the Soviet Union, other dissident trends of direct interest to the Italian Communist Party, not only in the sense that we support the freedom to express them, but also in that of supporting the programmes thus expressed.

Roy Medvedev, the Russian historian, has written a book, *Was the October Revolution Inevitable?*, which was published in Italian by our Party's publishing house, Editori Riuniti. We published it because Medvedev is a constructive internal critic of the régime. Or take the case of Mlynar. About a month ago De Donato Publishers in Bari brought out Zdenek Mlynar's book, *Prague— Open Question.* Mlynar is, as you know, a leader of the Socialist opposition in Czechoslovakia. Well, I wrote the introduction to his book. De Donato is a Communist, I am a Communist; and the Italian Communist Party is in complete accord with Mlynar's argument and with my introduction. This tells you something about our attitude to dissent in the Soviet Union and Eastern Europe.

Urban What, to be more precise, *is* your general line on dissent in these countries?

Lombardo Radice The Party's general line is as follows. The Socialist countries can claim credit for far-reaching, historic achievements. They have done away with private property, the exploitation of man by man, unemployment, inflation and illiteracy. They have exemplary systems of social security, health care and education. These achievements have advanced and matured the consciousness of the citizen who is now demanding, and rightly demanding, that he should be given individual freedom. Our Party believes that this must be the next phase of historical development. Without it there will be a regression in Socialist society. The Italian Communist Party does not believe that the demand for freedom is an expression of class-interest. There is, as you know, a great debate in progress in Italy whether pluralism, democracy, and individual freedom are of value only in bourgeois society, or whether they are also essential in a homogeneous society, that is, in one where classes have ceased to exist. We believe that liberty is absolutely necessary in a homogeneous society, too, because, although in such a society antagonistic class-interests no longer operate, there continues to be a great variety of opinions and perspectives which must be given free expression if only to maximise the chances of the further development of Socialism. Freedom is a tool for the creative advancement of Socialism.

Urban What about the freedom of those who do not want to use it for the advancement of Socialism? After all, the meaning of freedom is rendered nonsensical if you confine it to the 'advancement of Socialism'.

Lombardo Radice They should have freedom without any conditions. But let's look at the achievèments of Soviet society. With all its faults, the Soviet Union is a highly developed, modern Socialist country in which the vast majority of citizens want to stay loyal to the structure and institutions of Socialism. They have no wish to bring back the landowners and capitalists. Could such

a society be threatened, much less destroyed, by individual freedom? This would be an absurd assumption. Let Solzhenitsyn by
all means return to the Soviet Union, and let him say with all the
power at his command that the Soviet Union should pick up the
threads of Holy Russia and authoritarian rule. He could be no
danger to Socialism, absolutely no danger.

Urban   Why, then, is he not allowed to do so?

Lombardo Radice   This is precisely the problem.

Urban   Is it because the Soviet leadership, consciously or sub-
consciously, regards *itself* as the latter-day embodiment of Holy
Russia?

Lombardo Radice   I don't think it does.

Urban   There are certainly some striking parallels between the
two, especially in their shared predilection for obscurantism and
fear of light. Take the Soviet leaders' obsessive concern with
'revisionism'. Isn't this a re-run of the story of the Old Believers?

In the seventeenth century, the Patriarch Nikon reformed the
Orthodox ritual, correcting mistakes in the sacred texts. The
name of Jesus in particular was mis-spelled when it was first
translated from the Greek. This aroused passionate opposition by
the Old Believers who denounced the reforms as 'foreign innova-
tions' and an outrage upon the 'Third Rome', that is, upon the
authority of Moscow. Tito's Yugoslavia, the Prague Spring, and
Eurocommunism come to mind as tempting analogies. The Old
Believers were put down, but the spirit of Russian superstition
and obscurantism has survived to this day.

Or, take the celebrated dictum of one nineteenth-century
Orthodox bishop: 'Abhorred by God is anyone who loves
geometry—it is a spiritual sin'.

Doesn't, then, the spirit of Russia explain the Soviet leaders'
intolerance of Solzhenitsyn, Bukovsky, Amalrik, and any unau-
thorised interpretation of the sacred texts, whether by Rome or by
Prague Communists? I believe Marx *was* right in saying that 'the
tradition of the dead generations weighs like an incubus upon the
brain of the living'.

Lombardo Radice   I don't agree. There are no such inherited
national characteristics; there is no continuity of the kind you
describe. Today's Soviet citizens are members of an enlightened,
scientifically inspired, and technologically advanced civilisation.
The obscurantism of the nineteenth-century autocracy is dead
and buried. What we do have, however, is a persistent conservatism, an immobilism stemming from such very ordinary
characteristics as fear of change, fear of any kind of uncertainty. And this is as much at home in the West as it is in the
Soviet Union—

Urban   But in the West it has proved a little easier to correct than in the Soviet Union. . . .

Lombardo Radice   This is rather begging the question, isn't it? Even in the Soviet system there is a certain mechanism for self-correction. Khrushchev's report to the 20th Party Congress and the developments that followed it were liberating events of enormous significance. I was in Moscow in 1962. Why, it *was* possible to speak freely, and to write and publish with very few constraints! Solzhenitsyn's *One Day in the Life of Ivan Denisovich* was printed in that period. Then, in 1968, came the Prague Spring, Socialism with a human face, and a complete programme for the rejuvenation of Socialism in the spirit of liberty. There was nothing unnatural, much less anti-Socialist, about these developments. They weren't at all out of character. On the contrary: they corresponded to the real demands of people who wanted to safeguard the achievements of Socialism by changing and developing it from within.

Urban   Were the people demanding these things real Socialists or *the* real Socialists?

Lombardo Radice   They were Socialists who understood the historical necessity of freedom. Today, similar demands are being raised in East Germany, Czechoslovakia, and Poland. The Russian, East German, and Czechoslovak official press completely misrepresent the facts when they say that these demands are, by some mysterious sleight of hand, engineered and even paid for by the enemies of Socialism. Nothing could be further from the truth. The signatories of Charter 77 are true Socialists who understand that the development of Socialism demands liberty.

You see, after the recent East Berlin conference it was just impossible for the Soviet Union and the Socialist countries in Eastern Europe to go on as though nothing had changed. After all, at this conference the policy of our Party, and that of other Western Communist Parties, was put on the record; and although we agreed with the Russians to try to keep our disagreements within certain limits, the very fact that we exist—that strong West European Communist Parties support democratic Socialism (not, mind you, Social Democracy), that is to say, the combination of democracy with freedom—is enough to encourage and to support Socialist opposition in Eastern Europe. This can go quite far. My friend Wolf Biermann has composed a song on the note: 'The Federal Republic of Germany needs a Communist Party nurtured under the Italian sun. . . . ' Zdenek Mlynar and other signatories of Charter 77 have sent us messages asking us and the French and Spanish Communist Parties to support them in their predicament. We are doing this because Charter 77 represents a *Socialist* opposition.

Urban You know much better than I how accident-prone ideological and religious movements are—how easy it is for them to split and fall into disunity. I almost hesitate to quote examples as there are so many. However, let me quote one—Petrarch's observation on the great schism in the body of Christianity of his time: 'The Turks are enemies, but the Greeks are schismatics and worse than enemies.' Doesn't this strike you as being of great contemporary relevance? 'The capitalists (Americans, West Germans, Fascists, Zionists, etc.) are enemies, but the Eurocommunists (Chinese, Yugoslavs, etc) are schismatics and worse than enemies', a Petrarchian might write if he were sitting in the Kremlin in 1977.

Lombardo Radice I dislike talking of the work of the Communist movement in terms of Church history. With that said, the comparison has some validity, because it is our daily experience that the Soviet government doesn't at all mind having friendly and even far-reaching relations with American or German capitalists and imperialists but will have nothing to do with the internal opposition—your Greeks, if you like. I can explain this, though I would not want to excuse it. The Soviet state came into being at a time of almost insuperable difficulties, internally and externally. We know what these were, so I will not go into them again. The Bolsheviks' response to these difficulties was centralisation and dictatorship—étatism. What we have today in the Soviet Union—and I made this point in my book *The Accused*—is *state-Socialism*, not state-capitalism, but state-Socialism. The defence of this state-Socialist system has become a vested interest of the Soviet leadership and of the *apparat*.

But, of course, nothing in history is eternal. Even Soviet Socialism has to change. Therefore the struggle we can see developing more and more articulately today is between *conservative* Socialists and *progressive* Socialists. Naturally, the conservative Soviet position is extremely strong. Only yesterday I had a televised discussion with Alexander Chakovsky, editor of *Literaturnaya Gazeta*, in which Chakovsky was telling me that, as Soviet society was a classless society, there could be no conflicts of political opinion within it. Opinions critical of Soviet society were capitalist opinions. Well, this is not the way we see it.

Urban When the Russians condemn Charter 77 aren't they, in effect, also anathematising the schismatic views your Party advocates under the umbrella-notion of Eurocommunism?

Lombardo Radice Yes, they are, but it is a little simpleminded to talk of '*the* Russians', because we are sure that there are important contradictions, even struggles, within the Soviet Party itself. I have already mentioned Roy Medvedev—well, there he sits in Moscow, writing his books, sending them abroad, and getting them published abroad, and getting them published abroad without anyone worrying him. You cannot do this kind of thing in the Soviet Union unless you have political support. I understand he has such support.

Urban Inside the top echelons of the Party?

Lombardo Radice Inside the Party. But let me ask you a question: who knew the name of Alexander Dubcek in December 1967?

Urban No one did.

Lombardo Radice Yet a few months later his name became a by-word.

Urban So you think a similar possibility exists in Moscow?

Lombardo Radice Without a doubt. The struggle for *progressive* Socialism has popular roots in the Soviet Union. It is not a child of the imagination of frustrated intellectuals. It is a life-necessity.

Urban Let me try to summarise two important points you made in our conversation yesterday. First you said, quoting the testimony of Ernst Fischer, that if circumstances similar to those which obtained in the 1930s arose once again, you would act exactly as you then acted—

Lombardo Radice —*generally* in the same way—

Urban —generally in the same way, which I take to mean justifying Stalinism for fear of jeopardising the survival of the Soviet system. Second, you said that, if the Italian Communist Party as a governing party were asked to choose sides in a grave international emergency, it would, with qualifications, choose the Soviet side. . . .

Lombardo Radice It would be more precise to say that we would want to fight neither the United States nor the Soviet Union.

Urban Naturally, we both hope that the need to make an awesome choice of this kind will never arise. But we must, as realists, assume that a war-like crisis between the West and the Soviet Union *is* a possibility.

Suppose you were in the shoes of Cyrus Vance or Zbigniew Brzezinski and the United States President asked you to frame a policy to take care of the Italian Communist Party's possible rise to power or partial power—what would be your advice to President Carter? You would be facing the problem whether to tell the President that the Italian Communists were a safe bet in power, or whether to tell him that they weren't. Judging by what you told me yesterday, and indeed what you are now saying, the answer is clearly: No, they aren't.

Lombardo Radice   In the hypothetical case you mention—and it is extremely difficult to foresee under what precise conditions a war-like emergency could occur—the Italian Communist Party would probably not want to commit itself to either side. It would be for peace. It would (as I have already said) certainly oppose anti-Sovietism. It would be against any move to roll back the present frontiers of Socialism and *a fortiori* to destroy it.

Urban   The big debate going on in Washington and the West European capitals centres precisely on this point: Can the Italian Communists be trusted to uphold NATO, to be loyal allies in an emergency, to keep military secrets; or would they act as Trojan horses in the Western camp and, at the very least, paralyse the Western defence effort by insisting on debilitating cuts in military expenditure? Your contention that the Party would choose neutrality, and still more, that it would oppose any roll-back of Soviet hegemony, is to my mind an unequivocal way of saying that it would act against the interests of NATO, for a war-like emergency would undoubtedly be about the restriction of Soviet hegemony and very likely the destruction of it.

Lombardo Radice   Perhaps I ought to have expressed myself more clearly. My meaning was simply that in the unlikely event of a showdown, we as a Party could not be expected to work against the general interests of the Soviet Union, and by 'interests' I mean the historic achievements of Socialism, which we don't want to see destroyed or diminished.

Let me insist once again: Italy, France, and the other European members of NATO must be prepared to be 'loyal' to the common 'defence' of the alliance if that defence is based on *common decisions*. However, their obligation lapses if the United States ceases to respect the defensive character of the alliance and imposes on it decisions without the concurrence of the other signatories of NATO.

Urban   But as all NATO decisions have to be unanimous decisions, this would mean that a Communist or Communist-led Italian or French government would possess the crucial power of deciding for the rest of NATO what does or does not constitute 'defensive' action. And this in turn would, as Henry Kissinger feared, make nonsense of NATO.

Lombardo Radice   Let me come back to your provocative question: what would I, if I were a Western bourgeois adviser to the United States President, tell him to do about Italy? I would, in the first place, probably tell Mr Carter: 'Let's try to rescue Italy by capitalist means—by giving her large loans, beefing up her economy with investments and encouraging petrodollars to flow into the country'. (Gadaffi's recent investment in Fiat may well be a sign that the Americans or the Arabs or both are, indeed, thinking of a capitalist rescue operation.) But if, for some reason, this traditional form of rescue cannot be put in train and the collapse of Italy cannot be avoided—

Urban —the collapse of Italy as a country?

Lombardo Radice Yes, there is a danger of complete collapse in the sense that Italy no longer functions, corruption is rampant, and inflation may go through the ceiling again. Therefore, if the collapse of Italy, and the catastrophic burden this would place on America and Western Europe economically and politically, cannot be avoided by capitalist remedies, then I would, as a bourgeois adviser, tell the American President to put his faith in the Italian Communist Party, because this is the only force that can get the country back on its feet again. When the Agnellis of Italy give up in desperation, the only serious factor left in Italian society is the Communist Party.

Urban There are, as it seems to me, justified fears in Washington that the Italian Communists may be saying one thing while out of power and quite another *in* power. There is certainly nothing in the precedents of Communist rule to make us think otherwise.

Lombardo Radice The Americans understand neither the history of the Italian Communist Party nor the complexities of the current situation. It is, in a democratic society, impossible to advocate year in, year out, a pluralistic, free, democratic type of Socialism, and then, as soon as we are put in power by the votes of the people, to repudiate it, to suppress freedom and set up the dictatorship of the proletariat.

Urban This is not going to happen?

Lombardo Radice Of course it isn't. It is quite unreasonable to suppose that you can say one thing on Monday and do the opposite on Tuesday.

Urban But this is very much what you *can* do if you are a Leninist—

Lombardo Radice —I don't think I should go into your very peculiar idea of Leninism which you seem to conceive of as a confidence trick. Let me simply say that, while you can man-oeuvre one football team against another, you cannot manipulate and deceive millions of workers. They have voted for you because you have given them a certain programme. You can't suddenly choose to do the opposite.

Urban What you are saying is: You would advise the American President to ask the Italian Communist Party to rescue the Italian capitalist/bourgeois social order for the general good of the West?

Lombardo Radice   No, not at all. I would tell Mr Carter that this is the least damaging way for the West to cut its losses in Italy. For clearly the Americans have to lose *something* in Italy if they cannot, or do not choose to, rescue Italy by capitalist methods. If so, it would be better for them to lose a hand rather than a limb, or a limb rather than the whole body. The Italian Communist Party would not—let there be no mistake about this—save Italy for the benefit of capitalism. We would save it for the benefit of democracy and the prospect of Socialism. In this sense, our accession to power or partial power *would* damage the interests of imperialism—there can be no doubt about that.

But what alternatives do the Americans have? Suppose we join the government, and the Americans put us under siege conditions politically and economically—well, there would be an economic collapse. The Communist Party and indeed the other political parties would find themselves forced into the arms of the Soviet Union. Italy would go Socialist, perhaps on the Soviet model, because all other possibilities of working out a solution would have been denied.

We would then see a repetition of Cuba, and the Americans would owe the loss of Italy to the same short-sightedness and ineptitude as lost them Cuba.

Urban   Your party is in a bit of a dilemma, isn't it? Should you, for whatever reason, be catapulted into power to rule single-handed, Italy's unmanageable conditions and your insufficient electoral support would sink you even without active American disapproval. If, on the other hand, you are thinking (as I believe you are) in terms of Communist participation in an Italian coalition government, then my guess would be that you could not carry out a genuinely Communist programme, and you would therefore be gravely discredited in the eyes of your electoral supporters.

Lombardo Radice   It wouldn't be a question of putting into effect a Communist programme.

Urban   A compromise?

Lombardo Radice   No, it would be a question of advancing democracy, of taking the first steps towards injecting Socialism into Italian democracy.

Let me clear up a popular misconception. It is completely false to think of the 'historic compromise' as some nicely arranged agreement at the top between Berlinguer and Andreotti. If the Italian Communist Party does come to power, it will be in the context of some profound crisis which would, among other things, involve the Christian Democrats in abandoning many a long-held conservative position. To be quite candid with you: our participation in government would be an earthquake in Italian politics, not a carefully premeditated, peaceful happening.

Urban That would in itself, in my opinion, militate against Vance and Brzezinski accepting your advice. But wouldn't they have reason to worry also on a different score? Wouldn't the acceptance by the United States of the Italian Communists as *bona fide* partners in government have a devastating impact in France and possibly even Germany, so much so that it would undermine the entire legitimacy of NATO?

Lombardo Radice Well, the American politicians must learn to have a little hindsight and foresight. NATO is now almost 30 years old, the world has changed. The American domination of Western Europe is over; the submissiveness of Western Europe is over too. If the Americans have not learnt that much from experience and all their expensive international symposia, policy analyses, think-tanks and the rest, then they have learnt nothing.

Urban I think it would be a great deal easier to persuade the United States President to recognise America's changed position in Western Europe if Moscow could be brought to recognise *its* changed position in Eastern Europe. But this has proved patently impossible. It *has* been possible for Spain and Portugal to change from Fascism to democracy. The Americans have not stood in the way—in fact, they have aided the process. No comparable development has been permitted by the Soviet leaders in Eastern Europe. I would have thought there was room here for a little reciprocity.

Lombardo Radice Oh certainly. There must be change in the Soviet Union and Eastern Europe, but it is not true to say that change is impossible. There have been two important changes in Poland: when Gomulka came to power and when he was thrown out of power. There was Hungary in 1956, Czechoslovakia in 1968—all dramatic events of great consequence.

Urban I would say: there have been *attempts* at change . . . until the Soviet tanks rolled in and change was nipped in the bud.

Lombardo Radice Ah, but the suppression cannot last. These countries *have* to develop. The only question is: Will the change be peaceful or dramatic, even tragic? Of course, one hopes there will be no fresh tragedies; but change must come. Talking of possible American attitudes to Italy, let me give you another example of American unintelligence. It is beyond any doubt by now that Allende was overthrown and Pinochet brought to power with American assistance. Now, Allende was no Soviet stooge. In fact he failed to get any of the Soviet economic support he needed. Why was he overthrown? Because the Americans were thinking in simplistic terms ('a Communist is a Communist') and lacked intelligent foresight. Now they are paying a very high political price for their unwisdom and have a terrible burden on their conscience. They should have supported Allende!

Urban   The Americans probably had the warning of Cuba in mind. But I am a little hesitant to condemn the United States for Chile before condemning the Russians for Czechoslovakia. And if you look at the two from the perspective of great-power interests, you might argue that the Russians could no more afford to take a chance with the status quo in Czechoslovakia than the Americans could with Allende. Political conscience is a highly elastic quality—power-interests are not. They demand concrete action.

Lombardo Radice   I'm not defending the Soviet intervention in Czechoslovakia. It is well remembered that the armed occupation of Czechoslovakia was immediately and strongly condemned by us, and this attitude of the Italian Communist Party is firmly maintained. The invasion of Czechoslovakia was completely wrong and politically counter-productive. It has solved nothing, as we can well see today. The Russians traded a short-term gain for a long-term liability.

Urban   Is the Italian Communist Party planning to make a *principled* critique of Soviet rule in Eastern Europe? So far you have criticised isolated events (though you have done so very effectively). I would have thought the time was ripe for a critical appraisal of the entire structure of Communist rule in Eastern Europe.

Lombardo Radice   What we have in mind is not a critique of the *principle* of Socialism in Eastern Europe, for the principle is clearly right, but a broad historical/sociological analysis of the state of the game at the present time. Our current understanding of it is obviously inadequate. Some work in this general direction is already being done at the Gramsci Institute. (For example, there has been an important discussion on Stalinism between the historian Giuseppe Boffa of our Party and the French Communist, Martinet.) But much more needs to be done. We must try to re-define the nature of the societies that have emerged in Russia, East Germany, Poland, Czechoslovakia and Rumania. Are they Socialist societies? Are they transitional societies? What are they? They are clearly post-capitalist societies, for they have taken the means of production into public ownership, abolished private property and so on; but this does not tell us very much about their real character. As you know from our talk yesterday, my own description of these societies would be 'state-Socialism', but others may find a more adequate characterisation.

The general outline of our interpretation would be that these societies are suffering from a crisis of uneven growth: they have developed enormous heads intellectually, technologically and economically, but these heads are not supported by commensurate bodies in terms of political structure, cultural emancipation, civil rights, and so forth.

Urban Would you, then, say that the Leninist interpretation of Communism is both morally wrong and a practical failure?

Lombardo Radice Leninism is a complicated subject. One cannot reduce it to a matter of mere tactics, or some prescription for a mindless dictatorship, or a blueprint for dogmatism—all this is old propaganda. Leninism is a profound, scientific approach to revolution in a relatively underdeveloped country. It was the spirit and the engine of the greatest progressive socio-political breakthrough of our century. Far from being a failure one would want to disown, it was and is the most powerful motor for liberation in human history.

What I would say is that, for us today, the whole system of power-from-the-top, the entire idea of dictatorship, has become false, utterly false, even if in those early and terrible decades of Soviet isolation in a capitalistic environment and under Fascist attack, Leninism was the simplest way of maintaining unity at home and security abroad.

But the fact that we repudiate the idea of dictatorship does not at all mean that Socialism itself is false. Self-management, a much wider distribution of power, and participation rather than state-Socialism—these are the reforms most needed in Eastern Europe. But we must not ignore the fact that, historically speaking, Socialism in Russia has given the Russian people more real freedom than they had before the October Revolution, because it put an end to the exploitation of man by man, outlawed unemployment and inequality.

Urban Let me again probe into the extent of freedom you would be prepared to see established in Russia and Eastern Europe. Yesterday you said that every kind of individual freedom should be permitted as long as it does not involve conspiracy. But the freedom to read, write, publish, listen to broadcasts, meet and discuss without hindrance would sooner or later lead some people to demand a change of system. Would they be allowed to do so?

Lombardo Radice   This is not a possible hypothesis. For six months in 1968 there was complete freedom in Czechoslovakia; yet no one demanded a return to capitalism. Socialism was in no danger of being destroyed.

Urban   But if you talk of complete liberty, you must surely include in it the liberty of the individual to share his views with like-minded individuals, and if these like-minded individuals decide to call their association a political party—a social democratic party, for example, or an agrarian conservative party—they should, according to your definition, be allowed to do so and test the popularity of their ideas in free elections.

Lombardo Radice   You are thinking schematically—in the stereotypes of pre-Socialist forms of government. After a probably crisis-ridden liberalisation of Socialism in Russia and Eastern Europe the forms of government there might vary. There might be more than one party, there might be only one party, or there might arise something completely new—we don't know. But even if the single-party system came to stay, there would be wide-ranging debate within that party, there would be a progressive and a conservative wing—there would be internal democracy. We saw in Czechoslovakia in 1968 that the revival of Social Democracy just did not come up as a problem. There was something quite different—the beginnings of a new kind of democracy on the basis of the existing structure of Socialism.

Urban   But the Russians feared what I, for one, also thought might happen: the eventual collapse of Communism.

Lombardo Radice   The Russians feared highly unintelligently. They were fighting shadows.

Urban   But complete individual freedom necessarily implies the legitimacy of a variety of political programmes, including that of saying 'no' to Socialism. I'm sorry to harp on this point but it seems to me crucial.

Lombardo Radice   I don't believe any such thing would happen. Would any part of the population want to see a regression from Socialism, a retreat from a higher form of society to a lower? Can you see a Hungarian or Rumanian agrarian party wanting to return the land to the large landowners?

Urban   I don't think they would want to do that, but, on your principle of liberty, the possibility that such a programme might emerge must be kept open. Many Hungarians might say: 'We want to return to individual farming—we want to divide the lands of the cooperative and state farms', and the farmers might demand their own political representation. Moves of this kind were, in fact, made as early as Imre Nagy's 'new course', much before the Hungarian Revolution of October 1956.

which just goes to show that people may look backwards and desire a "retreat from a higher form of society to a lower". In times of stress this could be v significant number.

Communism with an Italian Face?   49

Lombardo Radice   Well, people may want to 'demand' all sorts of things. In Italy there are people who want to revive the monarchy! In Russia there may be people who would want to return to Solzhenitsyn's Holy Russia. But these are insignificant minorities; they are no danger to Socialism. Solzhenitsyn should be allowed to return to the Soviet Union and preach his gospel. The hollowness of his claims would be shown up at once.

Urban   I'm not so sure. I think he would have a large following, and there would be an even larger mass movement to his political right.

Lombardo Radice   Perhaps a couple of millions in an enormous land—no more. History is strong. Solzhenitsyn and Bukovsky and Amalrik and all the others, known and unknown, should be free to say what they like. We are, after all, talking of countries that have had Socialist rule for a very long time—60 years in Russia and 30 in Eastern Europe. It is entirely unhistorical as well as unreasonable to suppose that they would want to turn the clock back. The Hungarian events of 1956 were a different matter: Socialism in Hungary was a weak plant, only some seven years old, and there was a danger of a regression to capitalism.

Urban   1956 was a counter-revolution?

Lombardo Radice   I was in favour of Russian action in Hungary, and this is no secret—

Urban   —in favour of suppressing the revolution?

Lombardo Radice   —of controlling it, because the danger of counter-revolution was strong. There was Cardinal Mindszenty speaking for the former landowners; there was violence in the streets against Communist workers and so on. Socialism was as yet without roots, therefore the roots had to be protected.

But to talk of 'counter-revolution' in *Czechoslovakia* in 1968 is pitiful nonsense. In Prague no one even remembered the names of the former factory proprietors and landowners! The present tendencies to reform Czechoslovak Socialism are even more distinctly Socialist than were the reforms of 1968, if that is at all possible.

The Soviet leaders and the Czechoslovak Communists must learn to understand that it is impossible for Socialism to advance without taking risks. I'm a great admirer of Kafka, and I realise that the chances of human planning and reason being mocked and frustrated by unreason, perversity, or sheer accident are very great. But that does not absolve us of the responsibility of trying to advance from structures and institutions which have outlived their usefulness to others which are more relevant to our needs.

Urban   After the occupation of Czechoslovakia I published an article in an American quarterly under the title of 'Removing the

Hyphen', and my meaning was that the Prague reform-Communism signified the first important move by a ruling Communist party to cleanse Communism of its Leninist accretions by removing the hyphen between Marxism-Leninism and returning the movement to its original, Western inspiration. With the ballasts of Russian autocracy and the heritage of Byzantium lifted, the Communist movement might recapture its appeal to Western societies (or so I interpreted the essential meaning of the Prague Spring). Aren't your strictures on the rigidity of the Soviet system and your support of the Czechoslovak Socialist opposition tacitly based on a similar reading?

Lombardo Radice   Not at all. We are, and we have always been, anti-dogmatists, and that is also why we have been Leninists. Lenin defied the prevailing Marxist orthodoxy that a proletarian revolution could not be carried out before there has been a bourgeois revolution. He did, rightly, lead the Russian proletariat to victory despite the fact that the proletariat was small, the country minimally industrialised, the economy abysmally backward and the majority of people illiterate.

Urban   He was a revisionist of Marxism. . . .

Lombardo Radice   He certainly was that. Now Gramsci was a revisionist of Lenin; for example, Gramsci's notion of 'hegemony' (of the working class) is very different from Lenin's idea of the 'dictatorship of the proletariat'; and *our* programme of Socialism through democracy is a revision of Gramsci. We are all revisionists or, if you like, Marxists-Leninists in the sense that we have all adapted, changed, or ignored the texts according to the demands of the concrete situations in which we found ourselves.

There is, therefore (to say it again), no rupture, no sudden leap in our movement. In his explanation of the dialectic Hegel uses the word *aufheben*, which can mean both 'to invalidate' and 'to raise' or 'to hold up'. Our continuous revisionism has done justice to the Hegelian notion in both senses. We have superseded certain irrelevant ideas in the history of Socialist thinking, the better to be able to promote Socialism through relevant ones. We are all Marxists—Leninists—Gramsciists—Togliattiists—because they were all revisionists. I am very fond of a sentence in a famous letter of Galileo's: 'If Aristotle were alive today', he wrote, 'he would say I am his best pupil because I challenge his theories'.

Urban   A *tour de force* of Marxist thinking. . . .

Lombardo Radice   No, simple dialectics.

Urban   Your dogma, then, is the repudiation of dogma.

Lombardo Radice   No, it is not a dogma; it is practice.

Urban   Would you say that the Italian Communist Party has, for all practical purposes, ceased to be Leninist in the dogmatic

sense in which Leninism is interpreted in Moscow? Certainly the
Leninist formula—of a close-knit, highly disciplined, conspiratorial body of professional revolutionaries, who bring
revolutionary consciousness to the working class from outside
the working class and impose in its name the dictatorship of the
proletariat— does not seem to me an election winner in Italy in
1977.

Lombardo Radice   As I've just said: for us in Italy the Leninist
conception of Party dictatorship is utterly false. It wasn't, of
course, false for Lenin, because in Russia's particular circumstances in 1917, dictatorship by a small and ruthless Party was the
only way of having a revolution.

Urban   And Gramsci, who is often quoted against Lenin by
the Italian Communists, entirely agreed with Lenin. In July 1918
he wrote (in *Il Grido del Popolo*): 'In Russia . . . the proletariat has
taken over the direction of political and economic life and is
establishing its own order. Its own order, not Socialism. . . .
Dictatorship is the fundamental institution guaranteeing freedom. . . .'

Lombardo Radice   But Gramsci also said that the dictatorship
was to be a transitional phenomenon, to be dissolved as soon as
the revolution was guaranteed against *coups d'état* by factious
minorities.

In any case, we broke, in practice, with Lenin's theory of the
Party when Togliatti returned from Moscow in 1944, and we
decided to make the Italian Party a mass party, with broad popular appeal—no dictatorship by a small band of leaders, no *ex
cathedra* enunciations of the truth, and so forth. The basic Italian
criticism of Lenin was made by Togliatti.

Urban   I am a little puzzled. If you don't agree with the Soviet
insistence that Leninism is as valid in 1977 as it was in 1917—if
you are gravely critical of the rigidity of Communism in Russia
and Eastern Europe—if you reject 'State-Socialism' as a perversion of Socialism—and if you feel, as Berlinguer told us not so
long ago, better protected as a Communist Party behind the
defensive shield of NATO than you would outside it—why do
you dutifully go to all these international Communist gatherings?
Why do you sign their declarations? Why not make a clean break
and accept no tutoring by Moscow and no community of purpose
with it?

Lombardo Radice   The East Berlin conference may have been
the last of the traditional type we attended. But remember that
the East Berlin document has clearly spelled out the end of a
monolithic Communist movement and established every Communist Party's right to independent action. Remember further

that we had made our objections to a monocentric movement very clear long before East Berlin. For example, at the time of the 1971 Moscow conference, there was a long debate in our Central Committee—which I attended—whether we should put our names to the proposed communiqué. We decided to sign only the first part, which dealt in generalities, such as the necessity to fight for peace, defeat imperialism and the like; but we never signed the rest.

I have to object to your statement that we accept 'tutoring' from Moscow. This lacks all factual basis—it is propaganda. There is between Moscow and our Party a partial community of purpose based on issues such as the maintenance of peace, détente, and support of the national-liberation movements. But such links as we have with the Russians are freely chosen. Your advice that we should 'break' with the Soviet Union is a little too obvious, coming as it does from the bourgeois-conservative side, for it is given in the clear expectation that the Italian Communist Party would eventually transform itself into a classical Social Democratic party.

Urban   But it is true, isn't it, that you have, for many years, and despite your growing differences, attended all these conferences, sunk (or kept quiet about) your disagreements, and upheld the fiction (if fiction it was) that the world Communist movement is, with all its tactical difficulties, ultimately based on certain shared principles of which, until quite recently, the Soviet Union was the principal interpreter and spokesman?

Now I invite you to think of this spectacle from the point of view of the man in the street in Austin, Texas. He would not be conversant with the refinements of Communist philosophy, but he might well ask: If the Italian Communists now preach freedom and yet attend these international synods, they should surely see the logic of permitting Polish farmers and Czechoslovak Social Democrats to attend 'green internationals' or the meetings of the Socialist International with Willy Brandt and Olaf Palme and Helmut Schmidt and Bruno Kreisky. Why (he might reason) should these East European citizens not be allowed to go to Paris or London every two or three years, discuss common problems, sign common documents and benefit from the solidarity of *their* movement just as the Communists do from theirs? I wouldn't know how to answer him. '

Lombardo Radice   The answer is simple. They should be allowed to go to all these meetings in complete freedom. This flows automatically from what I told you about the Italian Communist Party's critique of the Socialist régimes in Russia and Eastern Europe. We are against all restrictions of freedom of travel, freedom of discussion, freedom of assembly.

Urban So these East European people should be allowed to confer with Schmidt and Palme and return home to put their ideas into action?

Lombardo Radice Yes, of course; we *are* for freedom.

Urban Including this kind of freedom to organise internally on the basis of a larger international understanding?

Lombardo Radice Absolutely. Of course, I don't think Helmut Schmidt's kind of Social Democracy would have the slightest chance of success in Russia or Eastern Europe. It has been overtaken by history.

Urban But your insistence that the Social Democrats, with their rival interpretation of international Socialism, should also be free to organise is mortally opposed to the Soviet position.

Lombardo Radice Yes, it is. Naturally, I don't believe that international meetings of bourgeois parties or groups could overcome the problem that history is not on their side. The Communist Parties' common platform is rooted in the supra-national character of the world proletariat. It envisages a supra-national and better world order as expressed in the *Communist Manifesto*. The bourgeois parties are caught in the contradictions of a heterogeneous social order. They have no vision of a better deal for mankind. I can, therefore, see no great danger coming from that quarter.

Urban To be completely frank with you, Professor Lombardo Radice, I would not, if I were a young Italian radical, with fire in my belly, vote for your Party or support it. For what have I heard you say in this conversation but words of caution, compromise and liberalism? You have reneged on the dictatorship of the proletariat. You are very doubtful about Leninism. You don't seem to want to take power single-handed. And your sense of revolution reminds me of nothing so much as Eduard Bernstein's old claim that in Marx's theory there is no room for revolution— the class struggle leads to class reconciliation, reformism, and socialist democracy, with the bourgeoisie and the proletariat melting into a mass of classless citizens. How could this satisfy me, seeing what a beastly mess Italy has got herself into? I would want to put a bomb under it and blow it sky high; but to do that I would have to go to the anarchists and Maoists, for there appears to be no room for revolution in the programme of the Italian Communist Party. Don't you think your eagerness to adapt has now reached a stage where your Party has lost its sense of legitimacy?

Lombardo Radice We had our problems with the radical students in 1968, and in a sense there was then a crisis of Italian

Communism because we seemed to be overtaken on our Left. But all that is over. Today it is not our Party that is in crisis but the Maoists and anarchists who are in complete disarray. Why? Because revolution is not about rebellion—it is a serious thing—

Urban —too serious to be left to revolutionaries?

Lombardo Radice Too serious to be left in the hands of anarchists. I am sick to death of being reproached by the bourgeois side that our Party is not revolutionary enough. This is clearly an attempt to blacken us in the eyes of the revolutionary youth. But more and more of these young people realise that in an advanced, late-capitalist society our Party's policy is the only effective one. Therefore a great many young Leftists have joined our Party or come back to our Party, and the anarchist groups are rapidly disappearing (witness, for example, the splitting of the PDUP). Unemployment has, of course, caused great social tensions, but the young Leftist rebels are politically confused and no challenge to our Party. To say that our apparent support of the institutions of bourgeois society and our willingness to compromise is a betrayal of our trust and weakens the appeal of our Party, is a misjudgment of our situation. Our electoral support, our strength in local elections and in the trade unions have grown parallel with our moderate policies which are, however, moderate only in appearance.

Urban Let me take you back to the early history of the Italian Socialist Party of which Benito Mussolini was one of the leaders. For it appears to me that your popular appeal in Italy in 1977 may have something to do with a simple but highly important discovery the young Mussolini made, as a Marxist Socialist, between 1910 and 1914.

Very briefly: in 1910 Mussolini edited a paper called *La Lotta di Classe (The Class Struggle)*. In 1914, having been ousted from *Avanti*, he decided to call his new daily paper *Il Popolo d'Italia (The Italian People)*. Why? Because in those four years Mussolini discovered that the international brotherhood of the working class was a pious hope of Socialist theoreticians. There were no real bonds between working-class people in France and Germany and England and Italy. (And, as we now know, Mussolini's foresight was amply proved right when, in 1914, the German Social Democrats patriotically voted for the Kaiser's war credits.) But what there was in Italian society, and ready to be enormously exploited, was Nationalism. This was Mussolini's profound discovery. His combination of Socialism and appeal to the *popolo* of Italy brought him to power and secured him the Italian people's consensus for twenty years.

I do not want to sound too offensive, but it would seem to me that *mutatis mutandis* the Italian Communist Party has made a similar discovery. While you do not make an appeal to Nationalism, you do, nevertheless, let it be known at every turn that you are an entirely *Italian, home-grown* party (which you are); and I would have thought your popular appeal is not so much due to your moderate policies, as to this consciously fostered image of Socialism *and* Italianism—Socialism with an Italian face.

Lombardo Radice   The analogy is false. As you know, our terms of reference are not nations but classes. We do not try to appeal to Nationalism; we are against it. Our principle is that the leadership of Italian society has to pass to the working class, and this is, you must admit, a very different policy from that followed by Mussolini who sought to vest the leadership of Italian society in the bourgeoisie—

Urban   —the Nation—

Lombardo Radice   —nominally the Nation, but in fact the bourgeoisie and, to be more precise, the more aggressive and powerful sections of the bourgeoisie. I do not regard your analogy as 'offensive' because it has simply no basis in fact. We believe that the leading role of the working class is of benefit to the whole community, 'nationally' (if you like) and internationally—to the intellectuals, peasants, artisans, and so on—and Gramsci's word for this role was 'hegemony'—

Urban   —meaning?

Lombardo Radice   —meaning constructive leadership in the spirit of revolution but deepening the concept of revolution. It means that Marx's prescription for overthrowing capitalist society by revolution is adequately met by the leading role of the working class. It does not require us to go on to the barricades.

Urban   There are, as I see it, two charismatic ideas in our time: Socialism and Nationalism. The combination of the two is potent stuff indeed. The Italian Communist Party has, in the course of time, come to see this—not in the sense of 'National Socialism', but on the perfectly respectable calculation that in the sophisticated and freedom-loving context of Italian society the libertarian content of Italian Socialism must imply independence from foreign models, foreign inspiration, foreign control.

Lombardo Radice   Socialism is a charismatic idea, and so is freedom; and it is the combination of Socialism with *liberty* (not Nationalism) that is the potent mixture you refer to. Nationalism is a spent force. We are fighting for the hegemony of the working class because the interests and historical consciousness of the working class coincide with the universal interests of mankind. There was, of course, a time when the Italian proletariat, too, was narrow-minded and parochial. Gramsci himself had to remind the Turin workers that it was their duty to stand up for the interests of Sicilian peasants—it didn't come naturally to them. But those days are behind us.

Urban What precisely does Gramsci's idea of 'hegemony' mean in Italian practice? The dictionary definition of the word is ambivalent. It may mean simply 'leadership', but it may, and very much does in current usage, also mean 'predominance' or 'rule' of one state over another, or one group over another.

Lombardo Radice Hegemony means that the general problems of society (whether political, economic, or cultural) can only be solved if the proletariat obtains the leadership of society—not in order to dictate to society, but to head it. And this leadership is exercised in the framework of an 'historical bloc' (to use Gramsci's phrase) in which the interests of the three main strata of society—workers, peasants and intellectuals—are fully represented.

Urban Would political parties be included in this front?

Lombardo Radice The Italian Communist Party's view is that today such an 'historical bloc' requires several truly independent parties. Possibly Gramsci did not envisage more than one party, but this isn't important for us today.

Urban But if and when you have achieved 'hegemony' in Italy, would you be willing to renounce it if the Italian people decided that it wanted no more of it?

Lombardo Radice I told you before: once we accept the rules of the game and come to power through the ballot box, we are committed to respecting those rules, whether they benefit us or not. We cannot have one yardstick before we come to power and another while in power.

Urban You would be willing to resign, peacefully accepting defeat through the normal democratic process?

Lombardo Radice I think we would if we lost the support of the people.

Urban But earlier you said: it would be an impossible hypothesis to suppose that a society which has reached a higher stage of development in the form of Socialism would want to go back to a 'lower form of development'—to Helmut Schmidt's Social Democracy, for example. Wouldn't the same apply to Italian society once the 'hegemony' of the proletariat has been established through the offices of your Party?

Lombardo Radice I'm no prophet; but once the working class has acquired hegemony and led Italian society out of its almost permanent crisis, it would be difficult to envisage anyone wanting a regression from a better state of society to a worse state.

Urban But should such an unreasonable view assert itself through the political process, would you bow to it?

Lombardo Radice It is in the logic of our policy that we would.

Urban 'Italy is truly prey to demoniacal spirits, impossible to control or comprehend: the sole principle of order is to be found in the working class, in the proletarian will to inscribe Italy concretely and actively in the world historical process. The principle of order can only express itself politically in a rigidly organised Communist Party, which sets itself a clear, unambiguous objective. . . . '

These words were written, not by one of your colleagues in the Italian Communist Party's leadership in 1955 or 1977, but by Antonio Gramsci in 1920. Having listened to you for two extremely stimulating mornings, I am inclined to concede that the continuity you have impressed on me in this conversation truly exists. Fifty-seven years after Gramsci, the 'demoniacal spirits' of Italy have still not departed and—unless I am gravely deceived—the Italian Communist Party has yet to be 'rigidly organised' and set itself those 'clear and unambiguous objectives' which Gramsci demanded. I don't myself think the Party is a 'principle of order' which will lead Italy out of chaos. Much rather is it part of the chaos itself. And that, I must confess, tempers some of my gloomier forebodings about the future of Italian democracy.

Fabio Mussi

3 A Communist View of Fascism

Urban Fascism, in the standard Soviet interpretation, is 'the most reactionary and openly terroristic form of the dictatorship of finance capital, established by the imperialistic bourgeoisie to break the resistance of the working class and all the progressive elements of society'. This is the definition given in the *Short Philosophical Dictionary* and repeated without change in the most recent Soviet literature. The picture of Fascism emerging from Renzo de Felice's work* takes issue with this interpretation, and I should imagine your Party takes issue with de Felice's analysis. To summarise him in a nutshell: de Felice says that Fascism enjoyed a great deal of mass support; that it inherited certain 'progressive' characteristics from the French Revolution and the syndicalist/anarchist origins of the early Fascist movement; that it rode to victory on the backs not of a petty bourgeoisie facing economic and social ruin but of one on the rise; and that Fascism was in most ways not comparable with National Socialism. Where does your Party stand on these questions?

Mussi Recent years have seen a great increase in the study of Fascism. We too have tried to re-think some of the conclusions drawn from our earlier analyses—judgments which have become stale through lack of critical attention. Of course, our concern with the study of Fascism is not dramatically new. Throughout the 1920s, both our Party and the Communist International spent a great deal of time analysing the precise nature of this phenomenon, but the interpretations of that period were in many respects erroneous. For example, until the mid-1930s, it was accepted thinking that Fascism represented the last violent pangs of capitalism and that the advent of Fascism was in fact speeding up the

* See: 'Varieties of Fascism', pp. 97–115.

58

coming Socialist revolution. This was, furthermore, related to another error—the error of believing that certain parties and movements which were, in fact, close to the Communist Party were more dangerous to it than the truly reactionary parties of the Fascist kind, because it was feared that these non-Communist left-wing forces might dilute the revolutionary essence of Communism, whereas Fascism (it was thought) could be clearly seen to be on the enemy's side of the fence.

Urban You are referring to Stalin's treatment of the German Social Democrats. . . .

Mussi Not only that; I am also referring to the manner in which we as a Party treated, in the later years of Fascism, the clandestine non-Communist parties—the Socialists for example—whom we considered to be our principal antagonists. This was the International's position, and we accepted it uncritically.

It is clear to me, and it was clear already in the 1930s, that in any realistic assessment of Fascism, two of its aspects must be interrelated: Fascism as a class phenomenon, and Fascism as a political phenomenon. The initial error we committed was that of thinking that politically the régime was simply built on terror and that, from the class point of view, Fascism was (as I have just said) the last desperate act of capitalism before its surrender to the Socialist revolution.

At the same time it is important to bear in mind that, of all the parties belonging to the International, the Italian Communist Party was one of the first to initiate a revision of this interpretation of Fascism. In his *Prison Notebooks* Gramsci observed that Fascism was, of course, a dictatorship, but one in which there coexisted a complex of social relationships—the state, civil society, a dominant social bloc, a political party, and so on. In other words, it was not a seamless affair—nothing to which a simple slogan could do justice. Also, in his lectures on Fascism which Togliatti delivered in Moscow in 1935, Fascism was described as a *mass* reactionary régime—counter-revolutionary, to be sure, but also a régime which succeeded in winning a good deal of mass support—

Urban —including support by the working class?

Mussi Yes, including that, for what choice did the working people have? As a result of severe repression by the régime, the Socialist Party was virtually non-existent and therefore rapidly losing touch with those classes which had supported it until the 1920s. The leaders and cadres of the Communist Party were under arrest and the Party was unable to function. True, some of our Party leaders managed to meet for our 4th Congress in Cologne in 1934, and there was a basic Party in existence comprising a few thousand members. In other words, the Party resisted; nevertheless it was reduced to a minority affair, above all in the industrial areas in the North.

Why was the working-class movement so effectively des- troyed? This was the starting point of the Communist Party's re-evaluation of Fascism; it also brings us to the controversy surrounding Renzo de Felice's analysis. In his biography of Mus- solini and his *Intervista* with Michael Ledeen, de Felice sees almost exclusively the element of consensus as the determining factor of the Fascist régime and loses sight of the social, economic and class elements which made up its real character. This is the main reason for our quarrel with de Felice.

Urban Arnold Toynbee once wrote that Communism was Christianity gone awry. Mightn't one say that, in one important sense, Fascism was Communism gone awry? For that seems to me to be de Felice's implication.

Mussi No. De Felice commits an error of ingenuity, a very serious error, in that he takes the documents and speeches of the so-called 'Fascists of the first hour', the proto-Fascists, who were mainly syndicalists and anarchists, and describes the nature of Fascism in terms of the programme offered by these men. These anarcho-syndicalist Socialists were a small group who founded, with Mussolini and others, the Fascist Party in 1919. Not surpris- ingly, their political vocabulary was identical with the language then current in the Socialist and Communist movements to which, in fact, some of them belonged.

Urban You have in mind Marinetti and other Futurists with their gospel of a 'proletariat of gifted men'—glorifiers of war as 'the world's only hygiene'?

Mussi Yes, this was a fairly influential movement for the rejuvenation of art. Politically, for many years, it was difficult to say which way it was going. Eventually some of its leading members merged into the Fascist movement—

Urban —but others became Communists—

Mussi —very few, and the fact that so few of them went into the Communist movement is probably one of the reasons why this utopian cultural-artistic vanguard, with its grotesque attempt to suppress history in the name of art, was so poorly received, and why realism was eventually vindicated.

In order to prove his thesis, de Felice is forced to manipulate some of his materials. He covers up or keeps in the background the Fascist régime's violence up to about 1928. As you know, the path to the establishment of Fascism was paved with arrests, torture and murder. In de Felice's reconstruction the 'Fascism of the first hour' dominates the picture and is arbitrarily separated from the main body of Fascist history, although it is well recognised in historiography that this 'socialistic' phase of early Fascism lasted only a few months as an autonomous movement. After the official foundation of the Party, Fascism was almost immediately taken over by the big landowners of the Po valley and by northern industrialists. This is well documented in every detail: who financed what, the moneys that changed hands, the people that were bought and so forth. The fact is that within a few months, the movement became the tool of a distinct social group.

Urban But surely you would agree that Mussolini was a leading Marxist Socialist, editor of *Avanti*—a man who commanded the respect of Socialists and Communists? Some striking utterances stick in my mind, such as Gramsci's description of Mussolini in his Socialist phase as 'our leader'; Lenin's reproach to an Italian Socialist delegation: 'Mussolini? A great pity he is lost to us! He is a strong man, who would have led our party to victory'; Trotsky's remark to the same group: 'You have lost your trump card; the only man who could have carried through a revolution was Mussolini'; and Togliatti's observation: 'Let us not forget that Mussolini was a Socialist party leader'. Professor Alberto Aquarone quotes a remarkable police report from 1931: 'The Duce is today more popular among the working classes than among the capitalist bourgeoisie. . . . The bourgeoisie complains that "Mussolini is slowly, sweetly and silently, moving in the direction of a form of Bolshevism".' (Can one, incidentally, imagine a confidential NKVD report in the USSR warning Stalin's Politburo that in the eyes of some sections of Soviet society Stalin was moving in the direction of Fascism?)

There was, moreover, a certain two-way traffic in personnel between Fascists and Communists, best represented by the ambulatory loyalties of men such as Bordiga, Cantimori, Bombacci, Labriola and Malaparte, to name only the best known. Surely there is something more profound behind this than the pendulum action of extremist temperaments, or some mistaken identification of Fascism for Socialism and vice versa?

Mussi I find this argument incomprehensible—whether it comes from you or de Felice. Among Roosevelt's New Dealers, who directed American economic and social policy after the 1929–30 world slump, there was a group of men with Marxist and Socialist backgrounds, including a number of orthodox Communists, some of whom had actually lived in the Soviet Union under 'War Communism' and in the NEP period. Does this entitle one to say that the New Deal was an offspring of Marxism? Or, to come back to Italy, many of the scholars and politicians who explicitly supported Mussolini and Fascism up to 1925 were

men of liberal political origins. They included a great part of the
liberal representation in the Chamber of Deputies who saw in
Fascism a handy tool for stopping the advance of Socialism. Does
this entitle us to say that Fascism was an offspring of liberalism?
Régimes are what they are. They do not depend on the biog-
raphies of a small number of personalities who become a régime's
leaders and supporters.

Urban   What you seem to be saying is that you do not accept
the standard Soviet definition of Fascism, but neither do you
agree with de Felice's definition of it. You are somewhere in
between.

Mussi   Yes, and this state of being 'in between' is something
that is happening to us nowadays not only in respect of our
definition of Fascism but in respect of the whole position our
Party has been developing in the last few years in the context of
Eurocommunism. But to stick to Fascism: de Felice has allowed
himself to be carried away a little by his admiration for Mussolini.
This is, to say the least, an ahistorical way of going about history
with which we cannot agree. The *liberal* interpretation of Fascism
as an historical accident, as it emerges for example from the work
of Croce, is for us another over-simplification. But, on the other
hand, we also reject the Soviet view which sees in Fascism the
direct outcome and culmination of bourgeois liberalism.

Urban   But don't the Russians go a little further than that?
They say Fascism is an openly terroristic despotism by the
'imperialistic' bourgeoisie, and what would nowadays be called
the 'gnomes of Zurich', over the honest working man in Milan.

Mussi   The Russians are, of course, right in saying that Fascism was a brutal and bloodthirsty affair. However, we in the
Italian Communist Party do not believe that the bourgeoisie, or
any part of it, was *fated* to take the road to Fascism. Rather do we
think that some of the responsibility for the rise of Fascism has to
be borne by the erroneous policies of the Socialist and Communist movements.

Urban   You said Fascism was, in the liberal interpretation, an
accident of history. If it *was* so regarded (and I am not so sure that
it was), support for it was surprisingly strong and articulate. On
10 July 1924, a month after the assassination of Matteotti, when
Fascist fortunes were at a low ebb and Mussolini's fall seemed a
strong possibility, Benedetto Croce endorsed the Senate's vote of
confidence in Mussolini in the following words:

> We could not expect, or even hope, that Fascism should sud-
> denly fall. It has not been an infatuation or a prank. It has
> satisfied some serious requirements, and has done much

good, as every fair mind must admit. It advanced with the applause and consent of the nation. So on the one side there is a desire to preserve the benefits of Fascism and not to return to the exhaustion and inconclusiveness which preceded it; and on the other there is the feeling that the interests created by Fascism, even the less laudable and beneficial ones, are also a reality and cannot be tossed away. We must therefore give Fascism time to complete its process of transformation. This is the reason for the Senate's prudent and patriotic vote.

This sounds to me like proof positive that in Croce's assessment the arrival of Fascism was neither accidental nor unwelcome.

Mussi This misjudgment of Croce's lasted only a very short time, and it was a delusion common to the leaders of the liberal movement. The laws of January 1925, which put an end to all political liberty, opened the eyes of this group too. Croce was a determined anti-Fascist—there can be no question about that. His house in Naples was even destroyed by the Fascists. Yet, as you rightly say, at one time he held the views you have quoted. But if you want to be hard on liberals, I might add insult to injury by mentioning the case of the liberal leader Giovanni Amendola, father of Giorgio Amendola, who was among those who thought and said that the March on Rome should not be opposed with force because Fascism was offering a useful balance to the Socialist movement. Later, however, he became one of the foremost promoters of the break with Fascism and eventually perished at the hands of the Fascists.

Urban Croce's logic is unassailable though, for he was saying pretty much what those who want to see the Communist Party come to power in Italy today are now saying: Italy is in chaos, the ruling parties are indecisive, factious and corrupt. Hence the single-minded rule of Fascism is welcome for a time, because it will enforce law and order and put the country back on its feet again. I would have thought this is also the rationale of *your* appeal for public support, or, at any rate, it is *this* side of your appeal that might hoist the Communist Party to power or a share of power. Would you say there is truth in this argument?

Mussi No, there isn't.. If it *were* true, I would take my hat and leave the Party. I work for a party whose rationale rules out any analogy with Fascism. Italy, as everyone recognises, needs a new social order. My whole reason for working for the Party is to see that this new order comes about with the greatest possible liberty for all and the emancipation of the working class, and not through the *denial* of liberty and through dictatorship.

Urban I doubt whether Lenin would agree with you, though

Marx might. Lenin said freedom was a bourgeois prejudice. Would you describe yourself as a Leninist?

Mussi I would prefer to say I am a Marxist, but to that I would willingly add that I am also a Gramsciist and Togliattiist. I consider Leninism as a great historical achievement in a given situation but one that can be measured only against Russian reality. Then, I am perfectly willing to skip over Stalin and Stalinism—

Urban —which is cutting out half of Soviet history—

Mussi —Yes, it is.

Urban Do these views represent the official thinking of the Italian Communist Party?

Mussi Yes, they do. The points I am making were publicly made and discussed at our January 1977 conference on intellectual affairs, where Berlinguer strongly denounced recent examples of the denial of freedom—not only intellectual freedom—in Eastern Europe. Talking of the Italian crisis, he showed why economic austerity was a necessity, on account of both our grave internal situation and the pressure of the oil-producing countries. This austerity, however, was an opportunity (he said) for restructuring our institutions and reorganising Italian society on the basis of justice and equality. But a task of that magnitude could not be taken in hand by a single party without the danger of authoritarianism—

Urban —do you mean to say the Communist Party, with liberty and pluralism pinned to its mast, is yet afraid that in a critical situation the incubus of the past might reassert itself?

Mussi In a period of crisis such as the present one, any *one* party that attempted to fashion society after its own image would inevitably run the risk of imposing its own brand of policies to the exclusion of others. For example, the Christian Democrats have done so for many years.

Urban But what *you* are saying is that the Communist Party might, even against the judgment of its rational self, somehow slide into doing likewise.

Mussi There is the risk of repeating the performance—with the signs reversed—of the Christian Democrats who based their power on anti-Communist discrimination, not only at the level of government, but in every compartment of the life of Italian society, whether administrative, social or cultural. This produced a society of the Christian Democratic ideological stereotype, that is, a society based on the rule of cliques of personal and economic interest. Here we have one of the causes of Italy's present troubles. The Communist Party is entirely different from the Christian Democratic Party in that it does not stand for the interests of cliques of any kind. Nevertheless we know that crises are more easily overcome if we can call upon the cooperation of various parties and various political and social forces than if we have to shoulder the burden alone.

Urban   You seem to be apprehensive of the attitude of your own left wing.

Mussi   Not at all—

Urban   —what your left wing might do once you are in office?

Mussi   No. My concern is rather that a country as strongly polarised in its politics as Italy is today might, under pressure, split in two and enter a series of confrontations from which there would be no return. Remember that the situation in Italy is not one in which the political process works smoothly and the parties alternate in government. It is an abnormal state of affairs.

Urban   I'm not sure that I can recall any time when the situation in Italy was 'normal'.

Mussi   There you may be right—it is hard to recall one in the last 200 years.

Urban   I have heard it said in Rome, mainly of course by people who are not your Party's well-wishers, that now is the time to encourage the Communist Party to form a government, but single-handed: the mess in Italy being what it is, Communist rule would soon be discredited, for the Party could no more correct Italy's deeply-rooted troubles than could the Christian Democrats. I realise that your ambition is not to rule alone for the reasons you have stated. But if you are content with sharing power with a number of other parties, including the Christian Democrats, you run another risk, no less devastating—that of being compromised and defeated by your allies.

I am reminded of Mussolini's bitter comment in November 1943, shortly after the establishment of the Republic of Salò (and I have quoted this to Renzo de Felice): Italian Fascism, he said, had not been able to do justice to its original Socialist inspiration because the country had been ruled by a 'dyarchy'—the policies of the revolutionary Fascist élite had been frustrated by a collection of conservative forces shielded by the Monarchy. Italy, he argued had in fact been run by two governments, and the socialist essence of Fascism had been whittled away and finally defeated. Are you not concerned that a similar fate might overtake the Italian Communist Party if it joined a coalition government which it could obviously not fully control?

It seems to me the Communist Party would be heading for trouble whether it came to rule alone or as a partner in a coalition government. Would it therefore not be in the Party's best interest to return to a policy of robust opposition, waiting to fight under more auspicious conditions?

Mussi I should like to think you are offering disinterested advice. . . . There is undoubtedly some truth in what you say. We could, of course, stay in opposition, putting our stakes on an aggravation of the crisis, in fact adding to it in the expectation of winning votes and support through the sheer act of opposition.

But this might bring ruin to Italy just as surely as might any inclination on our part to listen to those siren voices that would like us to govern by ourselves. Berlinguer, in his concluding remarks to our January conference on intellectuals, quoted a passage from the *Communist Manifesto* in which Marx says there are times when the struggle between the working class and the bourgeoisie can only resolve itself in the ruin of both—at such moments in history a compromise must be struck. Ours in Italy is such a moment.

Urban I am not sure whether Moscow would agree with you on this point.

Mussi It would not—nor would it with many other things we are saying, but Moscow's views are *its* responsibility, not ours.

As to your second thesis: in 1943 Mussolini had to find a scapegoat for the failure of Fascism; shifting responsibility for the defeat of one's plans is a standard reaction in history. We are, of course, trying to foresee how effectively we could have our policies implemented as members of a coalition government, and the kind of negative possibilities you have mentioned have been carefully weighed by us. At the same time, it is clear to us that there are everywhere around us progressive and democratic forces with which we can work. Unlike Mussolini, we do not divide the world into two: the good which resides in the movement, and the evil vested in the establishment and Italian institutions. For example, the Church recently took an important initiative by calling a conference on evangelisation and the advancement of the human personality. Its attitude was not one of old-fashioned conservatism, but rather a willingness to engage in an open dialogue, with the emphasis on social change. Or consider the nature of the Italian Constitution, which was the joint effort of several parties and cannot be claimed as a symbol of victory by any one of them over the other parties. Yet this collegiate enterprise—this written result of a 'coalition'—has not led Italy down to ruin, and it is quite possible that we are on the eve of another phase in the continuing reinterpretation of the Constitution. In other words, coalitions, cooperation and compromise are on the cards, and we intend to make them work.

Urban Speaking again as the devil's advocate—how will the Moscow conservatives react to all this? My guess would be that you will be condemned, first as reformists and Social Democrats, and in the end as Fascists.

Mussi So be it. But remember, our concern is not exclusively with the reaction of the conservative forces in Moscow; we are just as much interested in what the progressive Communists will think and do.

Urban You are implying that there *are* such in the Soviet Union.

Mussi Clearly there are, and we strongly believe that the very existence of Eurocommunism will strengthen them and encourage them to change certain outworn, rigid attitudes and rectify various abuses in the Socialist countries.

Urban What is your evidence that such progressive forces do in fact exist in Moscow?

Mussi We think the 1968 Czechoslovak experience is evidence enough that the possibility of self-correction is a real one in Eastern Europe.

Urban I would hesitate to infer from the potential for reform in *Czechoslovakia* that a similar opening exists in the Soviet Union.

Mussi Moscow's violent reaction to the Czechoslovak road to democracy and liberalism was an expression of the fear that changes in Prague would release the pent-up desires for democracy throughout Eastern Europe.

Urban You are saying, to be quite precise, that Prague was suppressed by the conservatives in the Soviet establishment because they felt that there existed, in their *own ranks*, Prague-like seeds of discontent?

Mussi That is my point. Soviet society is habitually described as compact and monolithic. Up to a point this is still true, but it is also, and increasingly, true that Soviet society is opening up in different directions. And this is only to be expected when you consider that the Soviet Union is no longer a society of *muzhiks*, but one in which the working man's living standard, his level of education and his life-style have greatly changed for the better in the last 30 years. The ranks of the white collar workers, of the technical and non-technical intelligentsia have grown, and we in Italy have no doubt that the kind of intelligence that goes into the problem-solving activities of an advanced technological civilisation will not stop at the edges of the drawing-board but must, sooner or later, assert itself in every domain of life. In other words, it is bound to exert pressure for political liberalisation. The whole sense of our policy is to demonstrate that Socialism has within it the capacity to develop along a road different from the one it has taken in Russia, and I find it significant as well as gratifying that the signatories of Charter 77 have specifically referred to the example of the Italian Communist Party.

Urban   Lucio Lombardo Radice said in a recent interview in *La Stampa* that the time has come to go beyond the criticism of individual episodes and subject the East European variety of Socialism to a principled critique.

Mussi   This has to be done, and we have already begun to do so. After the invasion of Czechoslovakia, at the 12th Congress of our Party, Berlinguer made it clear that the time was ripe for the uninhibited application of the Marxist method of analysis to Socialism too. Also, in our recent criticisms of the suppression of dissent in the Soviet Union, Czechoslovakia, and Poland, we have plainly stated that the root of the problem was structural: it could not be understood or put right in terms of isolated episodes but only as part of the malaise of the entire party/state system. Certain articles published in *l'Unità* on this topic have given rise to lively discussion, and there are important Italian Communist intellectuals who support Charter 77 and other manifestations of dissent in Eastern Europe. And, as we are sitting in the editorial offices of *Rinascita*, I might as well add that I have myself written a leader for tomorrow's paper on this very question.

Urban   Could you summarise it for me in a nutshell?

Mussi   The article deals with intellectual liberty and the right of dissent, but the real point I am making is that intellectual freedom cannot be divorced from freedom *qua* freedom— freedom for everyone and without qualifications, that is to say, from democracy. Nor can one be satisfied with saying that a consensus exists, because such a consensus, whether imaginary or real, still implies the repression of dissent, not only of intellectuals, but of workers, women, young people, and, in fact, everyone who happens to fall outside some, usually arbitrary, definition of what the consensus is about. Still more important, I emphasise that the problem of democracy and freedom is not something that concerns only Communists, Italian-style, but Socialists and Communists wherever they may be.

Urban   A schismatic statement if there has ever been one, a Lutheran or Calvinistic challenge to Rome, with this theological difference—that on the question of the freedom of man's will Luther and Calvin paradoxically denied the freedom of the will, whereas Catholic teaching said it existed.

Mussi   Whether we are, in fact, offering this kind of a challenge has yet to be seen, but your analogy is not entirely inappropriate.

Urban   A higher stage of 'polycentrism' developing in the country and party in which the word was coined?

Mussi   Its roots go back much further than Togliatti, to whom you are obviously referring. Gramsci's *Prison Notebooks* already contain certain very unorthodox ideas which put him outside the ideological framework of the Third International. Between 1943 and 1945 Togliatti initiated the idea of an Italian road to Socialism and a new type of Communist party, followed, after the suppression of Hungary in 1956, by the notion of polycentrism. Therefore our autonomy and originality are not of recent origin. They go back to the inception of the Party.

Urban I am still not quite clear how the revolutionary mystique of Communism can be sustained if you discard Leninism as an accretion peculiar to the condition of Russia in 1917. If you eliminate Lenin's insistence that the pathfinders and vanguard of revolution are a conspiratorial élite united in a regimented party which *brings* revolution to the working class if the latter is too slow to recognise the ineluctable will of history—what, then, is left of the legitimacy of the Communist Party, any Communist Party? Marx, as we know, had no intention of forming a party— much less a one-party state—and he rejected the very idea of 'Marxism'.

But I don't suppose you *have* written off Leninism in your daily propaganda. This morning, as I was approaching your Party Headquarters from the direction of the Palazzo Venezia, what did I see but walls covered in Communist posters featuring a heroic Lenin surrounded by the Petrograd workers in the act of making revolution—

Mussi I'm sorry; you would not have seen Lenin on *our* posters. The posters you have seen are the work of extremist groups, not the Communist Party.

Urban It seems to me you are willing the ends of Socialism but you are not willing the means. Of the trinity Marxism— Leninism—Socialism, I would regard Leninism as the most important tool. Without it no Communist party has yet come to power or stayed in power.

Mussi I do not agree that the future development of Socialism has to be made legitimate by reference to the authority of the alleged fathers of Socialism. This is a mediaeval type of methodology which we reject. We are not churchmen; we do not appeal to the sacred texts. In any case, throughout modern history, including Socialist history, the initiators of political movements had no 'isms' attached to their names in their lifetime. The pedestals were built later. For example, the phenomenon to which we nowadays append the tag of 'Leninism' consists of an element taken from Lenin, but it also incorporates a great deal of Stalin. This is, from an objective historiographical point of view, a gross misinterpretation of Leninism. We have in Italy already made a start in trying to distinguish between Lenin the political philosopher, and Lenin the revolutionary leader. And in doing so we are shedding the ballast of religious ideology which has been built up around Lenin's personality and handed down to us.

Urban I have spoken to knowledgeable Italian liberal Communists and former Communists who strongly believe that you cannot demythologise Communism without destroying the movement. If you repudiate Leninism, Stalinism, Marxism and the dictatorship of the proletariat—what is left of Communism that could not be advanced with far fewer obstacles under some other name such as Social Democracy?

Mussi The history of a political movement is not like some luggage that you carry on your back if your situation so requires but abandon in a dark corner if you feel it has become a hindrance. The ideological development of a party is always a matter for revision—you lose or de-emphasise certain items but keep others.

Gramsci's case is a good and topical example. It is true that Gramsci thinks within the framework of Leninism—and what else could be expected of him given the historical environment he lived in? But Gramsci is at the same time a step ahead of Lenin. Many of his concepts cannot be found in Lenin. We must keep a sense of proportion and observe that, of the stock we have inherited, some parts have lent themselves to development, while others had to be written off. The ideological/political transformation of a political party is a long and complex affair. It is most certainly not decided at the conference table. Much rather is it a function of the twisting and turning processes of society.

Urban Wouldn't those who stand to lose most from Eurocommunism—the members of your *apparat* and your card-carrying supporters—*demand* that you stick to Leninism as ultimately the sole legitimation of the Party?

Mussi I do not see Leninism as the legitimation of the Party. The Chinese Party, too, is a Communist Party, yet its history is remarkably different from that of the Soviet Party. It would be very difficult to list it under the rubric of 'Leninism'. As far as our own cadres are concerned—these have been totally renewed in the last ten years. Some of the largest local Party Federations—for example those in Milan, Turin, Venice and Bologna—are now headed by very young men. The Party Secretary in Milan is 34, the Secretary in Florence is also 34, the Secretary in Venice is 31. Moreover, the members as well as the Secretaries of our largest and most influential Federations—those with more than 100,000 members—are 22, 25, 27 or 29 years old. I am myself only 28, and I am in charge of the cultural department of the Party weekly *Rinascita*. The Stalinist period and the Cold War are things I had to read about in books and hear about from older comrades. They do not impinge on my consciousness as a personal experience, therefore I do not feel bound by their rules.

Urban Do you feel the Italian road to Communism—Eurocommunism—is being offered as a universal alternative to the palaeo-Communism of Moscow? In the current Soviet view, Eurocommunism is an imperialist invention, which is the Soviet way of saying that it is only one step short of the betrayal of Communism; and I would infer from this Soviet attitude that a polemic may soon arise between Moscow and the Eurocommunists which may be every bit as bitter as is that between Moscow and Peking.

Mussi That Italian Communism is entirely different from the Soviet variety I can vouch for, but I cannot answer your main question because the process is far from being complete. So far the results of our policies have been positive but partial. If we can create a new type of democracy it will surely serve as an alternative, not only to the system existing in Eastern Europe, but to the capitalist variety of democracy as well. Of course we cannot hope to construct a society that would entirely run counter to both the American, the Soviet and the West German models. This would be too ambitious. Our aim must be to offer a type of Socialism that would, by its innovative appeal, command maximum acceptance and expose us to the least amount of attack. This is what we are trying to do.

Urban I can only re-emphasise my suspicion that your interpretation of Communism will strike—indeed has already struck—the Soviet leaders as highly insidious. Add to that Berlinguer's formula that your Party feels better protected behind the shield of NATO than outside it, and you have rendered yourself ripe for Moscow's anathema—unless, of course, Eurocommunism is a feint, in which case the Russians will patiently put up with your ideological fireworks as long as you and the French and the Spanish Communists can deliver the goods: Western Communist Parties in office.

Mussi I think we can dismiss your hypothesis that Eurocommunism is a diversion, but I would not dismiss the possibility, indeed the fact, of Moscow's hostility. But that is precisely why we fervently support the idea of peaceful coexistence.

Urban In the Soviet interpretation, however, peaceful coexistence applies only between states with different social systems. A Communist Italy might come under a different rule, as the Hungarians and Czechoslovaks well know.

Mussi Unfortunately the Soviet stance on peaceful coexistence also happens to be the American attitude to peaceful coexistence, certainly as it was interpreted by Henry Kissinger, for the Americans seem no more willing to permit any real measure of polycentrism on *their* side of the post-war demarcation line than the Russians are on theirs. What Berlinguer said about our position on this side of NATO was realistic. But I invite you to remember that he added to the statement you have quoted that while there may be people in Eastern Europe who do not want us to build Socialism in the Italian way, it is also true that there are people in the West who do not want us to build Socialism in any way at all.

Our purpose, to sum up, is to create understanding for a model of society which would cure, both in the East and in the West, many of the diseases of the late twentieth century without cutting into the vital interests either of the US or the Soviet Union, that is, without changing the balance of power as it has been left to us since the end of the second world war. To claim more would be foolish; to claim less would be renouncing our political entitlement.

Jean Elleinstein

4 'The Skein of History Unrolled Backwards'

Urban   Is there, in the year 1978, a world Communist movement to which French Communists still feel themselves to belong?

Elleinstein   No, there is no such thing as a world Communist movement, therefore we can owe no allegiance to something that does not exist. There are, or should be, independent Communist parties which maintain bilateral relations with one another. There can be absolutely no question of resuscitating some Communist International—much less of subordinating one party to another. It is our firm policy that every Communist party must be totally independent. The French Party enjoys such independence but, regrettably, not every Communist party does.

Urban   I would have thought that attending spectacular and secretive international gatherings, where policy and doctrine are enunciated with the solemnity of papal bulls, was not the most convincing way of telling a sceptical French public that the world Communist movement has ceased to exist.

Elleinstein   The conferences you have in mind are in reality meeting places for bilateral relations—no more. They provide the diplomatic context in which the French, Italian, Spanish and Soviet parties (to mention only some of the most important) meet and talk on the basis of complete equality.

Urban   At what point did the world Communist movement cease to exist?

Elleinstein   It ceased to exist some years ago, but the turning point came at the East Berlin conference of Communist parties, in June 1976, where Georges Marchais clearly stated that there would be no more gatherings of this type. One can, of course, envisage common research, common policies and common action on specific problems—unemployment, women's rights,

73

health care and the like—but these must not amount to a 'movement' nor must they give any impression of being one.

Urban But you would agree, wouldn't you, that a layman might be forgiven for thinking that people who work up to their international conferences with preparatory meetings of all kinds, stretching sometimes over a period of several years, get together when they eventually do because they *have* something of serious and common concern to discuss? Bilateral relations, I should imagine, could be settled with much less pain and expenditure of time and energy on a one-to-one basis than they can in the presence of batteries of delegates. But that would take away from the vestigial but nonetheless real universalism of Communism as it has been handed down to us through the Russian experience.

Elleinstein As far as the French Party is concerned, these meetings have not concerned themselves with working out common positions, much less have they resulted in common positions. Nor would it be desirable for such common policies to be attained. Each party must lead its own political life and construct its own policies taking into account the particular problems which require solution in its own environment. There is certainly no community of purpose between the French and the Soviet Parties. On the contrary, the French Party is currently engaged in looking at Marxism with a fresh eye and re-examining many of its tenets in the light of the problems which have arisen in France in our own time. I have myself, as a Marxist scholar and historian, just completed a study in which I strongly criticise Lenin's attitude to democracy in the last few months of his life. Why have I written this study? Because, despite enormous pressure on my time, I can see that the entire future of French and Western Communism is in the melting pot, and because I strongly believe that we now have a chance of building a type of Communism that will shed its inhibiting Russian heritage.

Urban The *punctum saliens* of the East Berlin meeting was the use or non-use of 'proletarian internationalism' in the final communiqué. The Yugoslavs were particularly anxious for the slogan to be dropped and—remembering the fate of Czechoslovakia— with very good reason. After a great many preparatory meetings, the phrase *was* dropped, but almost at once 'proletarian solidarity' was put in its place. Every time the Soviet leaders now want to emphasise the continuing validity of the 'Brezhnev doctrine', they simply press 'proletarian solidarity' into service and go on, in fact, asserting 'proletarian internationalism'. One may, of course, argue that this is a sign of the breakdown of the world Communist movement—rather than of its continuing existence. My point, however, is that large political parties do not go to a great deal of trouble in order to re-define an ideological formula unless they feel that they are making sacrifices for something they hold in common and which is worth defending.

Elleinstein We in the French Communist Party see no contradiction between internationalism, of which we approve, and the complete independence of every Communist party, on which we insist. And internationalism for us does not imply unconditional solidarity with the Soviet Union. We disagree with the Soviet Party on a great many points—human rights, the occupation of Czechoslovakia in 1968, the Soviet concept of democracy and others. To take an example that concerns me personally but is generally valid: much before the Soviet attack on Carrillo in June 1977, *Novoye Vremya* strongly criticised my own writings, in January 1977, apropos my book, *Le P C*.

Urban An extremely outspoken attack by Yuri Sedov—

Elleinstein Yes—and the target of the Soviet attack was the entire evolution of French Communist thinking. Sedov accused me, in brutally polemical language, of having frontally challenged Marxism-Leninism, of having abandoned the proletarian class approach, of being illiterate as a historian, insulting to internationalists, and a vilifier of revolutionary theory. He said that I was little better than certain 'reactionary hacks', 'dishing out' anti-Soviet fabrications about the violation of democratic freedoms in the Soviet Union and alleging that the 'Marxist-Leninist teaching is not acceptable to France.' 'Seeking at all costs to make it appear as if Leninism were no longer valid . . .', Sedov opined, 'Elleinstein goes to the outrageous lengths of making assertions totally unbefitting anyone calling himself a Communist.'

Urban Were the accusations (quite apart from the language) false or far-fetched? I notice that *l'Humanité*, in an unsigned article, came to your defence, at least to the extent of saying that the *tone* of the Soviet attack was unacceptable.

Elleinstein Sedov, of course, represents Soviet official thinking—no other thinking appears in the Soviet press. My views and my analysis of history—both Soviet and French—strongly diverge from that thinking, which is enough to explain my unpopularity in Moscow. What I did say in my book, and have expounded in countless articles and discussions, is (to put it very simply) that Leninism is inevitably the product of specific historical conditions in Russia at the beginning of the century—conditions which were, in some respects, barely ahead of those that had existed in Western Europe in the Middle Ages. Here was a rural, primitive society which had only tenuously emerged from serfdom, with no democratic traditions and no sense of indi-

vidual liberty, trying to hoist itself into the twentieth century and
directly into Socialism. At the time of the Civil War 70 per cent of
the Russian population was illiterate, tens of millions of beggars,
vagrants and abandoned children roamed the countryside, ban-
dits flourished and the country was short of 13.5 million people
who had perished as a result of the war, civil war, famine and
epidemics. As the distinguished French historian Aulard admitted (in his *l'Histoire des Soviets*) in 1922: 'the night was darker in
Russia in 1917 than in France in 1789.'

Clearly, the condition in which Soviet Socialism was born has
nothing in common with French conditions in the late 1970s or
with the type of Socialism we could or would want to instal here.
We cannot go on hiding behind Lenin's utterances against democracy in Russia's particular conditions in 1918 and 1919 in order to
justify the dictatorship of the proletariat in French conditions in
1978! The seizure of the Winter Palace and Mao's Long March
may appeal to the revolutionary imagination, but they have no
relevance to the needs and realities of French society. The transformation of France will be slow, peaceful and conducted
through the ballot box—not the barricades.

Of course, we must not commit the contrary mistake of judging
the 1917–1922 period—Russia and the Bolshevik revolution—by
our own historical experience and our own criteria. Lenin was a
man of enormous and relentless dedication and energy. He could
see that, until 1917, all revolutions had been defeated because
they had not been carried out to their logical conclusion. 'One
should not spare dictatorial methods', he said, 'in order to speed
up the implantation of Western ways in old, barbaric Russia, nor
flinch at using barbaric methods to fight barbarism.' This idea of
'Russian barbarism' occurs like a leitmotif in everything Lenin
wrote of the revolutionary process in Russia towards the end of
his life. But as soon as he analysed the chances of revolution in the
highly developed capitalist countries, he maintained that these
could proceed to Socialism in a civilised manner. All in all, however, it is true to say that dictatorial repression in the Soviet Union
began, and was given ideological justification, under Lenin and
not only with Stalin. It is this conclusion of mine, and of many
leading French Communists, that has caused special offence in
Moscow.

Urban To stick to your analysis of Soviet history for the
moment—you are not saying that Lenin should have given up
power rather than repress the class enemy and instal Socialism,
no matter how imperfect that Socialism may in fact have
been?

Elleinstein Not at all. The Socialist revolution had

triumphed, by a quirk of history, in a very poor and culturally backward country. As Trotsky once said: 'The skein of history unrolled backwards.' The Soviet Union was the only Socialist state and had either to move ahead or commit suicide. She chose to move forward. It was a historic choice and was not much in doubt.

Urban Suppose a French Communist/Socialist coalition was voted into power at the next French elections or the one after. Suppose further that this coalition fell apart on some controversial point of policy (not a very unlikely contingency) and the Socialists decided to walk out, ruining thereby the ascendancy of the entire French Left. Would the French Communists not argue, as you have just argued on behalf of the young Soviet state, that French Socialism would either have to move ahead or abdicate? And wouldn't the French Communists, in that case, see themselves constrained by the impetus of their entire heritage to consolidate their power, first without the Socialists, and then *against* the Socialists, by Leninist means of repression? Wouldn't then your rather civilised French variety of revolution nevertheless end up producing a one-party state?

Elleinstein Your supposition is not unreasonable, but the conclusions you imply are false. My point is precisely that, for a developed and sophisticated Western society such as the French, the Bolshevik revolution and Soviet society cannot serve as models. The historical and cultural basis of the two are incommensurate—and so are, and must be, their respective Socialisms, existing and future. The French Communists are perfectly prepared to abide by the rules of parliamentary democracy and relinquish the levers of power if they lose the confidence of the public.

The Soviet experiences stem from a set of complex and very Russian historical circumstances. Principal among them was the non-participation of the masses and the supremacy of a small minority which led to the dictatorial road to Socialism and eventually to a very Muscovite and totally un-Marxist phenomenon: the quasi-religious cult of the leader. Hence the great importance of the 22nd Congress of our Party which made it absolutely clear that the French road to Socialism must be democratic.

Urban I have no difficulty in agreeing with you that Russia left its fateful imprint on Socialism, and this I should imagine poses for you a most important question: can one expect Soviet society to become genuinely democratic and, more particularly, has Stalinism served as a vaccine against the despotism of future leaders? If we could say 'yes' to these questions, the West European Communist parties might have a better chance of fighting off the baneful heritage of the Soviet past which is their principal enemy.

Let me quickly say that what evidence we have from non-Communist sources points in the opposite direction. One perceptive observer of the Soviet scene, Hedrick Smith, shows in his recent book (*The Russians*) that a considerable part of the Soviet population hankers after the tough discipline of Stalinism: 'Today ... those who are nostalgic about the good old days under Stalin yearn most of all for his style of leadership. Time has dulled the memory of his awful malevolence.... As the leader who forged a modern state, who steeled a nation in wartime to emerge victorious, and then made the rest of the world tremble at Soviet might, Stalin embodies power.... This language of power is the language many Russians use when they recall Stalin, for they like a powerful leader. In their most admiring moments, Russians praise Stalin as the ... strong master. He held society together in his grip and they liked that feeling.'

Elleinstein   The Stalin phenomenon arose from the Bolshevik revolution and flourished in the period of Socialist construction. By educational and cultural development and expanding the economy, the Soviet historical experiment under Stalin made a contribution to ensuring that democracy would be achieved in the distant future. And when you think of the Stalin phenomenon during the war, what strikes one as extraordinary is that millions of Soviet men and women, who had been the victims of Stalinist terror, played a heroic part in the struggle of the Soviet people. Why had their loyalty not been destroyed? Why indeed had the Soviet Union not disintegrated under the combined blows of Stalin's rule and Nazi attack? Because the basis of the Soviet state was Socialist and in most respects independent from the policies of the men who ruled it.

Far be it from me to defend Stalinism or, for that matter, Lenin's brutal onslaught on liberty and democracy in 1918. We know very well that Lenin had little time for either: 'The proletariat cannot achieve victory,' Lenin said in his 1918 Theses, '*without breaking the resistance* of the bourgeoisie, *without forcibly suppressing its adversaries*, and ... where there is "forcible suppression", where there is no "freedom", *there is, of course, no democracy.*'

My point is that, in Russia in 1918, this may have been a necessary recipe because it responded to specific historical circumstances—but it has no relevance to the situation in France in the late 1970s. History offers no second helpings. Leninism and Stalinism can offer no guidelines for us.

Urban I respect the distance you have managed to put between yourself and the Soviet element in the Communist past. At the same time I feel a little uneasy about two of your utterances which have a direct bearing on the question in hand. In *The Stalin Phenomenon* you quote, with a sense of approval, one of Voltaire's celebrated quips about St Petersburg: 'Back in the eighteenth century, when people protested about the way in which Peter the Great had built St Petersburg—100,000 serfs died building it—Voltaire replied: "Yes, but the town does exist." ' The implication of what you say is that Stalin may have been a dreadful tyrant but he did give us something worth having.

In another place you describe, with I think great courage, an event in your life that not many people in your kind of position would care to admit today: 'On 5 March 1953, I was hiding in a small house in the southern suburbs of Paris a few steps away from the Seine. I remember that I cried for a long time when I heard the announcement of Stalin's death on the radio.'

The question that bothers me a little is this: wouldn't the residual Stalinism of even the most liberal French Eurocommunists eventually get the better of them in a critical situation of the kind I have tried to describe? Wouldn't they be willing to force their conscience a little if their choice was between Socialism and relapse into the hated bourgeois order?

Elleinstein To take your second point first: it is easy, after a quarter of a century, to arrive at a calm judgement of how Communists ought to have acted after the Second World War. But remember that we did not act in a vacuum. The political mentors of my generation of Communists, and indeed the leaders of all the world's Communist parties, had been trained by the Comintern. One of the twenty-one conditions of membership of the Comintern was the unconditional defence of the Soviet Union. The latter was the only Socialist state, therefore the world Communist movement got into the habit of considering everything coming from Moscow as gospel truth. For a long time, Russia was a 'besieged fortress'—a weak state which had to be defended because Nazi Germany or British or Japanese imperialism threatened to or did, in fact, attack it. It became impossible to make fine distinctions between Stalin and the Soviet state.

This was the conventional wisdom handed down to me as a young Communist. And, in fact, in the years following the war, I felt very strongly that I was taking part in a great movement for the victory of Socialism. The Cold War was at its height, and my own Stalinism consisted in believing that until the war the Soviet Union alone had sought and found new solutions to the world's social problems and then played a leading part in the defeat of Nazism.

I do not feel that I sacrificed my youth for an empty ideal. I simply had to learn from bitter experience. When the myth of Stalinism exploded, some Communists of my generation felt that they had been cruelly deceived and left the movement. I could not share their disillusionment—it seemed to me that it was possible to dissociate Stalinism from Socialism, and that is the task to which I have devoted myself as a Communist and a scholar. Undoubtedly, Stalinism has left wounds in our hearts.

Coming to your first point—Voltaire on St Petersburg—this is a tricky one. An historian should never dabble in the 'might have beens' of history—yet I would risk the judgement that in Russia's particular conditions *a* kind of 'Stalinism' was virtually unavoidable unless Socialism was to be abandoned. Was there Socialism in the Soviet Union at the time of the death of Stalin? My view is that Socialism did exist there in 1953, but it had assumed a face which, though it can be explained, cannot be justified.

Urban What about those millions of men and women— twelve million in your own estimate—who were incarcerated and executed in Stalin's camps? Was the St Petersburg *they* built worth building?

Elleinstein Stalin's use of forced labour and the barbarisms associated with the purges were scandalous indeed but, as Deutscher has shown, this factor was marginal to the system because forced labour, even under the worst years of Stalinism, represented a bare 10 per cent. of the industrial labour force.

From the Western Communist point of view, Stalinism is, of course, entirely unacceptable. Those aspects of Soviet Socialism which are worth defending are not its distortions, or the specific forms it happened to take under Russia's particular spatio-temporal conditions, but its basic rationality and its social and cultural benefits. To these I would add Soviet economic achievement only with many qualifications because, despite impressive industrial progress in many fields, Soviet agriculture, for example, had failed, at the time of Stalin's death, to reach the per capita output of Tsarist Russia in 1913. Worse, the *kolkhoz* and *sovkhoz* peasants were bound to the land in almost serf-like conditions under a strictly enforced internal passport system.

I would therefore conclude that, although Soviet Socialism cannot be a model for French Communists, we cannot deny that it is nevertheless the first and most significant Socialist experiment in history. However tragic Stalinism may have been, it remains limited in time and space. Its evil consequences inside and outside the Soviet Union should not be permitted to obscure the rich hope of Socialism. It is now up to us, Western Communists, to build Socialism—as Marx foresaw—on the basis of a developed capitalist economy and in a milieu of democracy and freedom.

Urban You are implying that the Soviet Union, too, has put Stalinism well behind it. You owe me an answer to Hedrick Smith's observation that the Russian willingness to embrace some form of Stalinism is a congenital disease of the Russian people. Is it? Is the Soviet system beyond the hope of early reform and therefore unlikely to remove the odium attaching to the Western Communist parties?

Elleinstein Let me put it this way—I would not say that the Soviet system will *not* so reform itself. At some points of its history the Soviet system came close to becoming a democratic Socialism, but every time this happened the burden of the Russian past—economic and cultural underdevelopment, existing structures and institutions—sank its chances of success. Even today, the dead hand of Russian history inhibits the development of Soviet Socialism. That is why there is in the Soviet Union no democratic opposition, no free press, no freedom of association, no freedom of assembly, no freedom of opinion. That is also why State and Party coincide, and the Party cannot be, as it should be, disestablished.

Our criticism of the Soviet type of Socialism is accordingly severe, and it is shared, for the same reasons, by the Italian and Spanish Communists. That is also why the French Communist Party cannot take its cue from Soviet Socialism—while at the same time it does take full account of its existence and influence.

Urban Let me try to tackle this problem from a different angle. You have described the failures, errors and crimes of Stalinism more thoroughly than any Communist I can think of. Would you still say that Soviet society represents a basically superior social order to the one which exists in Western Europe today?

Elleinstein We do not pose the question in that manner. We examine the state of Soviet society in relation to what Russian society was like before the October Revolution, and seen in that perspective, Soviet society is, with all its many shortcomings, an improvement on its Tsarist predecessor. But it is senseless to compare Soviet society and French society as they are today. I can tell you that *I* would not like to live in Soviet society, because it does not guarantee those public and personal freedoms which I, and many French Communists who think like me, absolutely take for granted. For us the Soviet system is neither an example nor a model. It is simply an experiment in conditions which have nothing to do with those I myself experience and have to work in.

One could discuss the question of whether or not the Soviet Union and its client states in Eastern Europe are Socialist countries in our definition of the term—but that is another problem.

Urban Are they?

Elleinstein I would say they represent a certain type of Socialism—I would hesitate to say that they are *not* Socialist. There have been, since the middle of the seventeenth century, radically different types of capitalism—I don't see why there should not arise radically different types of Socialism under different historical conditions.

Urban I take your point that the Soviet model holds few attractions for Eurocommunists. Might *Eurocommunism* serve as a model for Soviet and East European Communists? Writing in 1920 (*'Left-Wing' Communism—an Infantile Disorder*), Lenin observed: 'It would ...be a mistake to lose sight of the fact that after the victory of the proletarian revolution in at least one of the advanced countries things will in all probability take a sharp turn—Russia will soon cease to be a model country and once again become a backward country (in the "Soviet" and the socialist sense). . . . '

Here is grist to the mill of Eurocommunists—if, that is, they feel, as you say they do, that the entire future of the Communist movement depends on their ability to cure the practice of Communism of the Russian disease and re-Westernize it. But my suspicion is that it would be asking a little too much of Soviet nature to expect the Soviet comrades to accept the truth of Lenin's statement and to agree: 'Yes, we shall from now on have to learn our Socialism from French and Italian models.' A schism in the movement, as serious perhaps as the Sino-Soviet split, seems to me unavoidable.

Elleinstein That would depend on the Soviets rather than on the French and Italian Communists. We in France are solely concerned with the future of *French* Socialism. We do not claim to be putting up a model. It may be that our policies will eventually serve as a model, but if so, it will not be because we have been consciously working for one. Our field of action is limited to France—we will measure our defeats and successes only against the goals we have set ourselves in our particular circumstances.

Urban But the Soviet Communists are extremely sensitive to non-Soviet models—declared, implied or even suspected. They took exception to Yugoslavia, China, Czechoslovakia. . . .

Elleinstein Indeed they are sensitive—they cannot see beyond their own model, and this is the greatest obstacle to the development of Socialism today.

It is also the principal factor behind the Soviet Communists' conflict with China. I am myself in sympathy with the Chinese—not because I always approve of their internal policies (in some instances I do, in others I don't), but on the question of their independence from the Soviet Union and the Soviet Socialist model they are absolutely right.

Urban But the Chinese, in so far as they do offer an alternative model (which they arguably do to the Third World countries), have nothing to do with Lenin's prediction as China is, from the Marxist point of view, an even more backward country than Russia was in 1917. But a French or Italian Eurocommunist alternative *would* challenge the primacy of the Soviet model on the strength of Lenin's own prognostication—and surely *that* must be most unwelcome in Moscow.

Elleinstein This may well be so. I can only repeat that we are not setting out to challenge Soviet Socialism. If our policies make sense to the French electorate and they eventually decide to put us into office through the ballot box, and if we subsequently do manage to combine Socialism with freedom and democracy—well, everyone is then free to draw his conclusions.

Urban Let me probe into the credibility of this whole notion of Eurocommunism—'good'—versus Russo-Communism—'bad'. Your problem as a Eurocommunist and my problem as a non-Communist is that I associate, because I am a realist, any kind of Communism with the only variety that exists—Russo-Communism and its subvariants in Eastern Europe. And no matter how many allowances I make for the backwardness of Russia and the dead weight of Russia's illiberal traditions, I cannot get away from the fact that the Gulags, the Great Terror, and the repression and extermination of all opposition have been, and still are, part and parcel of that system. Indeed, many would say they *are* the system itself. Whether this view is completely right or wrong—the image of Communism is as surely tied, in the West European imagination, to these facts as Nazism is tied to Belsen and Auschwitz. Therefore Eurocommunism has, as you know much better than I do, a very hard row to hoe. My suspicion is that you will not be able to muster the confidence of Western electorates until and unless you can show us at least one example of a Socialist country, Soviet style, having been peacefully converted into a free and democratic Socialist system. What I am suggesting is that your way to power in Western Europe leads through the amount of influence you are able to exert on the Soviet Union and especially on its soft underbelly in Eastern Europe. *Can* you exert the requisite influence? I am certain that a free Socialist *Czechoslovakia* would do more to catch votes for the French Communist Party than anything you can do in your election campaigns.

Elleinstein   This is a difficult one. It is much easier for us in France to work for a democratic Socialism, French style, than to promote or engineer change in Czechoslovakia. Socialism in that country is a function of Soviet decisions, and there is nothing much we can do about *those*. We can, of course, exercise some influence by our example and our actions—and that is enough to get the Soviet leaders hot under the collar—but we have, as I say, no means of telling the Soviet government to get out of Czechoslovakia or to adopt a different policy vis-à-vis the Socialist countries in East/Central Europe which are, as we all know, neither free nor sovereign.

Mind you, we can and we do say all these things to the Soviet comrades, and that is what I myself do in my writings—but so far my outspokenness has only got me into trouble with the Russian Communists. They look upon me as a renegade and shower me with abuse.

It is perfectly true that we are gravely handicapped by the history and image of 'existing' Socialism. All we can do to counteract it is to work out another type of Socialism and go on examining and criticising the Soviet model. The two hang together, and it seems to me that the combination of the two should make it possible for us to overcome the heritage of the Russo-Communist past. The Italian Party, which started doing all this much earlier than we did, commands some 34 per cent of the vote and is on the verge of sharing government responsibility.

Urban   You warn us in your books to be realists. Could you fault the French and Italian public if they summarised their thoughts on Eurocommunism in this fashion: The horrors of 'Socialism' are said to be due to the peculiarities of Russia; what is claimed to be good in 'Socialism' has yet to be shown to exist. The guilt of 'Socialism' is a reality—the good of 'Socialism' a mere promise. Therefore we can take no risks on behalf of 'Socialism'.

Elleinstein   This is certainly a great problem for us. But my reply as an historian is that it is intellectually untenable to argue that because something has so far not occurred in history it is destined not to happen in the future either. Suppose someone had stood up before the American Revolution and said that, because there had been no precedent for a successful colonial uprising, it was absurd to imagine that one could take place in America and lay the foundations of one of the world's greatest states. No—the future is open.

I think I need not repeat to you that I do not subscribe to the ideas governing Soviet Socialism; yet I don't see why, using different methods against a different background, we should not arrive at different but nevertheless Socialist results. Of course, one can have doubts, because one is breaking fresh ground. But in history everything that is new is put in question. Lenin himself, when he started the October Revolution, was severely criticised because what he was doing was not only un-Marxist but arguably anti-Marxist. He was a revisionist in relation to Marx; what we are doing is in the same tradition—it is revisionist, if you like, in relation to Marx and Lenin. If my writings have any merit, I would like to think it is this—that I clearly recognise our departure from received ideas and insist that what we are doing is legitimate.

Urban Suppose a latter-day spokesman of the proto-Fascist *Action Française* or of the *Croix de Feu*—a Charles Maurras, or a Colonel de la Rocque, or a Jacques Doriot—turned up among the restive students of the Sorbonne and addressed himself to the pressing problems of France in this manner: 'Hitler, with his Germanic barbarism, distorted the promise of a genuine French Fascism. We, civilised Frenchmen, would know how to combine the true values of Fascism—rootedness, energy, nationalism— with liberty and social justice.' Would you trust him? Would the French public trust him—remembering Dachau and Oradour? Yet such is the confidence you hope to win from the French public. You must surely have your own doubts whether Frenchmen of common sense could be expected to advance it to you.

Elleinstein Ah, but your analogy with Fascism is completely false—although frequently made! It is in the very nature of Fascism that it *must* lead to anti-semitism, intolerance, thuggery and concentration camps. There *cannot* be a 'good' Fascism.

What has happened to Marxism in Russian hands (and here I must repeat myself) was a deviation from Marx's thinking and, in extreme cases, a denial and repudiation of Marxism. But no one can say that Socialism is, like Fascism and Nazism, an evil doctrine in principle. Your comparison has a certain plausibility in the formal sense—and I say so in my books—because concentration camps are concentration camps whether they are in Auschwitz or Kolyma. It would be preposterous to say that a Nazi camp is a bad one while a Soviet camp has for some reason to be considered as a smaller evil. They are both evil— and so were the camps erected by the Americans in Vietnam and the French in Algeria.

But we must never forget that Nazism was an ideological and political form of modern capitalism, whereas Stalinism arose, in

Russia's particular conditions, from the Socialist revolution and flourished in the period of Socialist construction. Stalinism was and is no more the only form in which Socialism can exist than Nazism was and is the only form in which capitalism can exist— and I spell this out in *The Stalin Phenomenon* in some detail.

Urban I'm not quite reassured. You are implying, are you not, that the Gulags and the other horrors of Soviet history were a great wrong? Yet, side by side with every condemnation of Stalinism in your books we find some passage that seems to be saying 'Ah, but the sacrifices were, in the last analysis, made in a good cause!'

For example, after recounting the deportation and slaughter of millions in the Great Terror you observe (in *The Stalin Phenomenon*): 'Of the 1,827 delegates at the 18th Congress, only thirty-five had survived from the 17th Congress (about 2 per cent). At the same time, the Soviet economy had undergone an impressive transformation. A new society had been born. Illiteracy had been reduced.... Culture was widely spread among the masses.... The Stalin phenomenon had appeared and flourished in the soil of socialism....'

I cannot quite see how one can speak of the flourishing of 'culture' and praise the reduction of illiteracy when there was hardly a family in the whole length and breadth of the Soviet Union which had not lost a father or son or brother to Stalin's savagery. Can 'culture' flourish between the hangman and his victim? Can 'Socialism'? Aren't you, in effect, saying the sort of thing we have often heard said of Nazi Germany: 'Hitler's may have been a most objectionable régime, but he put an end to German unemployment, covered the country in *Autobahns* and restored the German people's self-confidence'?

And what is one to make of your claim that Nazism was a form of modern capitalism—a distortion, perhaps, of liberal parliamentary democracy, but basically the same kind of system Chamberlain was presiding over in London and Roosevelt in Washington? If that *were* true, then it might follow that Eurocommunism would be as different from the Soviet variety as British capitalism was different from Hitler's. But *is* it?

Elleinstein The comparisons you make have a great deal of force and I have repeatedly analysed them. Hannah Arendt held similar views, mistakenly, as I think, and I have tried to answer them. I dare say our search for a full answer is incomplete, and I hope that, as our thinking and research deepen, more profound answers may emerge.

I do not want to sound condescending when I say that to perceive analogies between Nazism and Socialism is typical of people who lack a certain intellectual imagination. We used to be asked at school: 'Which is the heavier, a kilo of lead or a kilo of feathers?' The answer is of course obvious—one is a kilo and the other is a kilo, yet lead is very different from feathers and is put to a very different use from feathers.

The goals pursued by Nazism and Stalinism were entirely different because the class content of the two was different. Both came into being as a result of a specific national and cultural history, and specific national thinkers and individuals—one Russian and the other German. But while Socialism is in principle internationalist, progressive and benign, Nazism is, in principle as well as in its practice, none of these. The massive evils of Nazism flowed naturally from the massive evil of the whole Nazi *Weltanschauung*—the evils of Stalinism, on the other hand, ran *counter* to the humanism of Marx's thinking and failed, in the last analysis, to stultify the progress of Socialism, although they distorted, decelerated and corrupted it, sometimes to the point of extinction.

The illustrations one could quote are legion. There were men like General Gorbatov, who had, in the 1930s, been arrested, deported and tortured. But after his release in 1940, Gorbatov fought most heroically right up to the river Elbe in 1945 as commander of an Army Corps under the same Stalin who was responsible for his sufferings. I have no doubt that this man fought for his fatherland and Socialism—not Stalin; he fought because he could see that the Soviet state was basically Socialist and because he could distinguish between Socialism and the men who were then in power. And this at a time when in occupied capitalist France former government ministers, admirals, generals, civil servants and a large part of the bourgeoisie happily collaborated with the Nazis. There was surely something the Russians had reason to fight for and the French didn't.

As to your point about culture in the shadow of the executioner: it is, of course, true that Socialism emerged damaged from Stalinism, but it had not been strangled. Paradoxically, it continued to make progress, and the most visible aspect of this progress was in the cultural field. I did not, of course, mean to refer to 'high culture' in the passage you have quoted—*that* could clearly not flourish under the Damocles' sword of bloody purges—but in the Asian republics, for example, new literatures were born and old ones revived; women threw off the veil; the study of national languages increased and educational institutions from primary schools to universities spread to the entire territory of the Soviet Union. This was certainly an odd phenomenon because it coincided with the omnipotence of the

MVD, violations of legality, and the rigorous imposition of Russification and centralism. Yet it did happen, and the historian's job is to record the facts as he sees them. Of course, one would have wished that Soviet culture had progressed under different conditions—but for the historian this is a theoretical question. Things happened the way they did. We can deplore the course of history but we cannot change it.

Urban We have now seen how the French Communists would like to be seen by the French electorate. How, in fact, is the French electorate likely to see the French Communists? What are the chances that the ordinary voter will take no account of the fact that the French Party has been rabidly Stalinist and Moscow-centric for almost the whole of its history—that in 1976 the dictatorship of the proletariat was unanimously voted out of existence by the same 1,700 votes that had been cast for it, year after year, also unanimously? Aren't these also hard facts of history which an historian may deplore but cannot change?

Elleinstein There has been, since 1975, fundamental change in the French Communist Party. Not everyone in France believes this change to be genuine, but many do. I am myself convinced that the coming years will see even more significant changes, so that the credibility of this reformed type of French Communism will greatly increase. The 22nd Congress of our Party, at which the dictatorship of the proletariat was voted out of the Party programme, was a turning point in our entire orientation. Inevitably, there is a time-lag between decision and execution. It is not true that the vote on removing the dictatorship of the proletariat from our programme was a mere formality. Extensive discussions had preceded it and some of the debate continues. Our task now is to re-work the whole concept of the state, power and revolution. This is what I am engaged in doing, and, as you know, I am developing the idea that, contrary to the Leninist conception of revolution, revolution in the West European countries, and especially in France, can only be peaceful, democratic, legal and gradual.

Urban Do you represent the thinking of the Party leadership in this matter?

Elleinstein When *l'Humanité* reviewed my *Open Letter* to the French public on the Common (Socialist/Communist) Programme (of 1978), it quoted my concept of revolution—the one I have just given you—with approval.

Urban Do Marchais and Kanapa support it?

Elleinstein You'd better ask them! I think they do—I can interpret *l'Humanité*'s attitude in no other way.

Let me add that the doubts which persist in some sections of the French public can be well understood. Even many French Communists are not fully convinced that the Party has changed tack. A reform as thorough as the one that is now being put into effect cuts across decades of ingrained thinking—three years have not been enough to change it. After all, by dropping the doctrine of the dictatorship of the proletariat we are in fact repudiating one of Lenin's basic propositions which the founding congress of the Comintern adopted in 1919 at Lenin's personal behest. What we in France are saying today about the democratic way to Socialism is undoubtedly contrary to Lenin's programme. It is, therefore, quite natural that the French Communists should have difficulty in understanding and assimilating so drastic a change. This goes equally for French opinion as a whole and *a fortiori* for British and American public opinion—the latter has always had a habit of identifying Soviet Communism *tout court* with Communism elsewhere in the world. Sooner or later it will become clear that we are hammering out an entirely *new* type of Communism—

Urban —which the Soviet Communists will like even less than the Eurocommunism they *know* and, as you have shown, dislike heartily enough.

Elleinstein That is their problem! It is for us, not the Soviet comrades, to decide whether Lenin's theses, which may have been relevant to Russian conditions in 1918 or 1919, are relevant to French conditions in 1978. We think they are not. France and Italy in 1978 have nothing in common with Germany in 1848, Russia in 1917 or China in 1949. If we look at the history of Socialism in the West more closely we see that revolution there has been a failure over the last hundred and fifty years. There was a kind of Socialism lasting a hundred days in the Paris Commune of 1871; there was a partial German revolution of sorts in 1919 lasting two hundred days, and a variant, of similarly short duration, under Bela Kun in Hungary. That is all. For a hundred and fifty years we have been chasing after a revolution that will just not happen. This has made us reconsider the whole idea of revolution in the West, and the only answer we can come up with is to say that 'revolution' must be redefined on the lines I have just indicated.

Urban But you would go on calling your variant a revolution?

Elleinstein Certainly, but it will be a civilised revolution—a revolution without violence. It will consist of a series of reforms which will modify economic conditions, social relations and transform people's consciousness—a cultural revolution, French

style. Some of this is already taking place, more or less spontaneously, under the technological and social pressures of the existing
French social and economic system. It will accelerate in the
framework of a free and democratic Socialism.

Urban   Where, then, will lie the difference between Social
Democracy and French 'Socialism'?

Elleinstein   The Socialists and Social Democrats, in France
and elsewhere, have been generally content to leave the fabric of
society unchanged. Their reforms were functional and
utilitarian—we, on the other hand, are attempting to steer a
course between the luke-warm reformism of Social Democracy
and the traditional policies of Communism. And therein lies our
difficulty. Our passage is uncharted and we are bound to run into
objections of the kind you have just raised, namely that Socialism
has always led to one disaster or another, Gulags and so forth.
And, as you know, I understand these objections. Yet, at the end
of the day, we are still faced with the necessity of putting our
shoulders to the wheel and pushing the cart of Socialism in a new
direction.

Urban   Wouldn't the internal democratisation of the French
Party be the most convincing evidence that the Party has
genuinely shed its Stalinist past?

Elleinstein   It is necessary and possible to improve the Party's
internal organisation. But, again, we must remember that we
have, as a Party, a certain past, certain habits and traditions
which cannot be overcome by the stroke of a pen. Great institutions, whether they are the Communist Party or the Catholic
Church, are always difficult to reform. But even if we succeeded
in putting through internal reforms with great speed, I don't
think that would suffice to persuade international or French
opinion that the Party *has* shed its past. Our heritage is such that
we will not shake it off easily. The Italian Communist Party had
the courage of tackling the problem of Stalinism much earlier
than we did—in 1956, in Togliatti's articles—and this has enabled
it to move ahead much faster than we have done. We must admit
that Thorez was, in the matter of Stalinism, quite wrong and
Togliatti was right, and I say so in my latest book.

Urban   You are, then, advocating an entirely free and democratic discussion inside the Party, with minorities fully able to
dispute majority decisions and stick to their views?

Elleinstein   Different points of view will certainly be put forward if the Party's internal life is democratised. This is already
happening, as witnessed for example by the differences between
Althusser and myself, and more is undoubtedly to come. But I
don't want to be misunderstood here: I am *not* saying that democ-

ratisation will, or should, result in the creation of majorities and minorities. What I am saying is that the present scope of debate will and should be broadened, that conflicting ideas should be expressed publicly and more clearly. But this does not mean that I would want to renounce democratic centralism. I want to see democratic centralism made more democratic.

Urban But isn't 'democratic centralism' the very source of the dictatorial system which grew up in the Soviet Party and was dutifully imitated by the rest of the world Communist movement?

Elleinstein We must conserve certain rules of centralism. It would be dangerous to introduce and formally legalise splinter groups and minorities, because these would divide the Party and impede decisive action. Such has been the experience of several French political parties, and we don't want to repeat their mistakes. We must, therefore, find a balance between greater internal democracy and effectiveness of action. This ought not to discourage public confidence—after all, we are not talking about rules for the organisation of *society*; we are talking about the reorganisation of the *internal* life of the Party. As far as society as a whole is concerned, we are, as I have said, for a plural society, that is to say, a democratic, multi-party system.

Urban You would, then, on the vital issue of minority opinion within the Communist Party, not go beyond the 1968 Draft Statutes of the Czechoslovak Party which had also made provision for the minority's right to formulate its views and have them recorded and periodically reassessed—but strictly under 'democratic centralism'; that is, the majority view was still binding and group activity was forbidden. And as the Czechoslovak Party, even in its much reformed state, was still *the* Party in a single-party state, the parallel is not reassuring.

Elleinstein Well, the 1968 Czechoslovak Draft Statutes, which were, or course, never put into action because the Soviet-led occupation forestalled the Extraordinary 14th Party Congress, was not a bad document. If you consider that it was the work of a Party which had to act within the political constraints of the Warsaw Pact, its liberalising provisions were remarkable. It foresaw a secret ballot for all elections to party organs; a time limit on holding office; a curb on the power of party functionaries and a rotation of party jobs; strict delimitation of Party from State; the right of members to leave the Party, and so forth. These may not strike *us* as being radical, but they were radical enough to get Moscow worried and to induce it to invade the country. Naturally, our reforms would be quite different and go much beyond what the Czechoslovaks thought they could get away with.

· **Urban** Would your conception of a plural society provide for a smooth rotation of political parties?

Elleinstein Yes, it would. I have just published an article on the need of rotation (in the journal *Le Pouvoir*).

Urban In other words, if you lost support in the National Assembly, you would resign and submit yourselves to the verdict of the electorate?

Elleinstein You are embroidering on an earlier question and I will repeat an earlier answer: Yes, we would resign. Better the risks of democracy than the tragedy of dictatorship—Left or Right!

Urban Why, then, did Marchais offer the East/Central European 'People's Democracies' as models of a multi-party system?

Elleinstein Marchais made that statement five or six years ago—he would not say so today.

Urban But you can understand, can't you, why the Frenchman in the street is a little confused about the precise intentions of your Party?

Elleinstein Certainly—but the French Communist Party is now firmly committed to a multi-party system—

Urban —which is, if we go back to Marx, not all that surprising as Marx never envisaged a Marxist party, much less a one-party state. How do you see the relationship between the Communist Party and the state?

Elleinstein The Party—all political parties—must be independent from the state. This is a necessary condition of democracy. An *established* party would be as grotesque and insufferable in France as an established Church. *We want democracy more than we want Socialism*. We want, to be more precise, *our* kind of democracy—a political democracy with all those public and private liberties which we have discussed in this conversation. And here lies the problem facing the Soviet Union, the East/Central European Socialist countries, China, Cuba and Vietnam. But while these countries can to some extent excuse themselves by claiming that, with the single exception of Czechoslovakia, they missed out the bourgeois revolution and are consequently lacking in libertarian traditions, no West European country can offer such an alibi. Hence West European Socialism must be an entirely free type of Socialism, or else there will be no West European Socialism at all.

Urban You stuck a pin into me when you said that your democratic reforms would 'transform people's consciousness.' One of the give-away signs of incipient totalitarianism is the ambition to change the nature of man. We could both produce dozens of quotations from early Socialist thinkers to Lenin and

Stalin to demonstrate that revolutionary fanatics are seldom content with regulating what people can do, but that they also want to control what people *are*. And this is extremely dangerous, for if you are obsessed by the idea that human nature is open to improvement by social and cultural engineering, then there is no indignity and no cruelty you cannot inflict, with an absolutely clear conscience, on individual men and women in the name of bettering mankind. How, then, are we to understand your suggestion for the 'transformation of people's consciousness'?

Elleinstein This is a complex problem. We envisage important changes—not so much in human nature as in human *behaviour*, but even that will be a long time in coming, and we are persuaded that it must not be promoted by violence, direct or indirect—not even moral, political or ideological pressure. Change as a result of a long evolutionary process is all we can aim for. The fundamental error of the Bolsheviks was to assume that one could modify consciousness instantly, by repression. That, of course, is a Stalinist Utopia. In his last writings Lenin himself stated repeatedly that it would take generations to transform the thinking and culture of the Russian people. He was too right.

Urban I am often inclined to think (and you may find this rather shocking) that Stalinism had a perverse appropriateness about it, because it demonstrated with exceptional clarity that the Stalinist/Leninist variety of 'Socialism' was so contrary to human nature that it *had* to rely on the firing squad and the Gulags as its *sui generis* method of government. So great a wrong could not be put into effect with any but the most evil means.

Elleinstein Yes, Stalin is remembered for his famous dictum at Lenin's funeral: 'We Communists are people of a special mould. We are made of special stuff.' It was bad enough that he believed this; it was worse that he wanted to mould others after *his* Communist model. All this was terribly Russian, with a modicum of Utopian Socialism to underpin it.

Urban Pascal said religion must be 'contrary to nature, to common sense, and to pleasure'. Isn't the whole business of Soviet 'Socialism' a religious type of construct in Pascal's sense?

Elleinstein Not the *whole* of Soviet Socialism. I think your joke should be on Stalinism alone. That is, alas, a large enough chunk of Soviet thinking and history.

Urban All that remains for me to do now is to ask you about the likely behaviour of a reformed French Communist Party in an international crisis. Let me put it to you, as I put it to Lucio Lombardo Radice, that in a warlike East-West emergency the

French Communist Party, if it found itself in office, would have to make a quick decision whether or not to come down on the NATO side of the fence, or possibly remain neutral, which would itself be a declaration of hostility to the Western alliance.

Elleinstein   This is an unrealistic hypothesis. The situation in the world today is firmly based on détente. The conditions for war between the Soviet Union and the United States do not exist, therefore for me the question of a warlike emergency does not arise. Moreover, my hope for a new Socialism of the type I was defining a moment ago is in good part based on the fact that détente is here to stay. Of course, East-West relations could be a lot better than they are, but, compared to what they were even ten years ago, they are, all things considered, not without promise.

I don't think we are committing the mistake (or misjudgement) which Jaurès committed before the First World War, of thinking that war could be avoided by the solidarity of the international proletariat. Jaurès did not foresee that war was coming and therefore his generous aspiration for the peaceful evolution of Socialism could not be fulfilled. Today, under conditions of peaceful co-existence, Jaurès' hopes, which are also ours, have a good chance of being translated into reality.

If a crisis between the East and the West should nevertheless arise, we would have to examine our position in the light of circumstances—one cannot take up advance positions in principle. But, as I say, your scenario is, happily, so unlikely to materialise that I am inclined to dismiss it, though I understand well enough your reasons for confronting me with it as you have done.

Urban   But surely we cannot exclude the possibility that a serious crisis *might* arise between Russia and the West (a) over the Middle East, (b) over Soviet expansion in Africa, (c) as a result of a succession crisis in the Soviet leadership, (d) over the eruption of discontent over one issue or another in Poland or East Germany, and it is quite possible that some of these, and others I have not listed, might coincide and indeed feed on one another. If so, peaceful co-existence would, at the very least, come under serious strain.

Elleinstein   I don't believe any of these factors would ultimately make much difference to peaceful co-existence. The world situation is based on the balance of power which is unalterable, certainly as far as Europe is concerned.

If there *was* serious tension between Russia and the West, I don't think we in the French Communist Party would necessarily embrace Soviet policies if those were warlike policies. But I don't see why the Soviet Union should pursue warlike policies in present conditions.

Urban But quite conceivably it might—indeed it did in Angola and does in Ethiopia.

But to return to Europe: How would the French Communists act, assuming they were in office, if the balance of power came under strain as the result of a Polish uprising or a Polish Communist reform movement?

Elleinstein The United States has turned human rights into an important instrument of its policies. I am basically in agreement on this point with Carter—he is right and Brezhnev is entirely wrong. No doubt Carter would be well advised to take a greater interest in the condition of human rights in those countries in which the United States has special influence—but I do not want to labour this point: fundamentally I agree with Carter that human rights, that is individual rights, should be scrupulously respected everywhere and at all times. Having said that— will Carter go to war with the Soviet Union to make *it* respect human rights? I would no longer support him if he did. If the Americans waged war on the Soviets on this score, I would suggest that France remain neutral. But, as I say, this is an impossible hypothesis. The hypothesis one *can* adopt is that East-West relations will, thank God, remain as they are and will probably get better.

Now if there were trouble in Poland, I'm convinced that the United States would do nothing that would amount to intervention, as she also refused to act in the cases of Czechoslovakia and Hungary. Let us imagine that the French Left had been in power at the time of the 1968 Prague crisis. We would have condemned the occupation of Czechoslovakia—vigorously, publicly, in the United Nations and in France— but would we have gone to war with Russia? Certainly not, no more than did the United States. If the Left were in office in France tomorrow and events of this kind occurred in Poland or anywhere else in Eastern Europe, we would criticise the Soviet Union with as much vigour as we criticise the United States when *it* carries out policies of intervention in a number of areas—but we would go no further.

Urban You are saying, if I understand you correctly, that the triumph of 'Socialism' in France and Italy presupposes the continuation of détente. Let me put it to you that the Soviet Union does not *want* to see you and the Italian Communists in office, not only because you are doctrinally divisive, but precisely because French and Italian Communists in power would *end* détente: the Soviet leaders realise that Communists in power in Western Europe would so upset the West's internal status quo and the

Atlantic Alliance, and so discourage American public opinion,
that the whole fabric of peaceful co-existence would at once come
apart and Soviet 'Socialism' would cease to be subsidised, and
indeed bailed out from its periodic economic crises, by Western
trade and investment. Détente requires, if my argument is correct, that the Soviet Union does nothing to help you—its interest
is, in fact, to keep you out of power though, for obvious reasons,
it cannot say so.

Elleinstein   You would alarm me if the future of Socialism in
France and Italy depended on the will of either the Soviet Union
or the United States. But is doesn't—it depends on the will of the
French and Italian electorates. If the Soviet Union is really
opposed to our rise to power, I wish it would say so loud and
clear. It would help us enormously!

Renzo de Felice

5 Varieties of Fascism

Urban Your scholarly work on the roots of Italian Fascism and the life and time of Mussolini have placed you at the centre of a national controversy in which Giorgio Amendola of the Communist Party, Leo Valiani of *Il Corriere della Sera*, Rosario Romeo of Rome University, and many others, both on the Left and the Right, have felt it necessary to cross swords and take up positions—positions, I might add, that tell us as much about the state of Italian politics in 1977 as they do about the origins of Fascism. Before going into the details of this debate, would you summarise your findings?

de Felice My first conclusion is a very general one: although common denominators certainly exist between various right-wing movements which have, wrongly as I see it, come to be labelled as 'fascisms', the national characteristics separating one from the other are more important than those which, for example, the Italian, French, German and English 'fascisms' have in common.

My second conclusion is that we must, when speaking of Fascism with any claim to accuracy, limit the concept to 'historical Fascism', i.e. the Fascism that existed between the two world wars, mainly in Europe, and specifically in Central and Western Europe. I don't think certain right-wing phenomena of a later period and in other parts of the world, for example, the first Peron régime in the Argentine, can be explained in terms of a Fascist model. Even less do I share the thesis (seriously entertained by certain scholars) that the régimes currently in existence in a number of third-world countries are 'Fascist' régimes.

It is equally misleading to subsume under Fascism the so-called neo-fascist movements in Italy and France; these are closer to Nazism than Fascism. For example, the Italian MSI (Italian Social

97

Movement)—the only sizable political association in any country that openly calls itself 'fascist'—consists of two sharply different sections. One is strongly neo-Nazi and has spawned movements such as the *Ordine Nuovo* and other terrorist groups, and the second conceives of itself as a party of traditional right-wing conservatism. There are, in effect, two parties in the MSI.

My third conclusion is: historical Fascism was essentially a lower-middle-class and middle-class phenomenon, and on this point I am in agreement with most scholars who have written on the subject; but whereas the majority of historians claim that Fascism was the response of these classes to the threat of proletarianisation and extinction, my conclusion is rather different. While it is true that certain sections of the lower-middle class and middle class did turn to Fascism because they found themselves in an economic and social crisis, the majority of Fascist support came, not from these people, but from the ascending middle class, i.e. the new bourgeoisie that had been forming before and during the first world war. This class constituted numerically the most important and the most dynamic element of the Fascist movement. In other words, Italian Fascism was not an expression of the *decline*, but of the *rise* of the bourgeoisie—a bourgeoisie that had already carved out for itself a significant social role and was trying to match it with a corresponding political influence. In this, Fascism differs significantly from Nazism. At the time of Hitler's gradual rise to power—in 1930, '31, '32—the German petty bourgeoisie is in profound crisis as a consequence of the 1929 depression. By contrast, the Italian bourgeoisie, which brings Fascism to power in 1919–1922, is for the most part a rising class.

A fourth conclusion may be summarised as follows: there is a radical difference between the authoritarianism exercised by the Italian Fascist régime, and all preceding authoritarianisms. Classical authoritarianism always sought to weaken or directly to suppress the masses and to re-establish a pre-existing social order.

Fascism on the other hand tried, even if demagogically and instrumentally, to activate the masses and attain its objectives through participation and consensus.

Urban   A point well recognised by Togliatti in his 1935 Moscow lectures and turned to good account after his return to Italy in 1944. *He* knew that Fascism had mass support, and that the Party would somehow have to justify this in theory and build on it in practice.

de Felice   This is so. A fifth and less general, but none the less significant, conclusion concerns the character of Mussolini's alliance with Nazi Germany. My long work on the political biography of Mussolini leads me to infer that Italy's entry into the war on the side of Hitler was not, as has been often maintained, due to any ideological affinity between the two régimes. The truth is that, almost to the day before Italy's entry, Mussolini was hesitant whether to come out on the side of Germany or against Germany. Mussolini's personal character and the whole tenor of his politics precluded neutrality; he was keen to be in the fight. Standing aside for him was a sign of degeneracy. When he did enter the war on Hitler's side, it was only because he misread the impending fall of France for the general victory of Germany, and was anxious to be on the side of the victor.

Urban Nevertheless, once his early diplomatic efforts to end the war had failed, Mussolini's main inclination was to fight France and England, not only because (as he put it to Ciano in January 1940) France and England 'have lost the victory', but because he had a deep contempt for the spineless and unpredictable ways of democracy with which one could not deal seriously. Germany was a different matter.

de Felice This is true, but the point I would emphasise is that there was no ideological solidarity. On the contrary, there was a great deal of suspicion, if not hostility, of a nationalistic nature; and there was a feeling on Mussolini's part of being slighted and ignored by a powerful and enormously self-confident Germany. I do not, of course, mean to say that there weren't factions in the Italian Fascist Party that decidedly supported an ideological alliance with Hitler's Germany in order to reinforce Fascism, and indeed to imbue it again with a sense of revolution, for the Fascist régime was widely accused by these people of having become far too bourgeois, anaemic and moderate.

Urban Let me pick up this sense of radicalism and jump as far ahead as the closing months of Fascism under the Republic of Salò. Here, in a twilight 'state' created with Hitler's support, Mussolini attempted to return to the revolutionary radicalism of the early Fascist movement, and succeeded in attracting a number of prominent anti-Fascists and even Communists. It is not always realised how far this went. There were voices raised in admiration of Stalin and the Soviet war-effort, with an emphasis on the common destiny of the Bolshevik and Fascist revolutions. Here, for example, is what one of Mussolini's close collaborators, Ardengo Soffici, said, in June 1944, at the Republic of Salò:

> Roosevelt's and Churchill's loquacity . . . invariably increases our respect for Stalin. We respect Stalin's seriousness, his simplicity, and the quiet, tough energy with which he gets to the point. . . . He had his people fighting with the style

worthy of a serious tragedy. . . . If the Axis were not to win,
most true Fascists, who escaped the flail, would pass over to
Communism and form a bloc with it. We would then have
crossed the gap which separates the two revolutions.

That sentiments of this sort were expressed in Mussolini's
entourage is surprising enough; that they were expressed under
Hitler's protective umbrella was either a sign of Soffici's enormous courage, or an outsize attempt at opportunism.

de Felice   There was a little bit of everything in the Republic of
Salò. Undoubtedly, there was a strong component of old Fascists
'of the first hour' who thought they would be able to do what they
had not been able to do in 1919–20—men of Socialist and syndicalist origins, who wanted to re-launch the 1919 Fascist programme.
On this basis they were able to establish links with people who
had, until then, occupied anti-Fascist positions, but now joined
the Republic of Salò. The most spectacular case was that of Nicola
Bombacci, one of the founders of the Italian Communist Party,
who had been a firm opponent of Fascism but found himself, at
the time of Salò, very close to Mussolini.

Soffici's was an interesting case. In the early years of Fascism
he had been a radical but withdrew from active politics much
before the 1943 capitulation. However, the Republic of Salò, with
its odd mixture of Nazi-type of intolerance and Socialism,
brought him back to the side of Mussolini. The speech from
which you have quoted is a truthful reflection of a certain type of
sentiment of which Soffici was not the only representative. There
is, to be sure, a good deal of self-justification and pseudo-
moralism in what Soffici says, but there is an even greater dose of
hatred and resentment of England and the United States. The
Soviet Union is built up in order to provide a telling contrast to
everything Soffici most disliked about the Anglo-Saxon powers.
He was particularly resentful of the wealth of America and the
carefree, ostentatious munificence with which it was pursuing
the war. What Soffici is really saying is that he has nothing but
admiration for the Russians' spirit and staying power, because
they were winning a difficult war despite their poverty and
scanty resources. The Americans, by contrast, were winning
because they were rich—not by dint of superior morality. He is,
by implication, also critical of the Italian people who were as poor
as the Russians but never matched the Russians' fighting spirit or
power of endurance.

Urban   Doesn't the concept of Italy as a poor and proletarian
country *par excellence*, fighting a large, rich but soulless enemy, go
back to the debate surrounding Italy's intervention in the first

world war? The Left's case for intervention, convincingly argued by the proto-Fascist Revolutionary Syndicalist, Filippo Corridoni, was based on the claim that Italy would fight the war as an under-privileged, proletarian nation against the German and Austro-Hungarian 'plutocracies'. The hardships of war would catalyse and abolish class differences and imbue the country with national consciousness.

A quarter of a century later, in 1941, the Christian-nationalist-Fascist writer Giovanni Papini claimed in a similar vein that Italy's war was 'a war against plutocratic domination . . . a war of the working nations against the rich nations, of the revolutionaries against the conservatives . . . of the future against the past' (with bits of anti-Semitism and barbs at Freemasonry thrown in for good measure). It would, therefore, seem to me that Soffici's admiration of the Soviet spirit was in a straight line of succession to earlier proto-Fascist utterances.

de Felice There did exist the type of argument you have quoted, though it would be a mistake to over-rate its importance. The interventionist debate at the beginning of the first world war went beyond the poor-nation-fighting-rich-nation type of controversy. The core of Corridoni's argument was that victory for the authoritarian, repressive régimes of Germany and Austria-Hungary would kill, or indefinitely delay throughout Europe, the hope of proletarian revolution. After the failure of 'Red Week'* it was no longer possible to envisage a successful revolution unaided by an international upheaval. Hence the demand for intervention on the side of the Entente powers. A large European war would inevitably bring about the weakening, or indeed the destruction, of the existing social order and unblock the road to revolution. This thesis was, of course, the common property of Socialist thinking in those days; it was shared by Lenin when he raised the demand: turn the world war into international civil war.

Papini's nationalism fed, like Soffici's, on anti-British sentiment. With the African war of 1935–36, Fascism succeeded in creating a lasting wave of popular emotion against Great Britain. There is evidence of this in a recently published collection of war-time private letters in which one can find no feeling of hatred for Greeks, Yugoslavs, Russians or Albanians; they were enemies, but they were not hated. The British were. Even today, the reduction of Britain to second-class status brings few tears to Italian eyes. Rather does it evoke a certain *Schadenfreude*.

---

*The general strike of 7–14 June 1914 accompanied by revolutionary uprisings in some parts of Italy [ed].

Urban The incomprehension of the British was certainly rife in high as well as low places. When Chamberlain and Halifax visited Mussolini in January 1939, Ciano's *Diary* carries the following entry for 11 January 1939:

> Conference at the Palazzo Venezia.... Effective contact has not been made. How far apart we are from these people! It is another world. We were talking about it after dinner with the Duce. 'These men are not made of the same stuff', he was saying, 'as the Francis Drakes and the other magnificent adventurers who created the empire. These, after all, are the tired sons of a long line of rich men and they will lose their empire.'

The interesting thing is that Mussolini harboured no anglophobic sentiments. The target of his real animus was the French whom he understood better and (perhaps therefore) hated more.

Urban But to return from the end of your story to the early and middle period of Fascism, there were—as you show—two, increasingly divergent, elements in Italian Fascism: Fascism as a movement and Fascism as government. While Fascism as a movement retained to the end some commitment, or, at any rate, a nostalgia for genuine commitment, to Socialism, Fascism as a régime was increasingly élitist and authoritarian and anxious to preserve the established social order. You argue, in fact, that Fascism as a movement has respectable credentials, that it derives from the traditions of the French Revolution and is, in principle at least, a partner rather than an adversary of Socialism. That Socialist and even Communist elements re-surfaced in the Republic of Salò is, then, more bizarre than ideologically surprising.

de Felice The history of Italian Fascism is the history of a continuous dialectic between the movement and the régime. What I mean by 'régime' is clear enough. When I speak of 'the movement' I am referring to certain changing groups in the rank and file of the Fascist Party; the same people do not represent the movement all the way from 1919 to 1945. Within this movement, then, there were, particularly in the 1930s, strong groups of young people who saw in Fascism a new form of mass democracy, undoubtedly with authoritarian characteristics, but at the same time with a socialistic and anti-liberal commitment. Fascism for them was a promise to renew the country through social transformation.

This socialistic undercurrent, which was never completely

absent from the movement, also explains certain differences between the histories of the German National Socialist Party and the Italian Fascist Party. Whereas the National Socialists suffered from very few (and untypical) desertions in favour of the Left—that is, virtually no National Socialist resigned from the Party in order to join anti-Nazi movements or the Communist Party—in Italy this is precisely what happened. There are many instances of Italian Fascists who, disillusioned by the pusillanimous social programme of Fascism, left the Party—sometimes simply to stay outside any commitment, but often to take up the fight as anti-Fascists and frequently as Communists. And this mutation from Fascism to Communism was a typical occurrence much before the crisis of Fascism, therefore it cannot be ascribed to mere opportunism.

Urban   This is, of course, an aspect of the Fascist-Communist nexus of which Soviet historians and propagandists have given us a much distorted picture.

de Felice   Certainly. The 'progressive' (if you like) content of Fascism showed itself in many other ways too. The early leaders, and the early rank and file, with Mussolini at their head, were Socialists and anarcho-syndicalists. They brought Socialist/syndicalist themes to the Fascist movement but in a national, and later nationalistic, orchestration. At the level of the Fascist *régime*, only very few elements of this tradition survived, but in the *movement* they persisted as a robust tradition. For example, Professor Ugo Spirito, author of the idea of 'the corporation as property', suggested at the 1932 Ferrara conference that the corporations should be owned and managed by the workers in the framework of a 'post-capitalist' corporative economy—an idea that would sound familiar to the protagonists of self-management in Yugoslavia today.

Urban   And it is intriguing that Togliatti, in his 1935 Moscow lectures to the Communist International, paid a back-handed compliment to Ugo Spirito's conception of workers' self-management.

> This interpretation of corporativism [he wrote] shows how the concept of corporativism allows Fascism to manoeuvre, inasmuch as it can cover any and all goods, even goods which can be considered 'subversive'—for example, the idea of the proprietary corporation, which inevitably must lead to the conclusion that it is necessary to expropriate the capitalists.

de Felice   Another example, less noted by foreigners but very important for Italians, was anti-clericalism. The Fascist *régime* entered compromise after compromise with the Vatican, but the *movement* remained strongly anti-clerical. Right up to the end, Mussolini expressed himself contemptuously about the Church and declared that he was a non-believer. Furthermore, the régime's coexistence with the Monarchy, too, sat uneasily on the shoulders of Mussolini, the erstwhile anti-monarchist.

Yet another characteristic of the 'progressive' nature of early Fascism, and one which had a noticeable though marginal impact on the régime, was a drive for the radical renewal of the ruling class. This was sought partly through the invigorating ethic of Fascist ideology, but partly also by insisting on what the Fascists of the early movement called 'the right of competence', i.e. by selecting people for responsible jobs solely on the basis of their knowledge and suitability. There developed from this, as Professor Alberto Aquarone has noted, a strongly technocratic tendency in the Fascist régime.

I would risk the generalisation that the socialistic aspirations of various groups in the Fascist *movement* were, throughout the history of Fascism, in substantial conflict with the conservatism, immobilism and monarcho-clericalism of the *régime*.

Urban In November 1943, just after the installation of the Republic of Salò, this duality in the history of Fascism was ruefully recognised by Mussolini himself. He said that for 20 years Italy had been ruled by a 'dyarchy'—a collection of conservative forces shielded by the monarchy, on the one hand, and opposed by a revolutionary élite within the Fascist Party, on the other. 'Plutocratic elements and sections of the clergy' waged a 'sordid and implacable struggle' against the revolutionary social and economic policies of Fascism. 'The capitulation of September', he said, 'signified the liquidation of the bourgeoisie as a ruling class.... The Republic of the Italian Workers [Salò] is the decisive realisation of all those postulates which, for 40 years, were inscribed on the banners of Socialist movements.' And a bare four months before his assassination, Mussolini instructed his Minister of Labour in the Salò Government to sow the fields of Italy with 'social mines'—deterrents (as he thought) against the return of monarchists and capitalists, whatever the outcome of the war.

Would I be right in saying that there is in Fascism—as Togliatti sarcastically hinted—a 'left-Fascism', meaning the socialistic aspirations of the early Fascist movement and their fitful survival all the way to the Republic of Salò, and that this 'left Fascism' had—as Togliatti would never admit—a natural kinship with Bolshevism? It is certainly remarkable, not only that Mussolini was a Marxist Socialist in his youth, but that he would make a point of stressing his early Marxism at the height of his power.

Talking to Emil Ludwig in 1932, Mussolini said: 'It was inevitable that I should become a Socialist ultra, a Blanquist, indeed a Communist. I carried a medallion with Marx's head on it in my pocket. I think I regarded it as a sort of talisman.'

de Felice One can sustain the thesis without sounding absurd. Quite apart from the Socialist and anarcho-syndicalist inspiration of the Fascists 'of the first hour', the Fascist régime paid great attention to, and in many ways followed the example of, Soviet economic planning. Indeed the feasibility of commanding the economy in certain directions as a means of achieving precise social and political ends, and the lessons to be learned from the Soviet experience, were regularly discussed by the Fascist government.

Urban It is intriguing that one can find in the history of the Fascist movement both attempts to eulogise the spirit of technological revolution—highly reminiscent of Lenin's formula 'Soviet power plus electrification'—and others to identify with the Soviet system because the latter was thought to run *counter* to the spirit of modernity. Some of both of these may, of course, have been simply due to the prevailing *Zeitgeist*, but the points of contact are thought-provoking all the same.

For an illustration of the first, I am reminded of certain ideas put about by Filippo Tommaso Marinetti, Mussolini's early and influential Futurist companion, with whom he had founded, in 1919, the *Fasci di combattimento*. In an essay rather appropriately entitled 'La guerra elettrica', this colourful and sybaritic proto-Fascist ('We want to exalt aggressive motion, feverish insomnia... ') expressed his longing for the kind of heroic technocracy which the October Revolution was soon to usher in—a technocracy where 'the energy of distant winds and rebellious seas, transformed into millions of kilowatts by the genius of man, would be distributed everywhere ... regulated by keyboards vibrating under the fingers of the technicians'.

My counter-example comes from the pen of that celebrated gadfly of the Fascist movement, the German-born Curzio Malaparte (his name is a heavy-handed pun on Bonaparte), whose admiration for the Soviet system was direct and vociferous. But, unlike Marinetti ten years before him, Malaparte ascribed the affinity between Fascism and Bolshevism to their common *opposition* to modernity:

> I believe that the phenomenon of the Russian revolution, which proceeds parallel to the Italian revolution in its hatred for and struggle against the modern spirit (which for us is the north-western spirit and for the Russians the European spirit),

is the complement of the phenomenon of the Italian revolution. Both are helping each other in their common task of destroying *modernity*, and one is not conceivable, possible or *right* without the other.

de Felice Well, Marinetti, despite his great early influence, was marginal to the lasting character of Fascism. But it is symptomatic of the common authoritarian thread running through Fascism and Bolshevism that both the Italian and the Russian Futurists were, in their role as romanticisers of the conquest of nature by technological revolution, relegated to the sidelines, and eventually absorbed.

Malaparte, who has fascinated many an Anglo-Saxon historian quite out of proportion to his political significance, was an entirely different phenomenon. By birth and culture, he was alien to the mainstream of Fascism. His non-conformist spirit and restless curiosity drove him into active Fascist politics between 1924 and 1926, but after that period his role was confined to work on the newspaper *La Conquista dello Stato*, and he represented no one but himself. His influence was ephemeral, but I can well understand why he appeals to the imagination, what with his many duels (he fought one with Nenni), his intrigues at the courts of Mussolini and Balbo, his editorship of and dismissal from *La Stampa*, the assault he suffered at the hands of Farinacci's agents in the Via Sistina, his *confino* (deportation) with his mistress on the island of Lipari, and his return to relative respectability under his new protector, Galeazzo Ciano. The transfer of Malaparte's admiration from Fascism, which he considered by 1929 to be insufficiently ruthless, to the fully totalitarian system of the Soviet Union, was an extremist's typical jump from one end of the political spectrum to the other.

Urban Malaparte's life would have lent itself handsomely to the music of a latter day Verdi—except for his unheroic end. Having constructed for himself an imaginary Fascist past to prove that he had participated in the March on Rome, Malaparte also constructed for himself, after his return from deportation, an anti-Fascist past. In 1943 he joined the US forces in southern Italy, and died in his bed in 1957 with the Pope's personal blessing, leaving his house in Capri—to the Chinese government.

Now your remark that Malaparte was attracted by the fully totalitarian qualities of the Soviet system is significant. Are you saying that Fascism was not a totalitarian régime?

de Felice The Italian Fascist régime was an incomplete totalitarianism. As we have already noted, Fascism had no control, and certainly no full control, over two other powers within the realm: the Monarchy and the Church. These reduced the chances of a seamless totalitarianism. While in Soviet Communism and Hitler's Germany the party is the supreme entity which stands above the state, in Italy the state retains its supremacy over the party. The local secretary of the Fascist Party is subordinate to the Prefect. The hierarchy is intact. But the ideological conception and practical execution of Fascist totalitarianism were also imperfect. One reason was the substantial preservation under Fascism of the old ruling class. While the Russian Communists exterminated or exiled the pre-1917 ruling class, and the German Nazis profoundly transformed theirs, in Italy, much to the dismay of the Fascist Left, a Fascist ruling class just did not come into being. The ideas and life-style of the generation that grew up in the 1920s and 1930s were firmly entrenched in the past.

Urban When one compares, for example, the state of personal and intellectual liberty in the Soviet Union in the late 1930s with that in Fascist Italy in the same period, one is struck by the relative ease with which direct opponents of the Fascist régime survived and prospered. One of the most famous critics of Fascism, the great liberal philosopher, Benedetto Croce, continued publishing in Naples throughout Mussolini's leadership. This at a time when (according to Raymond Aron) the monthly execution rate in the Soviet Union averaged 40,000.

Giorgio Amendola can hardly be accused of being an apologist of Fascism, yet this is how he describes the methods of the police state that existed under Mussolini:

> The type of repression carried out by Fascism was extremely flexible. The violence of the early years, the time when they murdered my father, was followed by a rational form of repression which soon took on the characteristic aspect of corruption. From 1926 to 1943 Fascist repression was essentially *corruzione*: 'Enrol in the Fascist Party', etc. There was nothing of the kind that happened in Nazi Germany.

de Felice Amendola's evidence speaks for itself. One might add that in Fascist Italy, in the 17 years between 1926 and 1943, there were only 26 executions, and these mostly for political violence in the Venezia-Giulia area. The comparison with Germany, and especially with the Soviet Union, is quite staggering. In Nazi Germany the mass massacres took place during the war. Between 1933 and 1941 there was undoubtedly a great deal of violence in Germany, but nothing comparable with the wholesale slaughters carried out, at a time of ostensible peace, under Stalin.

The Fascist type of repression, while never excusable, strikes one as an almost amateurish prelude to the ghastly deeds of the Führer and Stalin.

Now Croce's position under Fascism is explained by two circumstances—one general, the other particular to Croce. First, and more important, Mussolini was anxious to impress the world with a spectacle of normality in Italian life. He wanted to show that everything was in perfect order, everyone agreed with the broad outlines of régime policy, and there were no scandals. Explicit measures against Croce and other intellectuals would have undoubtedly created a great scandal. Mussolini preferred to allow Croce to continue to write and teach and publish his journal and even have a certain public influence, because he thought all these would be dissipated by time. His attitude to the less well-known intellectuals was based on the same considerations.

On the personal level, Croce's immunity was in some measure due to the fact that he was a senator, and senators were appointed by the king. An attack on Croce would have involved the régime in trouble with the monarchy, which Mussolini was always anxious to avoid. I remind you that Sforza, who was a senator and a knight of the *collare dell' Annunziata* (collar of the order of the Annunciation), though an active and violent anti-Fascist, was never deprived of his Italian citizenship, as many other anti-Fascists in exile were deprived of theirs. Even his salary, though he never collected it, was theoretically put aside for him and marked as 'paid'—all in order to avoid slighting a senator and a *collare dell' Annunziata*.

Urban But wasn't Croce's immunity also due to the fact that he rather welcomed—or shall we say, he did not at all condemn—the rise of the Fascist régime? Croce, like most liberals of his time, believed in a strong state. His liberalism was, as he put it, 'opposed to democracy when democracy substitutes quantity for quality, because, by so doing, it is laying the basis for demagogy, and, without wanting to, for dictatorship and tyranny, thereby destroying itself'. He approved of the Futurists' impact on Fascism, supported Gentile when the latter threatened to resign from Mussolini's government ('How long is it since we have had as willing and competent a Minister as Gentile . . . ?'), and defended the proposed single-list elections on the grounds that Mussolini must be given a fair chance to rule:

> I consider so excellent the cure to which Fascism has submitted Italy that my main worry is that the convalescent may leave her bed too soon and suffer a serious relapse. The heart of Fascism is love of Italy; it is the feeling of her salvation, the salvation of

the State; it is the just conviction that the State without authority is no State at all.

de Felice   There *was* this phase in Croce's life. But his conditional approval of Fascism came to an end in 1925. From 1925 on, his position is radically different—he is in opposition, not in any sense of planting bombs, but in that of trying to keep alive certain philosophical, cultural, moral and ideological themes as a counter-weight to Fascism. This detached intellectual resistance was highly significant and of great influence. I am convinced that in terms of effective impact, Croce's opposition was, right to the end of Fascism, of far greater importance than the bomb-throwing kind.

Urban   It is nevertheless a little disquieting to find so crass a break in the consistency of a man who has been held up to us for half a century as the very yardstick of integrity—even though Croce never admitted that there *had* been a break in his attitude. In October 1923 he was asked by a reporter from *Il Giornale d'Italia*: 'Is there not a contradiction between your faith in liberalism and your acceptance and justification of Fascism?' Croce replied: 'None whatsoever. If the liberals lacked the force and ability to save Italy from the anarchy which was rampant, they have only themselves to blame. In the meantime, they must accept and acknowledge the cure, whatever its source, and prepare themselves for the future'—a view which you may consider has an uncanny relevance to Italy in 1977.

de Felice   In 1923, it was not only Croce—a right-wing liberal—who would voice such sentiments; most left-wing liberals and democrats came out with similar statements. This was the time when Giovanni Amendola (father of the present Communist leader you have just quoted) tells those who press him to make a public stand against Fascism that the Fascists are carrying out a job of reconstruction and should be allowed to do what has to be done. Everyone considers Fascism a temporary phenomenon. Matteotti has not yet been murdered, nor has there yet been the 3rd January *coup d'état*.* Even the democratic Salvemini says it would be a stroke of bad luck if Mussolini died—he was in bad health at the time, and there were also rumours of plans to assassinate him. The public, too, feels that the Fascist broom should be allowed to sweep away the debris of the post-war chaos—when the job is completed, the work of building up a

---

*The assertion by Mussolini on 3 January 1925 of the authority of the state over the Fascist *squadristi*, and the beginning of the expulsion from the Fascist Party of its most violent elements, including the party secretary, Roberto Farinacci [ed].

democratic system would be taken up again. Such were Italy's expectations in 1923.

Urban Doesn't all this mean that, in that early phase of Fascism, Mussolini's credentials were, on the face of it, rather acceptable? For the Liberals he was the strong man who promised to enforce law and order. For the Socialists he was the author (with Marinetti) of the 1919 programme of the *Fasci di combattimento*, in which the following faultlessly revolutionary demands were made: abolition of the monarchy and the senate; confiscation of all church property and war profits; distribution of the land to the peasants; the abolition of all titles and of the political police; workers' self-management in industry; an eight-hour working day; freedom of conscience, of the press and assembly. I don't think the Italian Communist Party would, in 1977, need to be ashamed of such a programme—

de Felice —Oh, it is much to the *left* of anything the Communists would currently put their names to!

But Mussolini's original programme, which you have quoted, was already modified by 1920. The Fascists were at once confronted with the need to win over large sections of public opinion and to find areas of compromise with rival political forces. Their alliance with the Nationalists was not the most important of their steps to widen their base, because the Nationalists were not a strong political force. The Fascists' ambition, which they achieved, was to find acceptance within the existing political system. We must remember, shocking as this may sound to us in retrospect, that in 1921 the first Fascist parliamentary deputies were elected on common lists with Liberals and certain moderate democratic groups. Clearly, in order to form alliances of this sort, even though these may have been intended to be merely tactical, required the abandonment of the 1919 programme. The same goes for the winning over of certain bourgeois forces which did want social reforms but nothing like the sweeping measures demanded by the 1919 *Fasci di combattimento*.

Urban You have said that quite a few Fascists mutated into Communists, and we have now seen that this may have been due to the fact that a Socialist type of radicalism was part and parcel of the original programme of Fascism which survived, intermittently and under the surface, right up to the Social Republic of Salò. But if Fascists turned out to be Communists, would it then be too far-fetched to imagine that Communists—Italian Communists—might mutate into Fascists? (I am leaving aside the question whether Communists of the Soviet type *are* Fascists in the popular and pejorative sense of the word.) Communism painted in the colours of the Italian tricolor—would this not be a likely candidate for 'Fascism'? If the Italian Eurocommunist heresy goes far enough, I can certainly see Moscow calling it just that—which would, of course, prove neither that it is Fascist nor that it is not Fascist, but simply that it has become a thorn in the flesh for the Kremlin.

de Felice One can imagine a hypothetical type of National Communism which might assume vaguely Fascist characteristics. After all, Fascism contains, as we have seen, certain populistic elements which are also the key to the appeal of Communism. A Stalinist régime, such as the one in Rumania, conjoined with a rabid nationalism, would undoubtedly qualify for some tag such as 'fascism' in the imprecise sense of the word. But *would* the Italian Communists mutate into Fascists? I would hardly think so, except in the sense in which the Communists describe Pinochet as 'fascist'. But Pinochet is no such thing. His régime is an authoritarian, militaristic and reactionary regime, but it is not Fascist because, for example, he has never tried to mobilise the masses and harness them ideologically to his government, nor has he a party to lead society by its inspiration and discipline. It is anything but a Fascist régime if we look at it from the historical point of view.

Now if we want to go along with those who delight in corrupting the precision of historical analysis, or simply want to make propaganda, we can say that Pinochet's is a Fascist régime with the same kind of justification as we can call any authoritarian and nationalist régime 'fascist', including a 'nationalist' Communist régime. But this would be saying no more than that complete and incomplete totalitarian régimes have certain common characteristics, which the totalitarianisms of Mussolini, Hitler and Stalin had to widely different degrees.

Urban And yet, for the man in the street in Naples or Malcesine, how different from Fascism would Italian Communism be if it could assert its authority against Moscow only by wrapping itself in the protective colours of the national flag? The intellectual affinity between Fascism and Communism was well recognised by Mussolini. Addressing himself to the Communists in the Italian Chamber of Deputies on 1 December 1921, he said: 'We, like you, consider necessary a centralised and unitary State which imposes iron discipline on all individuals; with this difference, that you arrive at this conclusion via the concept of class, and we arrive there via the concept of nation'. As late as 1933, Ugo Spirito wrote: 'One does a disservice to Fascism in conceiving it as antithetical to Bolshevism ... if today the energies of the political orientation [of our time] find expression in Fascism and Bolshevism, it is clear that the future belongs not to that régime which negates the other, but that which, of the two, has shown itself capable of incorporating and transcending the other in a more advanced form. . . . '

For the man in the street it would make little difference whether he was forced into the 'iron discipline' of a centralised state in the name of class or in the name of nation, and in this broad sense (the sense you reject) I can well imagine a 'fascist' type of Italian Communism tempered by the same tendencies of corruption as also mellowed and made bearable the rule of Mussolini. It is all very well for historians to split hairs over the precise definition of one kind of oppression against another, but is enough thought being given to the common people who are at the business end of both sticks?

de Felice One can never completely exclude the possibility that something of the sort you have described might happen. However, the historical context today is so different from what it was between the two world wars that any similarities between a nationally coloured Communism and Fascism would be conspicuous by their dissimilarities. An American scholar of Russian birth has attempted to subsume various modern dictatorships under one convenient label and decided to call them 'syncretic régimes' for the same kind of reasons you have just put to me. Now if you throw your net as wide as that, you can naturally put all kinds of régimes into it, but whether it makes any sense to do so is another matter. Fascism, for me, is the Italian Fascist movement under Mussolini—no other.

The problem which your questioning seems to point to is rather this: all anti-democratic, anti-liberal régimes of our century are mass phenomena, socialistic phenomena and often nationalistic phenomena. As centralised, authoritarian and mass regimes, their methods of creating consensus, of running the economy, of enforcing discipline, of suppressing dissent are naturally very similar. They are dictatorships, and the use of these methods is precisely what dictatorship means. But beyond that I would hesitate to push your analogy.

Nationalism is the element that basically defines fascistic régimes. It is not fortuitous that when, under Stalin, Soviet Communism reaches the stage of complete totalitarianism, it embraces a good deal of Russian nationalism and weakens its links with internationalism. My impression is that totalitarian states, in order to become fully totalitarian, must pass through the nationalistic experience.

Urban 'Communism in one country' was Stalin's slogan at the time. At one stage Mussolini, too, said that Fascism was not for export.

de Felice Yes, but the time-sequences were reversed. Nationalism occurs in the Soviet Union in the mid and late 1930s when totalitarianism reaches its climax, and is then further promoted during the war. Soviet internationalism had been more characteristic of the Lenin period. In Italy, the slogan 'Fascism is not for export' is typical of the early 1920s, when Fascism was only groping its way towards totalitarianism. But when, in the 1930s, Fascism moves closer to achieving an incomplete totalitarianism, it begins to boast of an ideology destined to dominate the twentieth century. The historical reasons which account for these differences in Soviet and Fascist history are, of course, well known.

Urban Let me come back to some of the pressing problems of our own time. Wouldn't a conservative, authoritarian type of government—not fascistic, but perhaps a form of benevolent caesarism—offer a less hazardous solution to Italy's predicament than Communism, even (or especially) National-Communism? First, this would be a time-honoured and familiar recipe which might cope with the nation's troubles, and with which the nation would know how to cope. Second, it would be much less likely to be self-perpetuating than a Communist rescue operation, seeing that there are perfectly good ways of getting rid of 'fascist' and right-wing authoritarian régimes—witness the cases of Portugal, Greece and Spain—whereas no European country has yet been able to get rid of a Communist régime. At the very least, the onus of proof that this is not so is on the Communist Parties, although I don't think we should risk finding out.

de Felice As far as the freedom and dignity and integrity and welfare of the individual are concerned, there is little to choose between Communism and Fascism. Now, I would prefer not to give a direct answer to your hypothesis concerning a right-wing authoritarian resolution of Italy's many problems. I would rather invite you to consider the following: a Communist type of resolution of the Italian chaos could take either a *sui generis*, Eurocommunist course, or a Soviet course. The absorption of a Communist-controlled or partly Communist-controlled Italy in the Soviet bloc, with tacit American approval or through American helplessness, would remove all the question marks because it would make Communist rule in Italy irreversible as far as any of us care to foresee. Italy would become part of the Soviet sphere of influence, and its internal and external freedoms would be similar to those of Czechoslovakia. This is the less likely of my two scenarios.

What is much more likely to happen is the rise of an Italian Eurocommunist régime. This could not last, but while it lasted it would inflict great damage. It would probably have enough time to ruin the economy, isolate us from our natural friends and antagonise the great mass of the Italian people. Its rule would be ended by a sequence of events similar to that which brought Allende down in Chile, and it would be followed by a régime similar to Pinochet's—some right-wing authoritarianism taking us back to the base of the spiral where the Communists first came in.

Urban   So Italy's choice is between dictatorship and dictatorship?

de Felice   That is about right—except that I have not given up hope that Italy's present system can be sufficiently reformed to make it viable again.

Urban   There seems to be something in the socio-cultural specificity of Italian society that makes for the vicious circle you have described. Would it be due to the late arrival of Italy as a united, single nation? Or would it, on the contrary, be due to some prudent scepticism flowing from the lessons of a very long history? In other words: should we put the blame on the *nation* because it is too young, or on the Italian people because *it* is too old?

de Felice   I would say the superficial cause of Italy's recurrent malaise is a simple lack of orderliness and efficiency. But this is rooted in an interplay of a variety of historical factors. If you ask me to choose the most important of these, I would say it is the absence of a competent political class. After the fall of Fascism, Italy was without modern leadership. The people who occupied the commanding posts throughout the nation were the old Catholic ruling class whose contacts with modern life were tenuous. After the fall of Fascism the old political class tried, or stumbled into trying, a curious Italian hybrid: preserving the ways of the old bourgeoisie while superimposing on it a particularly Italian brand of Communism. This was meant to be something highly original—a third way—which didn't work. It may possibly work in the developing countries, but not in a highly industrialised state such as Italy, whose economic and social imperatives are of an entirely different order.

Urban   What you are saying is that the Italian ruling class attempted to avoid the sharp and angular solutions, and tried its hand at a shock-free transition. This is a very Italian *modus operandi* and one I would not condemn. I am rather taken by the thesis that the Italians' inability, or unwillingness, to do a thing 100 per cent right is the saving grace of Italian society. It is bad for industrial efficiency but good for human beings and a guarantee against the perfectionism of both Fascism and Communism. A nation that does both Fascism and Communism badly cannot be all bad.

de Felice I don't like this theory. Fascism *all'italiana* and Communism *all'italiana* can mean one thing only: postponing the crisis. The sequence of Communist-anarchy-leading-to-Fascism-leading-to-National-Communism-leading-to-right-wing-authoritarianism is a self-perpetuating evil. Somewhere the chain has to be broken. The danger is precisely that both National Communism and the right-wing authoritarianism that would follow its collapse would be far too bland and corrupt to make the Italian people realise the tragic precariousness of Italy's situation. The disease has to be cured at source, and that means neither a National-Communist nor a right-wing authoritarian expedient, but restoring, through hard work and a realistic appraisal of what is wrong with us, the present system's ability to find within itself the capacity for renewal. This is not a far-fetched idea; Italy's overall record as a modern nation since the Second World War is not a bad one. Italy is among the first ten of the world's industrial powers, but it will not remain in that league if the Communists come to power. For the Italian proclivity to do things badly would clinch the Communists' proven talent to wreck any economy.

Let me add one thing: you have rightly stressed the ordinary man's point of view. Clearly, the political and intellectual histories of Fascism and Communism are very different, and the régimes they have generated, or might generate in Italy, have been, and would be, different from one another when seen through the intellectually fastidious microscope of historical analysis. But for the man whose preoccupation in life is to stay alive, give himself and his family two hot meals a day, a roof above their heads and enough freedom to breathe like human beings and refuse to have their backs broken by tyranny, there is precious little to choose between the two. The difference between being thrown into the sea and being thrown into a lake is rather academic if you don't know how to swim.

Rosario Romeo

6 The Uses of Anti-Fascism

Urban What lessons are there to be learned from the reception of Renzo de Felice's re-examination of the history of Fascism? The subject is still uncomfortably close to the bone—if Benedetto Croce was right in saying that 'all history is contemporary history', it is perhaps equally true to say of the profound controversy created by de Felice's work that 'all contemporary history is current politics'. How then did Italy as a liberal polity respond to de Felice's findings?

Romeo The early post-war years saw the reinstatement, after 20 years of Fascism, of Italian liberal democracy, and of course the whole rationale of such a régime is the maintenance of liberty in the broadest sense. But, right from the beginning, the Italian interpretation of liberty was in some ways handicapped, because the midwife to our notion of freedom was an official anti-Fascist ideology which was not, and could not be, favourable to an untrammelled exercise of freedom. This official anti-Fascist framework limited the extent to which various issues of contemporary history could be dispassionately discussed. There was and is an inclination to think that friends and foes who made up our political/intellectual landscape some 30 years ago are still with us and must still be fought or defended. The struggle against Fascism has become a perennial anti-Fascism, which not only censors and tampers with the issues raised by recent Italian history, but also tends to prevent us from taking an independent scholarly look at the facts of Italian society as they are *today*. If you ask: What is the nature of the Italian state? To what extent is Italian capitalism capable of providing a ruling class that can effectively govern? What has prevented the problems of the South from being solved? What are the characteristics of class relationships in Italian society?—any and all such questions are immediately

116

grouped around and debated exclusively in terms of this official anti-Fascist ideology.

The basic tenet of this ideology is, of course, that Fascism was totally and execrably wrong, and everything opposed to it is to be applauded. De Felice makes an important point by showing that this cavalier interpretation of Fascism has led to a state of affairs where any criticism of Italy's present anti-Fascist régime is automatically branded as Fascist or something coming very close to Fascism. There is a tendency to say that any opposition coming from outside the perimeters of the official parties is a Fascist opposition.

Urban   Do the Christian Democrats share this ideology?

Romeo   They do, because they too subscribe to the idea that the womb of the whole democratic system in Italy was the struggle against Fascism. This framework has, as I say, proved very dangerous for intellectual liberty. Whatever the subject under discussion, your opponents can always try to silence you by conveniently saying that you are a Fascist. There has developed an atmosphere of gratuitous unanimity on what 'Fascism' is, even in respect of problems which have nothing to do with Fascism. The semantic catchment area of 'Fascism' has grown larger and larger until just about everything can be put into it if you want to be unpleasant to your neighbour. There is supposed to be a 'Fascist' manner of bringing up your children; there are supposed to be 'Fascist' ways of behaviour in the arts, in your attitude to women, your job, and even your choice of a haircut can allegedly display your Fascist inclinations. In brief, any attitude expressing authority is an invitation to be labelled 'Fascist' in the personal sphere, and any opposition to the existing system may earn you the same stigma on the political level.

For example, not so many years ago there was a serious discussion in Italy whether we should improve our poorly functioning parliamentary democracy by switching to a presidential system rather on the US pattern. But, after a few weeks of debate, the idea was branded as authoritarian, and not many months later anyone who still had the courage to speak up for presidential democracy was shouted down as a Fascist.

Urban   How did de Felice's work affect these attitudes?

Romeo   The arrival of de Felice on this scene was highly disturbing, for one of the many sophisticated observations de Felice makes is that Italian Fascism had certain characteristics which sprang from the general problems of Italian society, moving as it was in the 1920s and 1930s from agrarian backwardness to an urban and mass industrial society. The old élite of Italian liberal democracy could not (in de Felice's analysis) do justice to the country's problems. Thus, de Felice insists, we must understand that some of those problems which gave birth to Fascism have not gone away simply because Fascism has been replaced by another liberal-democratic régime.

The implications of these observations were most unsettling, for they amount to confronting our official anti-Fascism with the fact that, in order to find a solution to Italy's present problems, it is both reasonable and necessary to make a dispassionate analysis of what exactly had brought about Fascism in the first place.

De Felice's painstaking analysis of Fascism involved him in further controversial conclusions. He had the audacity to state that Fascism, like any other human phenomenon, had to be understood in its historical/political context, and that seen in such a framework, it could no longer be just asserted that it was purely the work of irrational, devilish forces. These, you must remember, were scandalous claims in an intellectual environment in which it had become *de rigueur* to profess that the sub-human nature of Fascism had been settled once and for all.

Not only that, but de Felice insisted on showing that in some important respects Fascism was a direct heir to the French Revolution. This claim was thought to be particularly monstrous, because de Felice's opponents could, in fact, truthfully say that the Italian Fascists had always repudiated the principles of 1789—the rights of man and the whole ideology of democracy. How then, it was asked, could de Felice make so grotesque a claim? But, of course, de Felice's claim was a much more modest one than his critics were prepared to concede. The connection he established between Fascism and 1789 was a partial one—he linked Fascism to the tradition of Robespierre and the Terror of the French Revolution, and not to Madame de Staël and the democracy of liberalism. Fascism, de Felice maintained, sprang from the entrails of mass-democracy, which was a violent and terroristic affair.

To make things worse, de Felice demonstrated that the mass support which Fascism enjoyed in Italy was essentially part of the same quest for democracy and participation which is asserting itself again today, though in different, but perhaps not entirely different, ways. Let me give you a humdrum but none the less relevant illustration. I know an old man who was an Under-Secretary of State in Mussolini's government. Talking to me about his career the other day he said: 'My father sold tobacco in a small town and was a very poor man. I did well at school and my father wanted to send me to the university. But as he couldn't find the money, he asked to see Signor Salandra, head of the then Liberal Government (Salandra came from our town and represented it in Parliament, so my father knew him a little). But Salandra wasn't impressed. "What's all this—everyone with any brains wanting to go to the university?!" he said; "Send your son out to work!" Of course, my father and I didn't like this a bit. I was a bright lad and I wanted to study philosophy; why should I be prevented from doing so?'

Ten years later, the same young man was the leader of the Fascist Union in Turin. He had found in Fascism a social escalator which gave scope to his talents and promoted him until he became Under-Secretary of State for Education. He could never forget that under the old Liberal régime the gates of the university had been barred to him.

There was yet another controversial element in de Felice's analysis—highly simple, if you think of it in its proper context, but it seemed revolutionary when de Felice first drew attention to it. According to the officially promoted theory of Fascism, Fascism was the work of capitalists and landowners mobilising the middle and lower-middle classes—former army officers and underpaid civil servants—who proved willing accomplices, because they felt economically and politically threatened by a rising working class. De Felice showed that this wasn't at all the case—on the contrary; at the time of the rise of Fascism the petty bourgeoisie was on the march. He produced incontrovertible statistical evidence that the lower-middle classes were steadily gaining in numbers, wealth and influence.

If you share, or profess to share, the official view of what Fascism has been about, it is impossible to go along with de Felice, for this would amount to the admission that Fascism was somehow moving in step with the march of history and not against it—a theological point, but one of great importance in Italy.

De Felice also had certain disturbing truths to say about the relationship between Fascism and the intellectual and artistic community. He made it clear that it was far too simple-minded a version of history to say that Fascism was something only brutish, untutored minds would embrace. He showed that a great many important Italian intellectuals, writers and playwrights—to confine oneself to the internationally known, one may mention, apart from Gentile, d'Annunzio, Malaparte, Pirandello, Giovanni Papini, and even Toscanini—actively supported or sympathised with Fascism—

Urban —and so did, outside Italy, many people of great eminence, although this alleged 'support' has become so mushy by propagandistic abuse as to be rendered virtually meaningless. One can adduce evidence of a kind to show that Austen Cham-

berlain 'supported' Fascism because he exchanged photographs
with Mussolini, or that Churchill 'supported' Mussolini because
he praised his statesmanship and proposed and signed in 1933 a
four-power pact with him for the peaceful revision of the Versail-
les treaties. But for many artists and intellectuals Fascism—or at
any rate certain élitist ideas one may vaguely associate with
Fascism—exerted a powerful influence. In France alone, the
names that come to mind include Charles Maurras, Léon Daudet,
Jean Cocteau, Jean Giraudoux, Sacha Guitry, Céline and even
Jules Romains, who wrote in 1933:

> We should not allow a natural antipathy for the outer appear-
> ances and many of the aims of the Fascist revolution in Italy
> and Germany to prevent us from realizing that it is not merely
> a return to the past, a completely negative episode of regres-
> sion and exhaustion, but also an attempt to find a possible
> solution to modern problems, precisely to those problems
> which Marxism has ignored or ridiculed.

Fascism, Romains wrote, 'is trying to erect a modern society in
which everyone is in his place and declares himself happy to be
part of it. . . . France should draw bold and wise ideas from
Bolshevism and Fascism'. (Jules Romains, I might add, left France
for the United States in 1940, and by the time I met him in Paris in
the early 1960s, his views had changed.)

But my favourite description of one side of the French people's
ambivalent attitude to 'Fascist' mentality comes from the pen of
Sartre. In *Chemins de la liberté: La mort dans l'âme* he depicts,
through the eyes of one of his characters, the entry of Hitler's
army into Paris:

> [Daniel] was not afraid, he yielded trustingly to those
> thousands of eyes, he thought 'Our conquerors!' and he was
> supremely happy. He looked them in the eye, he feasted on
> their fair hair, their sunburnt faces with eyes which looked like
> lakes of ice, their slim bodies, their incredibly long and muscu-
> lar hips. He murmured: 'How handsome they are!' . . . Some-
> thing has fallen from the sky: it was the ancient law. The
> society of judges had collapsed, the sentence had been obliter-
> ated; those ghastly little khaki soldiers, the defenders of the
> rights of man, had been routed. . . . An unbearable, delicious
> sensation spread through his body; he could hardly see prop-
> erly. . . . He would have liked to be a woman to throw them
> flowers.

This is, one might say, an early (1949) display of Sartre's *Schadenfreude* at seeing a meretricious bourgeoisie brought to its knees, but it does uncannily correspond with what, for example, André Gide recorded in more measured language in his wartime *Journal*, in 1941:

> I think it is good for France to submit herself to this imposed yoke of discipline. Just as she was incapable, at the point of moral relaxation and decomposition to which she had fallen, of winning a real victory over an adversary better equipped than herself, united, resolute, tenacious, fierce and wisely led by a leader determined to pass beyond all those scruples which enfeebled us, all the considerations which encumbered us, so I do not think that France today is capable of arising on her own. . . .

I will not mention straightforward cases such as those of Ezra Pound or Wyndham Lewis; but what is one to think of Sigmund Freud's little-publicised admiration for Mussolini?

In 1933 Freud sent a signed copy of one of his books to the Duce (it is in the State Archives in Rome) with this dedication: 'To Benito Mussolini, from an old man who greets in the Ruler the Hero of Culture'.

Romeo All this is true, and one could, of course, give a much more detailed picture of the mental processes that led distinguished people to approve of, or at any rate, to accept Fascism as a necessary, even though a transitional, form of government in Italy's predicament after the First World War.

To sum up: the general drift of de Felice's work was to show that Fascism expressed some genuine and popularly felt needs of Italian life; that many of the measures taken under Mussolini were legitimate and timely measures; and that similar measures were being attempted by different régimes in other countries. All this has had a salutory effect on the freedom of Italian intellectual discussion. The atmosphere which de Felice's work created has opened windows on the stifling conformity of Italian life since the war. It is now possible to argue, on respectable grounds, against as well as for the official ideology of anti-Fascism.

Urban How—to be more precise—did the reactions divide?

Romeo For a couple of months after the publication of de Felice's latest volume and his *Intervista* with Michael Ledeen, the main reactions came from entrenched left-wing radical positions. But there were others, such as an attack in *Corriere della Sera* by Leo Valiani, with whom both de Felice and I are on personally friendly terms, but who nevertheless strongly dissented from de

Felice's interpretations on a number of points. Valiani claimed that in de Felice's reading the Fascist movement's cult of violence for the sake of violence, the tyranny of the strong over the weak, was given insufficient emphasis, and that the indwelling evil in Mussolini's character and the criminality of the movement disappeared in de Felice's reconstruction. Furthermore de Felice was wrong, said Valiani, in drawing a demarcation line between Fascism and National Socialism. National Socialism, he argued, was certainly a far more destructive evil than Fascism, but that was due to the fact that Italians were not Germans—that the issues of race and anti-Semitism played no, or only a very late and marginal, part in Italian politics. But given the milder climate of Italian politics, Fascism was, said Valiani, entirely comparable with Nazism.

But there was more to come. De Felice told us both in the last volume of his life of Mussolini and in *Intervista* that Fascism rested on a good deal of consensus—that, in fact, it enjoyed mass support, including support by the Italian working class. This was, in Communist eyes, an especially scandalous thing to say, for it had been one of the unquestioned and unquestionable truths of post-war Italian social theology that the working class was and always had been anti-Fascist—it was Communist or at the very least Socialist. Here was a judgment running right in the face of official mythology. But it did more than that: it threatened to make nonsense of the reconstruction of recent Italian history by Marxist historians. Until de Felice came along, the main bits of mental equipment in that reconstruction were a red-clawed capitalist class defeating, between 1918 and 1922, the heroic struggle of the working class; but despite this setback, the struggle (not just the resistance) of the working class against Fascism continued for 20 years, until its final defeat in 1943. Now this edifying fable was disturbed by some of de Felice's unpalatable findings. Of course, most of de Felice's facts had been well known before, but he was the first to have the courage and scholarly integrity to say them.

What were the most offensive items in his 'revelations'? Well, he simply recounted the fact that every time Mussolini spoke from the Palazzo Venezia, millions gathered to hear him—and that they did not have to be shepherded; that in the Fiat factory and elsewhere thousands of workers assembled to applaud him—all this scrupulously attested by films, photographs and documents. For Marxist historiography this perspective was, as I say, not only offensive, but pulling at the foundations of the entire post-war ideological edifice. Naturally the photographs and films were declared to be forgeries, and the human witnesses, of whom there were millions, liars or Fascists.

Urban But didn't the Communists, especially Amendola, take a historically more accurate view, admitting, in fact, the mass appeal of Fascism, and trying to make the Party learn certain practical lessons from it?

Romeo Yes; and the first reaction on the democratic Left was to qualify rather than simply to reject some of de Felice's arguments. It was now said that there was no *general* consensus behind Fascism, that the working class did not give its *blanket* support, and if one could find evidence of working-class consensus, it was merely of a *passive* and *intermittent* kind. But it has to be said in fairness that the reasoning of Amendola and certain other leaders of the Communist Party was not really breaking fresh ground. As early as 1935, Togliatti, in his lectures to the Comintern school in Moscow, pointed out that the characterisation of Fascism as a purely bourgeois phenomenon was grossly misleading. Fascism, he argued, had a certain amount of mass support, even workers' support, albeit usually of a passive kind. With the demise of the Italian Socialists, the working class had lost its leadership and accepted Fascism as a substitute. The implication of this reasoning was that Fascism was a usurper of the loyalties of the working class—a false Messiah whose credentials went unquestioned because those of the genuine Messiah were no longer on view—

Urban —a useful argument, for it amounts to saying that the working class is without sin and the Party entitled to re-embrace it because the marriage between Fascism and the working class had never been consummated.

Romeo That was the meaning of Togliatti's reasoning, though your reading of it did not come fully into view until after the war.

De Felice denied that the Italian workers were the dupes of Fascism. He insisted that a large section of the working class were willing supporters of the Fascist régime because Fascism was a mass movement which opened the way for certain groups within the working class to participation and self-expression. There was also the social legislation of Mussolini's régime which carried general approval, so that, all in all, the consensus behind Fascism was, in de Felice's reconstruction, an active one.

To be fair to de Felice, he did not say that this consensus was strongly held, because the Party, especially as it got more and more identified with stable government, forfeited some of its rapport with the workers and particularly with those young intellectuals who had joined it out of a sense of idealism. After the murder of Matteotti, Mussolini purged and virtually destroyed the Party as a vehicle of revolution and national rejuvenation, and ruled through the traditional channels of the state—the swollen and hidebound ranks of the bureaucracy. From then on the Fascist Party had no political life of its own and its supporters lost faith.

Urban According to one school of thought, what we have after the Matteotti affair is not Fascism but Mussoliniism.

Romeo Yes, Mussolini as a person had a magnetic effect on large masses of the people. They would gather in the square to hear him, but there was, after the first years, no active political party behind him to provide the kind of transmission belt between the leader and the led such as the Bolshevik Party provided in Russia and the National Socialist Party in Germany. Mussolini's dictatorship was an externalised, one might almost say open-air, affair.

Urban Mussolini loved his image of Italy but was contemptuous of the Italian people—a nation, as he thought, of waiters, pimps and antiquarians. Like so many dictators before him, he felt the people didn't deserve a man of his qualities. He ordered the reforestation of the Apennines because this would (as he told Ciano) make Italy colder and more snowy: 'In this way our good-for-nothing men and this mediocre race will be improved'. His comment on a heavy air raid on Naples was: 'I am happy that Naples is having such severe nights. The breed will harden, the war will make of the Neapolitans a Nordic race', and when Italy did not feel the pinch of war visibly enough for Mussolini's taste, he ordered false air-raid alarms and the anti-aircraft batteries to go into action to toughen the population.

Élitist he was with a vengeance, yet his élitism, which comes directly from Pareto whose student he was in Switzerland, did not induce him to create a properly organised, much less a totalitarian, Party. Both Margherita Sarfatti and Emil Ludwig (friendly witnesses) stress Mussolini's loneliness which he had deliberately invited upon himself and found irksome to have to do without.

Romeo Mussolini liked his Party to be quiescent—he did not want too much activity from Party quarters. Ultimately the régime consisted of the Duce, the bureaucracy, and far removed from both, the people, whom Mussolini considered to be putty in the hands of the leader if he knew how to appeal to their interests and engage their enthusiasm. And, for many years, Mussolini knew how to combine the two.

Yet another irritant in de Felice's analysis was the evidence he produced of growing social mobility under Fascism, linked as it was to Italy's economic progress. Both, like his other principal conclusions, were totally inadmissible—inadmissible, that is, until Giorgio Amendola joined the debate with a major article in *l'Unità*, and said a number of things which came close to endorsing some of de Felice's findings. This, as we have seen, immediately caused some of the more radical and more scurrilous criti- cisms of de Felice to be withdrawn or modified.

Amendola made no bones about admitting that Fascism succeeded in enlisting the support of large sections of the population. Its victory, he said, and its ability to mobilise working-class support were political facts which had to be explained and not explained away by attributing them to physical terror. Why, he asked, did Fascism succeed in attracting so much working-class support? Could Communists avoid repeating the mistakes of the past unless they first answered that question? Anyone who saw in Fascism nothing more than a particularly virulent form of capitalist reaction knew nothing about the real needs and motivations of the working class.

What Amendola the political animal was, in fact, implying (and we have hinted at this already when we spoke of Togliatti) was that those Italian workers who had supported Fascism had set themselves the correct objectives, but chosen or acquiesced in the wrong means to attain them. In the given situation, he argued, they became Fascists for perfectly good reasons. And he added for good measure: 'It must not be thought that studying Fascism ... might lead, as some seem to fear, in some way to the rehabili- tation of it. . . . '

Urban   In other words, the workers erred in embracing Fasc- ism, but they erred for the right reasons and could be forgiven and indeed reintegrated in the only rightful movement of the working class—the Communist Party.

Romeo   Yes. And this paradoxical 'rehabilitation' of Fascism by Amendola produced some comic and highly Italian effects. An old Liberal friend of mine from Naples who would never touch Fascism with a barge-pole, said to me after Amendola's article: 'Now I will go back to Naples to look up an old buddy of mine who was one of Mussolini's Party Secretaries in the city. I was never a member of the Party, and I never asked him to do the slightest thing for me when he was in power. But now that I'm told, 30 years after the fall of Fascism, that there are only two legitimate ways of being an Italian—via either Communism or Fascism—I will go back to this old pal of mine and ask him to give it to me in writing that I, too, was a Fascist—a Fascist, mind you, (as Amendola says) for *good* reasons.'

Urban   There is something honourable about Amendola's courage in being frank about the Italian past. Your ex-Fascist

Party Secretary in Naples would probably think: 'This damn
Bolshevik is simply saying what we old Fascists have known all
along—that "Fascism is Communism with a human face" '; and
there is indeed evidence that as late as 1941 Dino Grandi expressed fear, after a particularly vehement anti-bourgeois out-
burst of Mussolini at a meeting of the Cabinet, that Fascist Italy
was facing the *'white* Bolshevism of Mussolini'. I find the phrase
significant.

Romeo   Well, the Communists in Italy claim that the human
face belongs to Eurocommunism. And, as far as Amendola personally is concerned, this is certainly true; he has an open
mind—there is nothing you cannot discuss with him reasonably.
But he is not the Party.

Urban   There is one, as I think, politically shrewd observation in
Amendola's article which has particularly attracted my attention:
'...ignoring the history of Fascism means condemning oneself
not to write the history of anti-Fascism.... ' What does this
mean? My interpretation of it would be that Amendola is anxious
to show that anti-Fascism in Italy was a predominantly, if not
exclusively, Communist affair, and that the other Parties which
now claim to have participated in the struggle were in reality
insignificant or non-existent. 'We have opened our files on our
past', Amendola seems to be saying to the other Parties. 'Will you
open yours and show us what exactly *you* were doing in those 20
years to combat Fascism?' Would you say this is part of the game
that has developed around de Felice's analysis?

Romeo   It is, and Amendola said words roughly to that effect
in his *Interview on Anti-Fascism*, which appeared soon after de
Felice's *Intervista*. What is interesting to observe is that, although
Amendola as a Communist leader is a much more important man
in Italy than de Felice, the latter's *Intervista* has had incomparably
larger sales than Amendola's. The reason is simple: anti-Fascism
has lost its drawing power, because for 30 years it has been official
dogma. Fascism, on the other hand, is news again precisely
because it has been either swept under the carpet or discussed in
purely Manichean terms.

Amendola's and de Felice's books were brought out in the
same series by the same publisher, Laterza in Bari (this tells you
something about the permissive climate of Italian politics), and
shortly before the publication of Amendola's *Intervista*, Amendola, de Felice, myself and some others had a meeting at Laterza's
to go over the issues raised by his book. In the course of our
discussion I raised with Amendola a point very similar to the one
you have just made: did he think that the illegal Italian Commun-

ist Party had made a greater contribution to anti-Fascism than the pen of a single man, Benedetto Croce? Would he agree that Croce's work inspired a more profound sense of anti-Fascism than the work of all the Communist Party organisations put together? Amendola said he was clear that Croce's was the more important influence but, he added, it was a long-range, non-combatant influence which didn't kill Fascists.

Let me say here in parenthesis that the background to our discussion was this: Benedetto Croce was a widely known and widely respected thinker who published and taught and was read in Italy throughout the Fascist era. A very large section of the Italian white-collar class, even many of those who accepted, on the political level, Mussolini's leadership, were culturally Croce's followers. This was the intellectual and moral matrix which prepared them for anti-Fascism and served to turn them, during the war, into active opponents of Fascism.

But there was no declaratory anti-Fascism in Croce's books; he acted at a more profound, seminal level. The Communist Party, on the other hand, was practically destroyed by the Fascist régime. Amendola, Spinelli and their colleagues were under arrest, and the Party's influence was virtually nil.

Yet Amendola in his book asserts that the Communist, and to a much smaller extent the Socialist, share in the struggle against Fascism was predominant, and he accuses Croce of being content with offering cultural/spiritual advice rather than a fighting opposition.

Now at our meeting with Amendola I said to him: You are accusing Croce of a fruitless, ivory tower type of resistance. But we know perfectly well that, with the sole Russian exception, every single Communist uprising or take-over between the two world wars was mercilessly defeated. The political mistake was made, not by the Italian radicals who knew better than to engage in hopeless revolution, but by those Communists in Finland, Munich, Budapest and Berlin who did so despite all the known odds. Therefore Croce was absolutely justified in warning that it was useless to try to unseat the system by revolutionary means, and that one had to wait for a favourable moment, which came with the defeat of Fascism in the war. He was not only wise as a philosopher but absolutely right as a political brain too.

Urban   It surprises me that a man of Amendola's reasonableness and liberal background should have so closed a mind on Croce's impact. What was his reply to your objections?

Romeo   He gave practically no answer. I was therefore not surprised to find that Croce's influence is barely mentioned in Amendola's book.

But, of course, Amendola's is an absurd argument. It is tantamount to saying that Solzhenitsyn and Amalrik and Bukovsky
are not anti-Soviet forces of the greatest potential, or that the
nineteenth-century Russian intellectual/literary opposition
played no direct part in the collapse of Tsarism.

Well—how does one go about showing that nine-tenths of
Italian anti-Fascists were Communists when, in fact, they were
not? You can do this by the simple expedient of ignoring the
entire intellectual community which provided the majority of
anti-Fascist leaders by saying that they were Croceans, not
Communists. And Amendola does just that; his reasoning is that
virtually the sole source of anti-Fascism was the illegal Communist Party. This kind of argument is unworthy of a serious politician, which Amendola really is.

There is yet another aspect of the grotesque claim that Fascism
was an unmentionable evil and the very study of it verging on the
criminal. When you say that Fascism is beyond the pale of normal
history and add to it in the same breath that Italy was the country
that produced Fascism—what in fact are you saying? You are
saying that here is a nation that has something fundamentally
wrong with it, for otherwise it could not have given life to so
boundless an evil. At that point the study of Italian history turns
into a private investigator's or geneticist's attempt to track down
those criminal instincts and particular chromosome structures
that account for the indwelling flaw in Italian society. Italian
history ends, on this showing, in Fascism; therefore Fascism is
the key to unlocking everything in Italian history. Now, once you
have adopted this point of view, the next step in your reasoning
must be: if Italian history is flawed at its base, we must do
everything to uproot the flaw and avoid repeating the mistakes of
the past. How do we do that? By beginning an entirely *new*
history—by having a revolutionary about-turn in Italian affairs.
These were the historiographical implications of official anti-
Fascism.

Urban   But this is surely a near-racist type of condemnation of
the Italians as a nation which doesn't sort well with an ideology
that claims to stand for everything opposed to racism and nationalism. It is, in fact, the kind of generalisation Mussolini used to
make about the Greeks (decadent), Albanians (servile), Croatians
(brigands), etc.

Romeo   The Italian Marxists tried to obfuscate some of the
crudeness involved in these judgments. Their line was, of course,
that Italian history was the history, not of the people, but of the
ruling classes, hence the latter alone were responsible. The liberal
bourgeoisie, they said, which had brought about the unification

of Italy, was unable to put in train a *social* revolution. Some of this theorising was further refined by elements taken from Gramsci. Gramsci, as you know, had spent time in Russia and brought back with him the idea that national culture resides in the popular consciousness, not the ruling classes.

Urban An idea inherited, via the Slavophiles, from Herder and other German Romantics—

Romeo —certainly, but from the Communist ideological point of view Gramsci's adaptation of it was important because it made it possible for him to say that those elements of nationalism which were acceptable to Communists were 'in the people'. Thus one could go on condemning the ruling classes, while at the same time upholding the legitimacy of a certain national consciousness vested exclusively in 'the people'—

Urban —not remembering what Marxists seldom care to remember, that in Hegel's view 'the people' was that part of the population which did not know what it wanted.

Romeo Yes, but this admixture of Gramsci's ideas deflected from the directness of the Marxist critique. Everyone could point to his *neighbour*, never to himself, as the target of the attack.

Urban What was the non-Marxist reaction to this blanket condemnation of the Italian past?

Romeo After 1945 there was practically no nationalistic political culture left in Italy. Volpe's three-volume *L'Italia Moderna* was perhaps the only significant nationalistic answer to the Marxist offensive, but Volpe was an old man and his influence was very small. Some liberal historians offered more effective resistance, but their problem was that the Marxist approach to Italian history—especially the slogan of 'national guilt'—was not the Marxists' approach alone; it was shared by most anti-Fascists, particularly those anxious to demonstrate—usually a little after the event—their impeccably anti-Fascist credentials.

Some of this thinking has, incidentally, rubbed off even on respectable non-Italian historians such as Denis Mack Smith. He, too, sees Fascism as the key to understanding the whole of Italian reality.

Urban I am impressed and depressed by the acrimony surrounding so much of the debate on de Felice's work. Not that this is unusual among historians, but in Italy it has acquired particularly ugly accretions. You have written: 'We have heard echoes of shameful rituals in the violence with which the scholar has been held up to public execration'. De Felice himself commented on some of the distortions which his statements had undergone in the press: 'Fascism did infinite damage, but one of the greatest of its damaging effects was to have left a Fascist mentality as a heritage to the non-Fascists, to the anti-Fascists. . . . A mentality which must be fought . . . a mentality of intolerance . . . which seeks to disqualify an opponent in order to destroy him.'

Aren't we (as I also put it to de Felice) facing a self-perpetuating evil: Fascism breeding anti-Fascism, and anti-Fascism breeding Fascism, *ad infinitum*?

Romeo   There is something in that. Fanaticism and exclusiveness are important elements in the Fascist way of thinking, but it is regrettably true that these characteristics are general features of our time; they are not restricted to Fascism. Contemporary intellectual life is powerfully attracted by crudely drawn, black-and-white presentations. Ours is an intolerant century, and our minds are Manichean minds—notwithstanding the lessons of Hitler and Stalin. Our time has seen the greatest religious wars in human history; and can there be a greater evil than religious intolerance?

One of the most sinister aspects of this predilection for the either/or type of distinctions is the magnification of every problem, whether small or large, into theological issues (and we have already briefly touched on this). If whatever you do or say in your day-to-day life is automatically chalked up as a plus or minus on some ideological scale of values, then you soon reach the point where you must conclude that you can't change *anything* unless you change *everything*.

This ideologisation of the trivial is especially virulent in Italy where, in the politico-intellectual vacuum left by the war, the Marxist interpretation of the world acquired prestige and influence far beyond the card-carrying members of the Marxist community. Why?

The liberal-democratic régime which preceded Fascism and was unable to prevent the rise of Fascism was, not unnaturally, held responsible for Fascism. Therefore, in the post-war elections, this once mighty political force shrank to insignificance (as it also did in Germany, and for similar reasons). This left the stage to the Marxists on the Left and the Christian Democrats on the Right. Of the two, the Marxists claimed to have the wind of history in their sails. They were self-confident; theirs, they said, was the promised land. They attracted the Italian intellectuals by the sheer smell of success. The contrast between them—the winners in the battle against Fascism, and the liberal democrats who had been defeated by Fascism—was overwhelming.

The Christian Democrats started off with many advantages, the most important being that they were not implicated in any failure to stand up to Fascism, because they had not been in office. They had the Church's support and attracted the votes of that very large section of the population which was against Communism and found in the Christian Democratic Party the only large force that carried any promise of opposing it. But Roman Catholic political culture has always been extremely weak in Italy. It has been heir to the fact that the Italian nation-state was created in opposition to the Papacy. It had few constructive ideas, and only the most tenuous links with what makes a modern society work. And because the Christian Democrats lacked an autonomous political culture (while sharing with the Communists opposition to the liberal democratic tradition), much of their intellectual furniture was borrowed from Marxist stocks. To this day articles in the Italian Catholic press and the utterances of Christian Democratic politicians are honeycombed with Marxist arguments. The attacks on de Felice from Christian Democratic quarters have brought this out very clearly.

To sum up: the Italian liberal democratic tradition has political culture but no votes; the Christian Democrats have votes but no political culture. The Communists alone have both votes and political culture. This explains their success.

Urban   I was surprised to learn that the publication of de Felice's *Intervista* with Michael Ledeen was deliberately delayed by the publishers until after the 1976 general elections. Was this, I wondered, simply the opportunism of a publisher who wanted to be sure which way the wind was blowing before coming out with a book that was going to damage certain left-wing interests and might hurt him in the process? Would he have had it pulped if the Communists had come to power? Or was it, more profoundly, a reflection of the fact that the whole of Italian political culture was so weak, not to say infantile, that a small and learned book could decisively sway opinions to the Left or the Right? And if it was the latter, wasn't libertarian democracy facing hopeless odds in Italy? Surely, I reflected, the whole idea of holding back the publication of a book because elections were impending would sound absurd in an Anglo-American context. Not so, however, in France where we have, in the French reception of Koestler's *Darkness at Noon*, at least one outstanding piece of evidence of how a single volume can influence a country's entire political climate.

Romeo   I am surprised at your surprise. I don't know why exactly the publication was delayed. It is possible (though I have nothing to prove it) that Mr Laterza, who likes being on good terms with the Left, preferred to avoid the accusation that he was publishing anti-Left propaganda at a decisive moment in our political life. This is the easy answer. The real answer has to do with the particular acoustics of Italian politics. Not to go over ground again we have already covered, let me just say this: the publication of *Intervista* shortly before the general elections would have shaken some of the fundamental assumptions of our post-war political ideology. What would the Italian public have read in, or read into, de Felice? That the present system is not the bearer of irrefutable historic truth; that many of the things our Parties say have happened in respect of Fascism did in fact not happen; that anti-Fascism is no more an unmixed blessing than Fascism was an unredeemable evil—all this from a university professor who has spent all his life studying Fascism and written thousands of pages on Fascism. I am not saying that any of this would have suddenly switched large numbers of votes from the Left to the Right—it would be ridiculous to assume any such thing in a country with 40 million voters—but it would have been enough to damage the credibility and the image particularly of those political parties on the Left which have built their entire legitimacy on anti-Fascism.

Questioning the anti-Fascist credentials of the Italian Left before general elections is like questioning the existence of God when a Catholic Party is running for office: it is not the most opportune moment.

Urban   What accounts for the vicious tone of the reaction to de Felice's observations?

Romeo   A lot of people had their peace of mind disturbed. Academic conservatism is a powerful strain, and you have to expect to pay a price if you run against it—

Urban   —facts interfering with a good theory?

Romeo   That sort of thing, but it has gone way beyond it. De Felice evoked some entirely emotionally motivated reactions. One was left with the impression that the heart of the matter was not an historian's investigation of *what* had actually happened, but the moral values surrounding or attributed to his interpreta-tions. Let me stress again: Fascism has been portrayed as *the* diabolical force in modern history. Along then comes de Felice and says: 'Just a moment. Thirty years have now passed since the struggle against Fascism ended, and it is now possible to say, without supporting either Left or Right, *who* had actually fought Fascism and *what* the Fascists had really done and said.'

Well, this threatened to puncture the unquestioned assump-tions of official anti-Fascism. It was no longer possible simply to tell the young that those at one end of some arbitrary political spectrum were the good guys, and those at the other the bad ones. A political faith was being questioned, and that is never without its ructions.

But I would go a step further. Words are powerful weapons. When you have nurtured a convention whereby you can brand anyone opposed to you as a 'Fascist', then you have become an extra-legal arbiter between good and evil. In post-war Italy the designation 'Fascist' has come to carry the same condemnatory undertones as 'Trotskyist' did in Russia under Stalin: the word is the verdict. There is no need to ask where precisely the accused man has erred, or whether he has erred at all—the charge is enough, and in the last 30 years nothing has been more dreaded by Italian non-Communists and anti-Communists than to be marked by that stigma. The Italian Communist Party owes a great deal of the fear and respect it inspires, especially among intellectuals, to this monopolistic power—the power to label you a 'Fascist' without further argument. A Communist in Italy is widely recognised as a man who has the power to point a finger at you and say: '*You* are a Fascist'.

Need I go further? De Felice has shown that these labels are meaningless because the true history of Fascism and anti-Fascism does not coincide with the one that has been taught and mythologised since the war. The Communist Party has lost or is about to lose its power to smear and to frighten by semantic blackmail.

Urban   The 'anti' weapon, I might add from personal experience, has had a similar history in Hungary where it was used, between the two world wars, with comparable mythological overtones but in a sense diametrically opposed to Italian anti-Fascism. Under the Regency of Nicholas Horthy it was of great importance that one should be able to demonstrate or construct a 'counter-revolutionary' past. If you could show that you were a man of 'counter-revolutionary merit', or the widow of a man so distinguished, you had a much better chance of obtaining a licence to sell tobacco, or run a public house or, during the war, to obtain scarce materials, to say nothing of enjoying superior chances of promotion in the civil service and the armed forces, than did other citizens. A minor peerage (*vitéz*) was created to distinguish men of special 'counter-revolutionary merit', and the school history-books incorporated the appropriate bias. I was myself rigorously taught such history and examined in it.

Romeo   Yes; the advantage of the 'anti' slogan is that you enjoy the benefit of having an official enemy without anyone pressing you to say what you are *for*. In Italy, if you are a certified anti-Fascist, you can articulate many ideas which you couldn't if you were not so identified. For example, Leo Valiani, who was a real anti-Fascist and spent time in gaol, can get away with saying a great many things without danger. Others, whose anti-Fascist past is a construct, can also speak with some freedom as long as the construct remains unchallenged. But if you have no such credentials, your freedom is limited. It is useful to be able to demonstrate an anti-Fascist past.

De Felice challenged the conventional tableau of Italian politics, and that was enough to expose him to a spate of despicable *ad hominem* attacks.

Articles were written against him which seemed to be saying that his books were a matter for the police; that it dishonoured the name of the University of Rome to have a man like *that* on its academic staff, and that publishing houses such as Einaudi and Laterza (which claim to be anti-Fascist) should never have stooped to publishing his work. The tenor of these attacks was also something to be marvelled at. It seemed that to know Professor de Felice was not a good thing for one's career or reputation—that de Felice should be isolated and treated as a social outcast. Soon after Amendola had written his famous article in *l'Unità*, some friends of the de Felices phoned Mrs de Felice: 'We are happy for you and your family', they said, 'because now that Amendola has written his piece you are no longer in danger'.

After Amendola had spoken there was (as I have said) a change for the better. Amendola himself, however, was still proving much more open-minded than other critics on the Left. There appeared a four-part series of articles in *Il Giorno* under the significant title of 'La Pugnalata dello Storico', 'The Historian's Stab-in-the-Back'—a direct transplantation of the *Dolchstoss* legend, de Felice being the wielder of the knife and anti-Fascism his victim.

Urban *Is* there going to be a break in this apparently self-replenishing cycle of Fascism/anti-Fascism/Fascism, under whatever name one or the other may surface?

Romeo The de Felice affair has made a difference. It is no longer quite so easy to say that the very attempt to understand Fascism historically is a crime. Of the articles so far published, about one third were in defence of de Felice and two thirds against him, and yet de Felice is alive. He has proved that it is possible to write the kind of thing he has written and to survive.

Urban Survive—but for how long? When I read some of the details of the attacks, I wonder whether the viciousness of the polemics isn't a matter of political temperament and therefore closed to any appeal to reason. Take the radical critic Giovanni Ferrara accusing de Felice of out-and-out perversion. Had not Croce laid it down (Ferrara wrote) that the entire subject of Fascism disgusted him, and was it not clear that someone who devoted his entire life to the study of such a repulsive subject was himself abnormal?

Romeo Yes, I read the article and I know Ferrara well. Alas, my good friend Ferrara chose to quote only part of what Croce had written. Croce's position was that he, as a private person, was free not to study Fascism, because he did not like Fascism and did not want to spend time writing its history. However, *if* (he said) he decided to study Fascism, he would try to understand why so many people—people who were neither particularly wicked nor fools—chose to become Fascists, and he would also try to show what historically positive elements were incorporated in Fascism. De Felice's were (as I've said) not the first books on Fascism, but they were epoch-making in the sense that they are backed up by a staggering amount of research, archival evidence and the rest. It has become very difficult to brush him aside by branding him a liar. He has the materials on hand.

In this sense the de Felice controversy has promoted a more rational atmosphere. Whether it can last is an open question. If the Communist Party came to power it would be useless to hope that the de Felice type of phenomenon could survive—

Urban —you feel that his freedom to study Fascism independently would be jeopardised?

Romeo Eurocommunism, as you know, is said to be a special kind of Communism which claims to be liberal. But I don't think that even under Eurocommunism intellectual life would be permitted to be free enough to accommodate the kind of work de Felice has done or the discussion he has generated.

Urban You are saying—if I may offer an interim summary of your argument—that the publication of de Felice's work and the subsequent controversy have, on balance, enhanced the state of Italian freedom, first, because de Felice's painstaking research has demolished some old shibboleths and, second, because the Communist Party has, in the person of Amendola, tried to direct the controversy into constructive channels.

Romeo Yes, but we are talking of one particular case only. The de Felice affair is not coextensive with the intellectual life of Italy. We are discussing a limited historical problem which is, however, very important because it is also a political problem. Amendola's position has undoubtedly helped to give the discussion a rational outcome. It is in this sense, and in this sense only, that the Communist Party has, in the person of Amendola and not that of other Marxist intellectuals, contributed to the growth of a more permissive intellectual atmosphere.

Naturally, this 'liberalism' of the Communist Party must be seen in the context of the Party's problems and general policy. We must hand it to them that this is not the first time that the Party has defended liberal positions. There have been many instances in the recent as well as the less recent past. But, of course, it is easy to be liberal when you are in opposition or, at any rate, not in power. What I am curious to know is: how will the Party behave when in power?

Urban   I am intrigued by your reference to Ferrara as 'my good friend' and to the apparently amicable personal relations which exist between de Felice and Amendola—whereas we know perfectly well that Amendola is one of de Felice's and your deadliest political opponents. Is this part of the rather attractive Don Camillo syndrome of Italian life, or is it purely a matter of good public manners?

Romeo   There are some 12 million people in Italy who regularly vote Communist. Almost one out of every three adult Italians is a Communist supporter. If you felt personal animosity for every Communist you encountered, life would become impossible.

Many of us went to the same schools and universities; we have known each other since we were small boys, and as we are not living in a state of civil war, we can, by observing the courtesies and civilities of life, manage to live together. Naturally, when blows are exchanged in academic or political argument, the atmosphere is less sweet and reasonable. Valiani's attack on de Felice ruined their friendship for a time—

Urban   —I'm told their wives stopped having coffee together—

Romeo   —I think it went a little beyond that. De Felice's good personal relations with Ferrara have also come to an end, so that the Don Camillo analogy does not always apply. Nevertheless, one of the features of democratic society—and we still have that to some extent in Italy—is that antagonistic views and their holders can coexist with one another in a climate of mutual tolerance.

But let me quickly add that a good deal of the philosophy of live-and-let-live also obtained under Fascism—certainly among the Fascists. You must remember that Fascists were ordinary people, no different from today's Communists or Christian Democrats. They had among themselves the fiercest disagreements, personal rivalries and dislikes. But as long as shared interests predominated, these disagreements and hostilities were ignored or controlled. But when they ceased to operate, the friendships came to an abrupt end and the killing started, as for example after September 1943. People change as their situation changes.

Urban There is a photograph in Edda Mussolini Ciano's recent book, *My Truth*, of Ciano putting a friendly arm around the shoulders of one of his closest friends, Alessandro Pavolini—the same man who demanded and obtained Ciano's head under the Republic of Salò as Secretary of the Republican Fascist Party. . . .

Wouldn't you say that Italy is, by virtue of the temperament of the people and the conservatism of her institutions, in a state of permanent but far from malign, much less bloodthirsty, civil war? Professor Hans Selye has recently noted that 'man has an innate tendency to go up to the maximum of his stress tolerance'. The Italian people's stress tolerance in terms of political intrigue and crisis is very high. I would therefore hazard the observation that Italy is strongly inclined to have, indeed it probably enjoys having, a near-disastrous socio-political crisis, whether or not it is actually warranted by facts.

Romeo I would hesitate to describe our situation as civil war even in the benign sense in which you have tried to depict it, but it is certainly true that we are always on the brink of precipitating a serious crisis. Why this is so is something very hard to understand if you are an American or even a Briton. The contest of parties at a general election in Italy is totally unlike anything you have at American Presidential elections. The recent choice in the United States was between Ford and Carter. Well, the voter wasn't faced with a tragic alternative. He did not have to search his heart and look deeply into past American political experience, and infer from the ideological pronouncements of Ford's or Carter's party which way he should vote. Indeed, the catalytic nature of the choice affected him so little that vast numbers of American citizens did not think it worth their while to go the polls. But in Italy the difference between having Berlinguer and a Christian Democrat at the head of the government is a matter heavy with consequences for the entire future of the state and the nation.

I know Americans who think the Italians exaggerate, that the PCI is really a Social Democratic Party, that there would be nothing very terrible in having Berlinguer as Prime Minister.

But this is misreading our situation. Since the 1968 upheavals in France and Italy, our country has never returned to normality. We are suffering from what could be described, with some exaggeration, as a permanent general strike. There is continuous agitation at the schools, universities, railways, airports, post offices, in the press and in the factories. And the strikes are more and more often clinched by violence and the threat of violence. Our economic life, civic security and international position have all been deeply affected. You have to live in Italy to get the full measure of this: it has become practically impossible to manage public institutions or private enterprise, because the legitimacy of all authority has been challenged and defeated. We have examples of this every day. At the moment we are suffering from the suspension of the law in favour of terrorists. There are two principal left-wing terrorist groups in Italy: the Red Brigades in the North and the Proletarian Armed Guards in the South. Some members of these gangs have been arrested and put on trial in Turin and Naples. But when the arrested men's colleagues began attacking the police and the judges, the trials were halted and no more arrests followed. The terror is being successful—both the judiciary and the police are frightened of being shot in the streets, as some have been. The most recent (May 1977) example of the defeat of the law has been the abandonment of the trial of a group of Red Guard terrorists in Turin. The intimidating effect of threats and recent murders has been so thorough that no jury could be found to sit at the trial.

Or take another kind of disorder. You have no doubt read in the Italian papers that so-called 'young proletarian committees' have set up house in the University of Milan. They occupied the university, stopped all teaching and research and went on a rampage, destroying books, documents, scientific instruments, as well as wrecking the premises. The Rector did not call in the police, and when asked why, he said he was anxious to avoid more serious incidents which might have included loss of life. And you could see what he meant: when you call in the police to expel young people armed with iron bars, knives and Molotov cocktails, the possibility of someone getting hurt or killed can never be ruled out—it has happened in the past—and if a student gets killed, the Rector is held responsible, for wasn't he the one who had called for police protection? At that point up goes the cry in every radio and television programme and in every newspaper in the land that the university teachers do not understand the young—and look what has happened: they've caused the death of a student! There then follows an emotion-packed funeral which thousands attend, and the sight of which on the television screen further magnifies the demand for the Rector's head. The Rector is, by now, completely alone. The political ruling class have disowned him. In fact, they reinforce the charge that he alone was responsible. Can you blame the Rector for refusing to assert his authority? The irony is that in our latest round of troubles the extreme Left has started armed attacks on members of the Communist Party, and the Communist press is calling for police protection. And while this is going on, Berlinguer continues to demand power for his Party on the grounds that 'without the Communist Party it is impossible to govern Italy'.

Or take the increasingly institutionalised censorship of intellectual work at the universities. (I have a letter in my pocket from a professor at the University of Rome which I will present to the Minister of Education when I see him next week to discuss with him the rule of the unions at the University.) The unions have decided that no funds shall be made available for university teachers to publish their work without the permission of an 'Institute Committee'. This Committee is a kind of Soviet, composed of a variety of people, including caretakers, nightwatchmen, cleaning women and so on. Since all these people are members of unions and take orders from their unions, the power of deciding what sort of book is fit to be published by the scholars of the University of Rome might soon be vested in the unions. And this, of course, would mean that you could write what you liked for your private drawer, but your writing would never see the light of day unless you were in with the unions. And the unions are, of course, appendages of the Communist Party.

So when Americans tell me that the Italian Communists are Social Democrats or social reformers, we tend not to be in complete agreement. I have long given up trying to explain Italian politics to Americans.

Urban I am strongly, and perhaps wrongly, under Luigi Barzini's influence in thinking that the basic good nature and opportunism of Italians would somehow take the heat out of, or at any rate corrupt, the extremism of any Italian political party. Professor Milton Friedman has recently argued that even in an even-handed liberal-democratic polity the 'political market' is heavily weighted against democratic decisions, whereas the 'economic market' is not. And he demonstrates this principle by a simple example. Suppose, he says, that the question at issue is whether neckties should be red or green. If this is to be decided by the political process, everyone votes, and if 51 per cent of the electorate vote that ties shall be red, 100 per cent of the people get red neckties. In the 'economic market', everyone goes to the shops separately, and if 51 per cent of the people vote that ties shall be red, 51 per cent get red neckties and 49 per cent green neckties. And the current tendency is, Friedman argues, to subject, entirely out of their proper context, more and more issues that immediately affect ordinary people's lives to the Yes/No type of vote of the 'political market'.

Now in Italy, under a Communist or part-Communist government, the number of Yes/No type of decisions would immeasurably increase, and the tyranny of the 'political market' would become all-pervasive.

But *would* it? If my Barzinian image of the Italian character is correct, even a vote much larger than 51 per cent in favour of, say, the Communist Party would not result in a 100 per cent Communist rule, because the Italians would always know how to play and outplay the system both inside and outside the Party. One may call this Italian wisdom, sophistication, cynicism, corruption, opportunism, what you will, but it is clear to me that even a 100 per cent vote for this or that extremist party would be nibbled away at the edges, watered down, reduced to ridicule, or manoeuvred into a cul-de-sac. It was so under Fascism, and I feel confident it would be so again under Communism.

Romeo I have heard this argument before and I'm far from certain that it is true. Where *is* this great humanity of the Italians? Italy is, and has always been, a country of violence. Some of the most famous assassins in world literature are Italians, usually imported for their skills. There are cities and entire regions in Italy today where murder is an everyday occurrence.

Only yesterday I was talking to a former student of mine who is now a member of the regional government of Calabria. He said:

> There are 2 million people in Calabria, of whom only 80,000 have gone to school, and even these have no work commensurate with their qualifications. One of the results is that anyone with a little money in the bank is exposed to blackmail: if you are a shopkeeper or a lawyer or a doctor or anyone suspected of having savings, you are made to pay protection money if you want to stay in business. If you are known to be rich, your chances of being kidnapped and released only against large sums of money are high. The situation is completely out of hand. Recently we and the Communists [the man is a Socialist] organised a mass demonstration, with red flags and a great deal of worker-participation, against the spread of this evil. A few days later the police tried to arrest some of the criminals involved—there was an exchange of fire and one of the wanted men was killed. A funeral was arranged and the Mafia let it be known that it expected the entire population of the small town where the man was to be buried to be present. Well, all shops were dutifully shut, all offices were closed for the day and the entire population appeared in the funeral procession—not because they had any sympathy with the dead extortioner, but because they were frightened of the consequences of not doing what the Mafia had ordered them to do.

Where, I ask you, is the exceptional wisdom and humanity of the Italians? In Lombardy and Piedmont, for some years after the war criminality was rampant. In Emilia there was a 'triangle of death', composed of the cities of Reggio, Parma and Bologna, where the assassination of landowners and capitalists for no other reason than their 'class' was a common feature of life. These were all Communist strongholds. Even now, if you go to Turin or Milan or some of the other large industrial centres, the atmosphere is so thick with political hatred that you can almost touch it with your hands. And you say the Italians are kindly folk?

Naturally, there is good and bad in every nation. There is a bit of the brute in all of us as well as some faint glimmer of the gentle Jesus. But to say that the Italians have a special knack for sinking their differences and letting reason prevail does not make sense to me. It is an old truth that it takes two to make peace but one is enough to make war. Of course in Italy, as elsewhere, the man in the street is a good-natured fellow. He is happiest when he is left alone, for his concerns are a secure job, a roof over his head, a satisfactory sexual life and the odd weekend at the seaside. But it isn't this sluggish majority that makes things tick in history. The Fascists weren't the majority of the Italian people, but they took power, and it was not very easy to say to them: 'But what has become of your good nature?' They had simple answers to complicated questions and the power to tolerate no others.

Today, again, we have a determined minority waiting in the wings to exploit the first turbulence in our political, economic or social equilibrium. And if this were to happen I would not vouch that civil strife could be avoided.

Urban The slow retreat of the freedom of the press, radio and television at a time when Communist or part-Communist rule is only a vague possibility is perhaps the most worrying aspect of Italy's troubles, and the one least realised abroad. Luigi Barzini's inability to take up his appointment as director of *Il Messaggero* represented, symbolically at least, the point of no return. What exactly prevented him from fulfilling his contract?

Romeo Barzini's story can be told in a few words. For many years Barzini was (though he is no longer) a Member of Parliament for the Liberal Party. When he was appointed director of *Il Messaggero*, a left-wing 'redaction' committee of the paper, which claimed to represent the 'workers', declared that Barzini was unacceptable to them because he was a repressive agent of the capitalist class; giving the direction of the paper to Barzini, they said, was an attack on 'democracy'. Barzini, you will recall, was imprisoned under the Fascist régime and barely got away with his life. The Liberal Party, to their eternal discredit, didn't utter a

word. Rather than protest that it was inadmissible and preposterous to allege that a Liberal Member of Parliament, especially
one with Barzini's record, could be 'against democracy', the Party
assisted, through its calculated silence, in making a sacrifice of
Barzini and the principles he stood for. The Liberal Party has
done many stupid things in its time, but this was its worst and
most self-damaging blunder.

Barzini's case was a watershed. It demonstrated that whatever
the Italian law may say, it is no longer possible for the legal
owners of a newspaper to appoint an editor if a Left-oriented
group of employees is against him. This state of affairs has now
been written into the law. There are people who argue that the
Italian press is freer than it has been precisely because it has
become Left-oriented. I have participated in several discussions
to examine this claim, and the point I have always made was that *I*
could see no sign of this increased freedom. While the prevailing
wind was anti-Communist, the press, too, was predominantly
anti-Communist; now that the government depends on Communist support and the Communist Party is widely thought to
have the future on its side, the press too is trimming its gear to
Communism. If an abject service of power or anticipated power is
what the freedom of the press is about, then, but only then, can
we say that the Italian press has gained in 'freedom'.

Urban   I know from Luigi Barzini that most Italian papers,
including for example *La Stampa*, will not publish him for the
reasons you have mentioned. His son has recently been refused a
place at an institute of higher education because of his father's
class background. When one adds these small pointers to your
formidable catalogue of civic unfreedoms—can one still say that
Italy is a free society in the West European sense of the term?

Romeo   At the moment, but decreasingly and with many
qualifications—yes. But at the same time we must make the world
aware that the body of classic democratic liberties has shrunk and
is on the point of rapidly shrinking further. The expectation that
the Communists will win and the fear of being found on the
wrong side of the future wielders of power have inspired many
an act of pre-emptive cowardice by omission as much as by
commission. There are factories and offices all over the land
where the workers are silent because they are frightened of
opposing the dominant unions; there are universities where it is
safer to say nothing than to invite the anger of 'proletarian committees' and other self-appointed groups of radicals; and in the
newspaper world it is virtually a requirement for survival to toe
the line, because refusal to do so soon relegates one to a place in
the dole-queue. There are thousands of Italian teachers who dare

not speak their minds to our 13 million school children and students because they feel unprotected, because whatever they say may be held against them if and when political power changes hands, and because their superiors and their superiors' superiors have the same preference for a quiet life and for the same reasons. The retreat of liberty is universal, and the cause of the retreat is fear of the Communist Party, assisted, as I say, by a feeling that if the rape of Italy is inevitable, timely consent might make for a more tolerable bed-fellowship.

Urban But how does this picture accord with the Communist Party's claim to be a liberal force in society? The Party's official and much publicised support for dissent in Eastern Europe and its promise of complete individual freedom in a Socialist Italy would be ill served by the practices you describe.

Romeo Since 1968 the Party has learned two things: first it has adopted, at the level of its leading cadres, a liberal Eurocommunist position. But, second, it has, further down the line, also learned something from the Chinese experience—namely the technique of beating or blackmailing your opposition by mass assemblies through the fear generated by a few ringleaders and the denial of the secret vote. The psychology of the 'mass struggle' (to use a Chinese phrase) has rubbed off, and with great success, on the local Communist secretaries. In every corner of Italy, day after day, assemblies are called to discuss some problem or other about the organisation or personnel or politics of your school or office or factory. No vote is taken; resolutions are adopted by consent after the activists have harangued you and put fear into the hearts of the opposition. All questions are presented in a Yes/No manner, and upon you be it if you say No, for the wages of dissent is the immediate accusation: *'You* are a Fascist!'

Now (to repeat) the man in the street is not a heroic character. He wants to do his work and go home. If keeping a judicious silence promises to give him a quiet life, he will adopt the resolutions, sign whatever he is expected to sign, and turn his mind to the next football match and his girl friend. It is through this fine combination of liberal promises at the top, Chinese techniques at the bottom, and a consummate popular apathy that the Italian Communists have infiltrated the whole of Italian civil society.

Urban If I were an Italian liberal Communist leader I would see all this in an entirely different light. I would say the interests of the proletariat coincide with those of the whole of Italian society (excluding, of course, a handful of capitalists and landowners whom history has relegated to oblivion). Therefore the freedom of the working class is ultimately the freedom of everyone. Hence (I would argue) what is really happening in Italy is a prudent understanding on the part of certain habitually wavering elements, of the politically immature, and those marginally still under bourgeois influence, that their future depends on the extent to which they are willing to identify their own liberty with the liberty of the working class. If, however, I were a more orthodox type of Communist leader, I would simply say: The Italians are learning to live with the dictatorship of the proletariat—Italian style.

Whatever the rationale, Italy's *Gleichschaltung* appears to be well under way.

Romeo   The Italian Communists—at any rate those who take the public platforms these days—don't say either. At the grassroots one may hear voices about the dictatorship of the proletariat, but not at the level of evangelicising Eurocommunism. Here all the talk is about democracy and freedom. And I think the current leadership is genuinely convinced that after the Stalinist experience one can no longer argue that the 'freedom' or the 'interests' of the proletariat coincide with those of the rest of mankind. Giuseppe Boffa, a former Moscow correspondent of *l'Unità*, has argued in the first volume of his history of Stalinism that the 'freedom' of the proletariat is a corrupt notion because it permitted Stalin to exterminate in its name nine-tenths of the Central Committee of the Soviet CP and to kill off millions of innocent people. Who, he asked, could possibly call himself free in such a society? Therefore the Italian Communists would find it difficult to argue that proletarian freedom is coextensive with the freedom of man. And they don't—not any more.

Urban   But Lombardo Radice does put forward that argument in this series of discussions.

Romeo   He is the exception that proves the rule. But even though the good of the proletariat is no longer identified with the good of mankind, let us be clear that the Italian Communists' notion of freedom is highly ambivalent. It has every appearance of meaning a liberal democratic polity if you look at the obverse side of the idea, but it will strike you as standing for a very different kind of 'democracy' if you inspect it from the reverse side. For every Lombardo there is an Ingrao. Signor Ingrao, now President of the Chamber of Deputies, has, together with Signor Natta, let it be known that it is perfectly possible to have a democratic parliament *without an opposition*. It is, he says, a bourgeois idea to think that parliament must always consist of a majority which forms the government, and a minority which is in opposition. Parliament properly conceived is a 'unitarian' institution where different social groups—schools, universities, workers' organisations and so on—find their rightful places and end their differences. This 'unitarian' parliamentarianism is, Ingrao claims, a higher form of democracy. In it the differences and contradictions characteristic of society at a lower level of development are absorbed and terminated.

Urban   Stalin would have no reason to demur at this formula.

Romeo   He would not—in Stalin's Russia too there were 'trade unions', and the Soviet state was 'unitary' with a vengeance. Ingrao's view is, of course, no freak of Italian Communist ideology. A recent issue of *Critica Marxista*, the Party's theoretical journal, clearly spelled out the thesis that it is possible and desirable to have a democratic parliament without an opposition. This was endorsed by Professor Giovanni Berlinguer, a relation of the Party leader, in the Party's official weekly *Rinascita*. It was clear to him as a constitutional lawyer, he wrote, that from the constitutional point of view it was perfectly feasible to have parliamentary democracy without an opposition.

Naturally, Ingrao, Natta, Giovanni Berlinguer and the others protest that they would not want to repeat the mistakes of the Stalinist past. But this is scant comfort for those whose memories are long enough to remember how Lenin went about destroying the constituent assembly (it lasted one single day), the uses to which parliament was put under Mussolini, and the sort of multi-party system that is allowed to exist in Poland, East Germany, and Czechoslovakia.

Urban   'We learn from history that we do not learn from history'?

Romeo   When the story of our time comes to be written, this may well prove to be the verdict of our successors—

Urban   —an old wisdom that strikes every generation which experiences it on its own skin as depressingly new. Arnold Toynbee once said to me that he found this unwillingness to learn from the misfortunes of earlier generations the most alarming aspect of human affairs. But de Felice's work is surely a source of hope— some of the fog has lifted.

Romeo   If de Felice's work has achieved nothing else, it has certainly made it a great deal more difficult for us to throw ourselves blindfolded into the arms of any kind of totalitarianism. From one eye at least the blindfold has been removed.

Domenico Settembrini

7 Mussolini and Lenin

Urban One of the least known and least advertised aspects of the interplay between Communism and Fascism is their shared roots and, in some important respects, parallel developments. From the Communist point of view, this is a delicate matter—the Italian Left's reaction to the work of Renzo de Felice has given ample evidence of their sensitivity, and of the undiminished importance, as a force in current politics, of both Fascism and the study of Fascism. Why should this be so more than three decades after the collapse of Fascism?

Settembrini The common matrix of Italian Fascism and Italian Communism is pre-1914 Italian Socialism, and the common denominator between the two leading Marxist revolutionaries of the time—Mussolini and Lenin—was their hatred for the betrayal, as they saw it, of the revolutionary message of Socialism by Social Democrats. Remember that the majority of pre-1914 Socialists were moderates who believed in improving the working-man's lot by trade unionism and gradual reform, and adapting the movement to the rules of parliamentary democracy. But this was not what Mussolini and Lenin understood by Socialism; this, for them, was selling out to the bourgeoisie. *Their* purpose was to destroy it. Italian Fascism and Italian Communism both set out to confound the official theoreticians of revolutionary Socialism who, while paying a great deal of lip-service to revolution, seemed as incapable of putting it into action as they were rightly suspected of being unwilling to do so. The remarkable thing is that Mussolini and Lenin shared this contempt for the official Socialism of their day and set about imposing on it a revolutionary programme without any knowledge of what the other man was doing. Some students of the period insist, and I would agree with them, that between 1910 and 1914

146

Mussolini was in many respects the more radical revolutionary of the two. Indeed Professor Ernst Nolte asserts, rightly as I see it, that Mussolini was the first historically significant European Communist.

Lenin's *What is to be done?*, in which he outlined the need for a disciplined, élitist, conspiratorial party organisation in order to provide a sluggish proletariat with determined leadership has, at least in the formal sense, its analogue in Mussolini's personal magazine *Utopia*, in which he articulated his dissent from Italian official Socialism.

Why did Mussolini need a separate mouthpiece? Because, as editor of *Avanti*, he was confined to representing the approved line of revolutionary Socialism, while privately he began to realise that the facts of Italian society were rendering the official canons obsolete: the *reality* was that Italian democracy was a going concern, that the living standards and social conditions of the masses were improving, and as a consequence of these, the spirit of revolution was sagging and, in fact, disappearing. None of this could be *officially* stated, for any admission that—contrary to dogma—the pauperisation of the proletariat was a non-fact and capitalism was improving the social conditions of the entire population would have robbed Socialism of its historical legitimacy.

Now Lenin, too, could see that the pauperisation of the proletariat had come to an end, and with it any hope that the masses would impel themselves into revolution had to be discounted. But whereas Lenin was working on a country which had experienced no renaissance, no reformation and no bourgeois revolution and was, therefore, ripe, as he rightly thought, for the *imposition* of revolution by a small band of self-appointed revolutionaries, Mussolini was active in a land where the bourgeois democratic revolution had in the main been accomplished and where following the Marxist doctrine to the letter would have meant relegating himself to the spectator's enclosure of history. The publication of *Utopia* was a symbol of these realisations. Mussolini now uses anarchists as his collaborators and, without repudiating Marxism, he nevertheless questions some of its accepted interpretations. He tries to return to the voluntaristic views of the Marx of 1848, while Lenin, working as he is in an entirely different social context, insists on the doctrines of orthodox Marxism.

Urban Whether Lenin's programme in *What is to be done?* is orthodox Marxism is rather open to question. I would have thought Lenin *protests* his orthodoxy but, in fact, the idea of a rigorously disciplined and centrally organised party *pushing* the cart of history in a direction in which it would not go of its own momentum as Marx predicted, was the negation of Marx's central doctrine. So, to a lesser extent, was Lenin's notion of injecting into the consciousness of a backward and self-seeking proletariat the will to revolution and power. As Leonard Schapiro put it:

> Lenin probably realised [in *What is to be done?*] . . . that the theories of Marx and Engels in their pure form do not lead to revolution. The logical issue of the analysis which Marx and Engels produced is simply that society develops along a pre-ordained path and there is no room for upheavals. In other words, revisionism as portrayed by Bernstein is, as it were, built into the system. And indeed there is a passage in Engels where he says that there is an inherent contradiction in 'our theory', for if the proletariat becomes class-conscious enough to make a revolution then it is not neccessary for it to make a revolution: if it does not become class-conscious enough to make a revolution, then it would be disastrous if it did.

Settembrini   The idea of bringing revolution to the proletariat from outside the proletariat comes from Kautsky, but there are also indications in *The Holy Family* that Marx was, in 1845, not completely confident that the proletariat *would* automatically recognise its class interests. He was intimating that, more important than what the proletariat *is* and thinks, is what the proletariat *must do*. In *What is to be done?* Lenin was certainly forcing Marx's views. The theory of a Leninist party is a mere possibility in Marx which Marx would have repudiated if his socio-economic theory had been confirmed by facts, and which he did in fact repudiate when he maintained that his theory *was* being confirmed by reality. We must remember that at an earlier period in his life Marx was a Jacobin. In 1902 Lenin realises that the facts do not tally with the central doctrine of Marx's mature theory—that the consciousness of the working class alone will produce no revolution, certainly not in backward, agrarian Russia. Hence he returns to the Jacobin Marx of 1845 and writes his blueprint for the practical realisation of revolution in Russia—theory or no theory.

Lenin, unlike Mussolini, could not *openly* repudiate Marxism, for he needed Marxism for the legitimation of revolution; Mussolini, on the other hand, had no choice but to subject it to a fundamental critique. In Italy, unlike Russia, the bourgeois revolution had been accomplished, and the official Marxism of the Socialist Party led by Turati was a highly conservative force from which Mussolini could not hope to elicit a revolutionary response.

So where did Mussolini look for his inspiration? He looked for and found some of his answers in nineteenth-century idealism which arrived with a great and sudden impact in Italian culture at the turn of the century. This idealism, and it was, of course, principally German idealism, carried a useful message. It said that each nation, each state, each class and each race carries a 'telos' of its own—that they are sovereign entities which have a higher claim to realisation than the individual. The individual is there to serve as a building stone in a larger edifice, but his inherent worth hinges entirely upon his usefulness in the design of the state, nation or class.

Urban It would be hard to think of a single passage which more accurately prefigures the law-sanctioned lawlessness of the twentieth century than Hegel's observation: 'Moral claims that are irrelevant must not be brought into collision with world-historical deeds and their accomplishment. The Litany of private virtues ... must not be raised against them. The History of the World might ... entirely ignore the circle within which ... the ... distinction between the moral and the politic lies.'

Settembrini The practical implications of this Hegelian notion had symmetrical consequences on the Left and Right. On the Right it was interpreted as a call for the sacrifice of the individual on the altar of the nation; on the Left on that of class and Socialism. In either case, liberal democracy was the common enemy, and it is this shared hostility to democracy and its institutions that provides the link between the pre-1914 revolutionaries—both Marxists and anarcho-syndicalists—on the one hand, and the post-1914 Communists and Fascists, on the other.

The idea that in the state, the nation, or the revolution resides some virtue which can rightfully claim to override the interests of individuals because it bodies forth some *Geist* or inner purpose of its own is, of course, at least as old as the French Revolution. Robespierre is said to have confronted a mob clamouring for more bread and cheaper living conditions with the warning: 'But will you ever learn to concern yourselves with something more elevated than fodder for your bellies?', or words to that effect. Lenin's contempt for trade unionism and mere 'economism' and Mussolini's similar contempt for the mob which expects to be and enjoys being dictated to stem from the same sentiment. Both believed, and said, that the proletariat is too short-sighted, too immersed in the gratification of pedestrian needs, and too uneducated to see the larger historic framework which it is their duty to fill with significant but preordained action. Hence the duty of bringing the proletariat's submerged consciousness to the surface falls to a group of organised individuals who articulate the laws of history in the name of the proletariat. Mussolini and Lenin enforced this interpretation of nineteenth-century idealism, each in his own way, with great and awesome consequences.

Urban Mussolini, to do him justice, was always prepared to acknowledge his debt. Both in the Chamber of Deputies, and talking to his biographers, he frequently underlined the psychological and systemic affinities between Fascism and Soviet Communism. For example, in his conversation with Emil Ludwig, in 1932, the following exchange took place:

> [Ludwig] Before the war . . . you once wrote in *Avanti*: 'Socialism is not an Arcadian and peaceful affair. We do not believe in the sacredness of human life.' Is not that Fascism?
> Yes, it is the same thing.
> You have also written: 'Unless Fascism were a faith, how could it arouse the fire of enthusiasm?' Is not that Communism?
> He nodded assent, saying: 'Such affinities do not trouble me.'
> 'It follows then, does it not, that the faith which both you and the Russians demand and find distinguishes your respective systems from all others?'
> 'Yes', he said 'and more than that. In negative matters as well we are like one another; both we and the Russians are opposed to the liberals, to the democrats, to parliament.'

An even more significant episode occurred in the wake of the Ribbentrop-Molotov Pact, which the Italians disliked intensely and Mussolini was at a loss how to serve up to his Party. Ciano records on 16 October 1939: 'The Duce was very much affected by certain documents and information on Russia which have come into our possession, and wants to begin a press campaign to explain to the Italians that Bolshevism is dead and that in its place is a kind of Slavic Fascism.' How right he was. How revealing of his mentality that he thought Stalin's Russia could be realistically presented to the Italian people as a form of Fascism!

Settembrini Yes—one could list a whole series of similarities, partial similarities, divergences and returns to a parallel course in the history of the two movements. Let me look at the question of 'interventionism'.

Mussolini as a revolutionary syndicalist of the Sorelian school and Lenin as a revolutionary Marxist both realised that syndicalism—that is, trade unionism—does not produce revolutions. The masses have to be *led* to revolution, and that requires a party. Quite independently from each other, the two men drew up plans for an élite leadership to propel the masses into revolution and to guide it. But while they realised that the party could be instrumental in radicalising the masses and shaping their responses, it could, on its own, not *create* the basic precondition for revolution—the collapse of the capitalist social order. Whatever Marx had said about the spirit of revolution automatically emerging from the impoverishment of the proletariat and the consequent inability of capitalism to sell its goods on a shrinking market, the fact was that the proletariat was not getting poorer, that the spirit of revolution was conspicuous by its absence, and the capitalist order was expanding rather than facing bankruptcy. A substitute had, therefore, to be found for Marx's supposed self-triggering mechanism, and that substitute was—war.

Mussolini, after the fiasco of Red Week in 1914,* was very conscious—and I would say he was more conscious than Lenin—of the limitations on what any combination of political and industrial action could achieve in stirring up revolution in a serious but not universal crisis. He realised that without the armed forces joining an uprising, no revolution could, in fact, take off. Hence he retreats in good time without completely compromising himself, and draws a conclusion which we might today paraphrase in the Maoist tag: 'Revolution grows out of the barrel of a gun'. Here again, Mussolini is close to Lenin's thinking. A year before Red Week, at the time of the second Balkan War, Lenin wrote to Gorky: 'It is much to be hoped that the war degenerates into a European war. This would certainly promote revolution, but we cannot expect that Nicholas or Franz Joseph will do us that favour.'

Lenin's language is significant, for it amounts to an admission that neither Socialists acting on orthodox Marxism nor Socialists acting on its voluntaristic interpretation were capable of actually propelling Europe into revolution: both found themselves constrained to wait upon the whims of the Autocrat and the Emperor, hoping but not expecting that they would present the revolutionaries with the coveted opportunity of war.

The Tsar does Lenin the favour he was hoping for—Nicholas is among the first to enter the war, but the Italian government denies Mussolini a similar favour and decides on neutrality—in good part at Mussolini's own behest, because throughout the summer of 1914 Mussolini himself was a determined advocate of neutrality on the then universally accepted Socialist principle that the refusal of the proletariat to be cannon-fodder in the predatory wars of capitalism constituted the strongest proof of the interna-

* For explanation of Red Week, see footnote, p. 101 above.

tional solidarity of the working class—a principle on which the German, French and Belgian Socialists were soon to disappoint him.

Urban   Indeed one remembers nationalism asserting itself in the heart of that doyen of international Socialism, G. V. Plekhanov. In August 1914 he summoned Angelica Balabanoff to Geneva to enquire of her what her and the Italian Socialist Party's attitude was to the war. The question amazed her, and she answered that the Italian Socialists would, of course, do their utmost to prevent Italy from entering the imperialist slaughter. Wasn't that (she argued) what he, Plekhanov, had taught countless Marxists, including Angelica Balabanoff herself, who had sat at his feet as admiring students at the People's House in Brussels? Plekhanov was (as we know from Balabanoff's memoirs) visibly angered by her reply. 'So you would prevent Italy from entering the war?', he asked. 'Where is your love of Russia? . . . so far as I am concerned, if I were not old and sick, I would join the army. To bayonet your German comrades would give me great pleasure.'

Settembrini   Yes, and Mussolini was to follow a similar course. The slogan of 'absolute neutrality' of July 1914 gave way to 'active neutrality' by September, and soon Mussolini finds himself in the grip of a psychological tug of war between his patriotism as an Italian and his revolutionary hopes as a Socialist activist. Between July and November 1914 he undergoes a remarkable change of heart from militant neutralism, on the principle that war and Socialism were 'antithetical and irreconcilable', to interventionism under the slogan: 'Today it is war, it will be revolution tomorrow !' 'Our intervention', he writes in 1915, 'has a double purpose—national and international. By a singular historic circumstance our national war may help towards the realisation of vaster aims of an international order. *Our* war, I say, and not the war which the governing classes of Italy may be preparing.' And he went on to say that the war would bring about the downfall of that bulwark of reactionary Europe, Austria-Hungary, and perhaps lead to a revolution in Germany and Russia, contributing a great step forward in the cause of liberty.

Now Lenin's attitude to the war is in many ways strikingly similar. The 1907 resolution of the International Socialist Congress said that the Socialist Parties had decided 'to exert every effort to prevent the outbreak of war'. But 'should war break out none the less', the duty of Socialists would be to exploit the resulting crisis in order to 'rouse the peoples and thereby to hasten the abolition of capitalist class rule'. The intention of Jaurès and Rosa Luxemburg in putting forward this resolution was to serve notice on bourgeois governments that the wages of war would be revolution. But when, in 1915, it looked as though the war might end in a peace without victors, without vanquished, without defeat or revolution, no one agreed more wholeheartedly with Mussolini than Lenin in treating the pacifists as rabble and in wanting the war to continue to the bitter end for fear that otherwise 'the incipient revolutionary ferment', as Lenin wrote to Wijnkoop, 'would be suffocated by an idiotic "peace programme" '.

Urban   How did Gramsci look upon Mussolini's *volte-face?*

Settembrini   Gramsci was entirely behind Mussolini's interventionism. Why? The revolutionary Socialists had believed and expected all along that the capitalist system would succumb, and succumb soon, to its internal contradictions. This is what Marx said, but this was precisely what was not happening. Along then comes an unexpected windfall—war—which bids fair to blow up the capitalist system more surely and more swiftly than one could expect from the laborious workings of the Marxist dialectic. When this is realised by Mussolini and Gramsci, both conclude that continuing to endorse Italian neutrality, as the Socialists led by Turati were still doing, was betraying the hope of revolution. Gramsci therefore fully supported Mussolini's *volte-face*. He wrote in *Il Grido del Popolo* that it was now absolutely necessary to free 'the Socialist Party from all the bourgeois incrustations which fear of war had fastened on to it'—the only way open to anyone who did not want 'the proletariat to stand by as an impartial spectator of events'. The gulf between Mussolini and Gramsci did not become unbridgeable until October 1917, when the sweeping events in Russia appeared to Gramsci to promise a better prospect for revolution than 'interventionism', which had involved him in awkward concessions to nationalism and inter-class solidarity. But Gramsci, who shared Mussolini's cultural background—Bergson, Sorel, idealism and voluntarism—was quick to recognise that Lenin's programme, like Mussolini's after 1915, was a voluntaristic affair and a negation of Marxism. On 24 December 1917 Gramsci saluted the Bolshevik revolution in a memorable article in *Avanti* as 'the revolution against *Kapital*': 'The Bolsheviks reject Karl Marx, and they affirm with the testimony of action . . . that the laws of historical materialism are not such iron laws as might be thought and has been thought. . . .'

It is one of the less known curiosities of Gramsci's place in Communist history that his support of Mussolini's interventionism set him gravely at odds with the Socialist Party, so much so that when the Italian Communist Party set up house at its Livorno Congress in 1921, Gramsci was not among the speakers, because for many of the delegates his name had become a symbol of

interventionism—a fact which has, until quite recently, been
tactfully neglected by the Italian Communists.

Urban Didn't Gramsci feel it necessary to resolve or to obfuscate the contradiction in Leninism between Lenin's show of loyalty to Marx's 'laws' of history, and Lenin's own free-booting revolutionary activism?

Settembrini He did, and he did so using a revealing analogy.
On 12 January 1918 he wrote: 'Before Marx, Giambattista Vico
said that faith in divine providence worked positively in history,
acting as a stimulus to conscious action. Therefore faith in determinism could have the same effect for Lenin in Russia and elsewhere for others.' This is an important articulation in its own
right for it reconciles Marx with Lenin—at any rate to Gramsci's
satisfaction; but it also underlines a point I have already made,
namely that Lenin could, despite his practical non-Marxism,
keep faith with Marxism on the theoretical grounds which
Gramsci indicated. Mussolini, on the other hand, could not. He
had to break with the Marxist-determinist tradition, and so had
his disciples, even those who became Communists. Their reason
for doing so was very simple: in Italy the Marxist tradition was the
property of the official Socialists. These, of course, were
evolutionists and thus opposed to revolution.

Urban This is perhaps where Bergson and Sorel come clearly
into Mussolini's politics.

Settembrini Sorel more than Bergson, for Sorel made no
bones about stating that the collapse of capitalism as diagnosed
by Marx in *Das Kapital* was a myth. He did, however, also say that
if the masses *believed* in the collapse of capitalism, they would
make it come true. Here again is the link with Mussolini.

But, to return to 1915, Mussolini's decision to demand intervention invalidates any further parallel with Lenin's attitude to
the war. Mussolini's interventionism is repudiated by the majority of Italian Socialists. His career is now forced on to a new
trajectory which is to carry him far away from the Socialist Party,
though not, as he saw it, from Socialism. Lenin, too, is momentarily isolated from the Party through his theses on 'revolutionary
defeatism'. But because Russia, unlike Italy, is defeated in the
war, and because Lenin's theses are close to the traditions of the
Zimmerwald programme, and not least because of Lenin's
enormous prestige and powers of persuasion, Lenin's position
and that of the Party eventually converge again, while Mussolini,
who is also anxious for a reconciliation with his Party, is unable to
bring one about. By 1919 Mussolini is completely isolated and
determined to start a new venture. As the Socialist Party's conservativism prevented him from leading the working class to

revolution, he now decides to try what, in fact, turned out to be the Fascist alternative.

Urban One might, I think, mistakenly infer from your analogy that Mussolini did approve of the Bolshevik revolution as a model Italy might follow. But this was not so. From the very beginnings of the *Fasci* in 1919, Mussolini rejected the Bolshevik example (particularly after the demonstrations in Milan by the Leninist faction of the Socialist Party), and he rejected it on conservative grounds, using a language that strikes one today as distinctly libertarian:

> . . . the masses . . . need a hero [he wrote in *Il Popolo d'Italia* in 1919], they must have someone to believe in. For the old idols they must set up new ones. But we, as individualists, cannot bow down before the new gods. We cannot fail to criticise the creed of the new revelation and to refuse to bow before the Russian icons which the populace now adore. . . . We believe in the conservative instinct which holds by western civilisation, which clings to the rights of the individual, which upholds his freedom, freedom of the mind which does not live by head alone, freedom which can no more be crushed by the dictators from Russia than it was by the dictators of Prussian militarism.

At this juncture, as Margherita Sarfatti reminds us, the *Popolo* changed its subtitle from *The Socialist Daily* to *Journal of the Fighters and Producers*—and one can see why.

Settembrini Mussolini realised that, although Italy had formally won the war, she had also lost it. The devastation in human lives and the disorganisation of the country were extreme. But he also knew that the Socialist hope of founding a Communist republic on these ruins was unrealistic. The institutions of the state were intact: the Monarchy was respected, the army was strong, and capitalism was in its place. And although (as I have said) he would have liked to lead the working class to revolution, he was, by 1919, convinced that the Russian model was inapplicable and that his revolution would somehow have to be held within the framework of existing institutions. But the libertarian sentiments you have quoted were, to put it no lower, merely tactical. Not many years later, in 1924, he preached the opposite: 'Fascism throws the noxious theories of so-called liberalism upon the rubbish heap . . . It has already stepped, and, if need be, will quietly turn round to step once more, over the more or less putrid body of the Goddess Liberty.'

We must surely not be surprised by the tergiversations of

politicians: Mussolini saw the Bolsheviks mount a demonstration on what he considered to be *his* beat in Milan—and he was against it; hence his protestations of individual liberty. But as soon as he is in power, he consigns liberty to the 'rubbish heap' of history, helping himself without embarrassment to the well-worn Communist metaphor.

Urban   One is not suprised; some of the lies and low cunning of politicians border on the sublime. One could indeed think of many more examples confirming the aptness of your parallel with Lenin. Sticking to mendacity, at the time of the Provisional Government, Lenin proclaimed: 'Our Party alone, by taking power, will assure the convocation of the Constituent Assembly.' But when the elections of 25 November 1917 gave the Bolsheviks only 175 seats out of 707—the great majority going to moderate Socialist Parties—Lenin changed his mind. The Assembly met on 18 January 1918, and as it refused to do the will of the Bolshevik minority, Lenin had it disbanded. It lasted 24 hours. It took Lenin one single day to frustrate the hopes of generations and wipe out the results of Russia's first and so far last genuinely free elections.

Mussolini's behaviour at the time under review is confusing if one is not familiar with his fiercely combative spirit and his affinity and friendship with those curious evangelists of Italian aestheticism—the Futurists. Mussolini strongly felt that the union of Hegel, Marx and Engels with the dark and Byzantine traditions of Russia produced a singularly unappealing offspring in Bolshevism. I am myself inclined to find the psychological clue to Mussolini's attitude to Bolshevism in his observation (in 1919): 'Bolshevism will never flourish in Italy, never, never! With this sunshine, it can never take root in our country . . . !' Mussolini was decidedly a 'Eurofascist' (or Eurocommunist?), with Buonarotti, Babeuf, Proudhon and Sorel as his apostles, and the aesthetics of Ruskin and William Morris as his guides for the future. Today he would feel more at home with Berlinguer and Carrillo than the ageing mandarinate in the Kremlin.

But, to take you back one step again, I am intrigued by the discrepancy between the myth of Gramsci currently put about by the Italian Communist Party, and the picture of Gramsci emerging from your account of his relationship with Mussolini.

Settembrini   Before I comment on that I should, I think, point to the close intellectual and ideological affinities in Mussolini's, Gramsci's and Bordiga's thinking, and I propose to do so by simply putting certain quotations side by side with one another and letting you draw your own conclusions. The first caption under my Mussolini-Gramsci diptych is: 'The destruction of democracy by determined élites'. Here, then, is Mussolini writing in February 1913:

> We must choose between democracy and Socialism. The struggle in human society has been and always will be a struggle of minorities. To aspire quantitatively to an absolute majority is absurd. One will never be able to incorporate the majority of the proletariat . . . in economic and political organisations. The class struggle is essentially a struggle of minorities. The majority follows and obeys. Violence, as Marx says, is the midwife of society. Do you want to avoid Socialism? Then take away the violence.

And in April 1913, dealing with the question of what constitutes 'common sense', Mussolini said:

> Common sense is conservatism. And listen, Socialists, common sense is the philosophy of the class in power. Revolutions are mad, violent, and bestial. They kill, destroy and sack. They are a cataclysm of men, and this is their beauty. Compare a page of Marx with a page of Bonomi or Turati. You will see the abyss. Common sense is an insidious voice, he who listens to it will never be courageous . . . Men must go beyond the limits of their physical and moral possibilities and challenge the unknown and die if necessary.

This was one of my two pictures. Now here is Gramsci, a disciple and admirer of Mussolini, writing in February 1917:

> It has been said that Socialism is dead because the image of society the Socialists have been creating was no more than a myth to deceive the masses. I, too, believe that the myth has collapsed, but its dissolution was necessary. The historic law, the preordained course of events, have been replaced by the determined will of man. One's soul must burn red-hot and throw off thousands of sparks. To wait . . . for the majority is the way of the cowardly spirits. They alone will wait for the donation of Socialism by royal decree, signed by two ministers.

Finally, here is another veteran Communist, Bordiga, writing in 1924 shortly before the assassination of Matteotti:

> Democracy has run its course. The liberal geese will cry a different song when they see how a real revolution deals with

democracy. Instead of restoring the ideas which Amendola, Turati and others of the same ilk babble about, the revolution of the proletarian masses ... will treat them to a merry-go-round of kicks in the ass of holy democracy. And this alone will deserve to be called liberation.

(Amadeo Livorsi, Bordiga's Communist biographer, writing in 1976, refers to this quotation as expressing an 'agreeably desecrating' view. Desecrating of what? Representative democracy, of course!).

One can see why, after the murder of Matteotti, the Italian public was reluctant to unseat Mussolini, for Mussolini's fall would have saddled them with the Communists, whose contempt for democracy was at least as rife as Mussolini's and, going by the evidence of the Bolshevik revolution, much more savage and irreversible.

Urban What you are saying is that Mussoliniism and Leninism are comparable deviations from Marxist Socialism. But you are implying more than that. I would infer from your reasoning that the Fascist movement in its first phase is the Italian version of Leninism, and Mussolini the Latin Lenin.

Settembrini That is what I'm saying. Both saw the sterility of Marxist dogma and the uselessness of Marxist prognostications. We have already examined the reasons that led them to these conclusions: the solidarity of the international working class was a figment of the International's imagination; revolution was not on the march, capitalism was not collapsing.

Urban Both were good revisionists in the sense of Bernstein: 'Peasants do not sink' (as he put in a famous note scribbled on the back of an envelope); 'the middle class does not disappear; crises do not grow ever larger; misery and serfdom do not increase'.

Settembrini Yes, for both men loyalty to the doctrine meant the death of the movement, and as both Mussolini and Lenin were activists and firebrands, their escape from the dead-end of Marxist dogma followed a similar route. Both knew in their bones that, Marx or no Marx, history was the story of the will-power of strong men. The masses were passive, waiting to be led and relieved of the dilemmas of the freedom of choice.

Now if such are your assumptions, your next step is to incorporate these ideas in a rigorously centralised, small party and, eventually, to place all power in the hands of one man—your own. Thus was totalitarianism born in the Soviet Union and in a milder form in Italy. Mussolini wants power, but once he is in possession of power he is more or less happy to let things go the way they have always gone. He is a dictator, but his totalitarianism is incomplete. His rise to dictatorship is not over the ruins of the existing social order—he has to learn to live with the Monarchy, the Church and the institutions of capitalism. Lenin, by contrast, has removed all these impediments. His totalitarianism is merciless and complete. I have no intention of whitewashing Fascism when I say that of the two Fascism was incomparably the smaller evil. Why? Because Mussolini never set out to change the nature of man, whereas Lenin believed, and the Soviet Leninists have never ceased to believe, that the radical change of society requires the radical change of human beings. This is an open-ended and lethal doctrine which implies and has provided legitimation for the most monstrous crimes that have yet been perpetrated in history in the name of freedom.

Urban Mussolini's attitude to race, at a time when Hitler was about to seize power in Germany (1932), confirms what you say. Not only had Mussolini no ambition to create 'Fascist man' on the analogy of 'Soviet man', but he was also entirely unselfconscious about race as an attribute of Italianness. 'Race!', he said on one occasion, 'It is a feeling, not reality; 95 per cent, at least, is a feeling. Nothing will ever make me believe that biologically pure races can be shown to exist today. No such doctrine will ever find acceptance here in Italy. National pride has no need of the delirium of race.' Mussolini's official biographer and long-time political associate, Margherita Sarfatti, was a Jewess. So was his early friend and mentor, Angelica Balabanoff. Aldo Finzi was a member of his first cabinet, and Guido Jung was his finance minister for many years—both Jews. There were many Jews present at the foundation of the Fascist Party in 1919. In 1941 Mussolini said he 'could never forget that four of the seven founders of Italian nationalism were Jews'. During the war he interceded with Hitler on behalf of Bergson. None of this, however, prevented him from eventually delivering the Italian Jews to the Nazis.

Settembrini There has never been any question in my mind that the proper analogy is between Mussoliniism and Leninism and not between Fascism and Nazism. But, if we want to be historically accurate, we must keep reminding ourselves of the limits of this analogy. In 1918 Mussolini realises that capitalism is far from being a spent force—indeed, to it, he thinks, belongs the future. He therefore completely abandons any idea of overthrowing it in his lifetime. That in itself was enough to set him on a road that could never lead to complete totalitarianism. Think of the reasons that made Stalin abandon the NEP experiment and collectivise agriculture: he was aware that NEP allowed the peasants and small traders to accumulate a certain wealth and gain a modicum of independence that goes with property. Such people could not be controlled. A capitalist social order, even one based on a mixed economy, is a safeguard against totalitarian régimes. One can have under capitalism a ferocious dictatorship, but not a completely totalitarian system. Mussolini understood this. He would gladly have done without the Monarchy and the Church, but he was convinced that capitalism was there to stay. Before the March on Rome, that is, before the failure of the attempt to find a *modus vivendi* between Fascism and Socialism in 1921, it was still possible for Mussolini to become the leader of a radical reformist movement. From his writings of 1920–21 it is very clear that he was anxious to win the Socialists over to his position and gain their respect and support, and that he resented not being able to do so. He used threats of violence in the hope that the Socialists would yield. He tried to set the pro-Soviet faction, which he thought he could not win over, against the Centre-right which he thought he could, and he repeatedly tried to draw Turati into government. When Turati was eventually persuaded that it was necessary for the Socialists to join the government in order to use the power of the state to defeat Mussolini's incipient Fascism, Mussolini threatened: 'Don't think you'll find it easy to destroy us. We will not shrink from allying ourselves even with the Communists in order to defend ourselves against you'. By 1921 Mussolini was convinced that he could take power only over the dead body of the Socialist Party. Yet, even after the break with the Socialists in 1921, he still hoped to come to terms with the Confederazione Generale del Lavoro, the trade-union federation controlled by the Socialists and Communists.

Urban   But to return to the similarities, didn't Togliatti himself recognise a certain parallel between Mussolini's and Lenin's efforts to get their organisation right?

Settembrini   From a fairly early date, Togliatti differed from the Communist International's interpretation of Fascism by saying that Fascism was born of the alliance of Socialists and syndicalists on a democratic platform, and that it was in no way *destined* to become totalitarian. Togliatti asserted that even after the March on Rome it was not inevitable that Fascism should become a dictatorship, and he suggested that part of the blame for its degeneration into dictatorship had to be borne by the erroneous policies of the Socialist and Communist movements. But— and this comes closer to your question—Togliatti recognised a certain (as he thought) creative innovation in the manner in which Mussolini—like Lenin—organised his party.

After the assassination of Matteotti, Mussolini's choice was either that of trying to survive in the existing democratic framework and risk being defeated by the anti-Fascist forces (and the risk of that was very great indeed), or that of becoming a captive of the violent Fascist *squadristi* whom the Party had inherited from revolutionary Socialism and syndicalism. He chose neither; he chose dictatorship. Writing in 1935, Togliatti observed that there was an analogy between the Leninist party and the party that was now created by Mussolini: 'We have stressed that a characteristic element is the absence of any form of internal democracy ... For this reason Mussolini's claim, borrowed from Lenin, to have created a new *party* has some justification. This element of liquidation of every form of democracy, of adapting the party to the forms of dictatorship, certainly gives some new features to the party.'

The analogy goes, in fact, much deeper than Togliatti would concede. In 1921, before instituting NEP, Lenin abolished all internal party democracy to avoid being attacked by his Left who saw in NEP a concession to capitalism and were bitterly opposed to it, just as the Fascist Left, after 1924, considered Mussolini's reconciliation with the state and the Monarchy as the betrayal of the revolutionary programme of Fascism.

For the student of Fascist history, Togliatti's recognition that Fascism and Leninism are in some respects near-identical twins is nothing very new. Togliatti was, in fact, simply endorsing Mussolini's statement to the Chamber of Deputies in December 1921: 'I recognise that between us and the Communists there are no political affinities, but there are intellectual affinities. We, like you, consider necessary a centralised and unitary state; with this difference, that you arrive at this conclusion via the concept of class, and we arrive there via the concept of nation.'

Urban In 1921 it was perhaps too early to say whether the affinities were, in fact, only intellectual—in any case, I doubt whether political affinities can be divorced from intellectual ones. Also, in 1921, Mussolini's whole programme rested on the denial that political affinities with Communism did or could survive. Yet the continuing two-way traffic between Fascist and Communist politicians (and I have discussed this in some detail with Renzo de Felice in 'Varieties of Fascism') shows that they could and did. Let me borrow from one of your own essays the celebrated example of the Communist, but formerly Fascist, historian, Delio Cantimori. He described the revolutionary hopes which had led him to Fascism in these words:

I entered the Fascist Party in 1926. I was in a state of mental

confusion and had really no excuse for it. In fact I had read
Gobetti's *Rivoluzione liberale* ... and Salvemini's *l'Unità*
... But I was convinced that Fascism had carried out the true
Italian revolution and was still doing so, and that it should
become a European revolution; and I believed one had to work
along these lines.

Settembrini   Yes, and the wisdom of Togliatti was to perceive
that the intellectual impulse that leads a man with revolutionary
sentiments *into* the Fascist Party can also lead him *out* of it and
into the Communist Party; as indeed it often did. The intolerance
and sectarianism which have governed so much of Italian culture
since the second world war can be explained in no other way. The
same mentality predominates—only the shop signs have been
changed.

Cantimori's was, of course, only one of many similar cases.
Throughout Mussolini's rule the voices of 'Socialism betrayed'
were never completely silent in the Fascist Party and, indeed, in
Mussolini's personal surroundings. For example, Ruggero Zangrandi, a close friend of Mussolini's son, Victor Mussolini, retails
some highly revealing facts about the political sentiments in the
Duce's own family. He tells us in his memoirs that according to
Victor Mussolini one of the constant topics of conversation in
Mussolini's home was the disappointed expectations of
revolutionary Fascism, and that almost all those Fascist 'dissidents' who maintained political ambitions later joined the Communist Party and often rose to important positions, especially in
the cultural field. Mussolini himself was in touch with the Left
wing of his movement, mainly through Ugo Spirito, but in the
1930s he also encouraged Victor Mussolini to run what might be
called an 'opposition' newspaper in order to create a platform for
the young Fascist left-radicals.

Urban   In March 1942 there was a 'super-Fascist' insurrec-
tional movement at some Italian universities which—so Ciano
tells us—set out 'to eliminate all rightist or conservative elements
in the Party, and to impose on the Duce a violent socialistic
policy'. That in 1942 the Duce was still thought capable by these
students of heading a Socialist renewal of Fascism is remarkable.

Settembrini   On a different level there is the celebrated case of
Angelica Balabanoff (and we have already referred to her), who
was Mussolini's friend, assistant, admirer and reputedly also his
mistress at the very beginning of his career as a Socialist in
Switzerland—

Urban   —and, according to rumour, mentioned but denied by
Edda Mussolini-Ciano, she was also Edda Mussolini's mother—

Settembrini —yes, but in this case I tend to believe with Edda Mussolini that the rumour was false. In any case, here is Angelica Balabanoff—a devout revolutionary who follows Mussolini to Italy, assists him in editing *Avanti*, is eventually expelled from the Italian Socialist Party, becomes an enthusiastic supporter of the Bolshevik revolution, joins Lenin's immediate circle and is made Secretary of the newly formed Third International. She then becomes disillusioned again, this time by Lenin's and Zinoviev's duplicity and callousness, and returns, after the second world war, to Italy to join Saragat as a Social Democrat. Her *Impressions of Lenin* are the finest testimony of the inescapable clash between two Socialist temperaments: Angelica who really believed in serving the people, and Lenin who believed only in manipulating the people.

Urban The fact that this highly sensitive, intelligent and idealistic woman found it entirely possible to switch her loyalties from the Socialism of Mussolini to the Socialism of Lenin tells us a good deal about the close affinity between Fascism and Bolshevism, at least in the early stages of the two movements. In the end, Angelica Balabanoff regarded both Mussolini and Lenin as renegades of Socialism. Her memoirs of Mussolini appeared under the title *The Traitor: Mussolini's Rise to Power*, and of the betrayal of the hopes of revolution by Lenin she wrote: 'When those who under Tsarism had fought against infringement upon liberty began themselves to violate freedom, when independent thinkers were persecuted by the Bolshevik government and the prisons filled with men and women the Russian people considered innocent, the suspicion arose—it was to become certainty later—that nothing had changed, and things were as before, even worse.'

Angelica Balabanoff believed to the end of her long and puritanic life (she died in 1965) that Socialism is a protest against the 'misery that is the lot of the many'. So perhaps it is. The mistake she made was to believe that the monsters Mussolini and Lenin were rearing had anything to do with Socialism.

Settembrini Angelica Balabanoff's case is a spectacular example, but one could go on extending the list of personalities who changed camps almost indefinitely. In the 1920s and 1930s, the Italian Fascist journals of law and philosophy devoted a great deal of space to the study and exaltation of the Soviet Union. The similarities between Fascism and Bolshevism were a constant theme. But the admiration was reciprocated. Consider the famous observation of Maxim Gorky, quoting an even more tell-tale remark of Trotsky's, after the 1924 elections. Gorky, who was living in Capri at the time, was invited by a correspondent of *Il*

Corriere della Sera to comment on the results of the 1924 elections which, as you know, had been heavily rigged by the Fascists. And this is what Gorky said: 'From the governmental acts of Mussolini I have come to know his energy and I admire him, but I prefer Trotsky's opinion to mine—"Mussolini carried out a revolution; he is our best pupil".'

Urban The yearning for utopia was, in reality, the common denominator behind the creative minorities of both Fascism and Bolshevism. The canvas was broadly conceived; the details were often interchangeable. Speaking in 1943, before the July coup that deposed Mussolini, no less authentic a Fascist than Gentile said: 'Whoever speaks of Communism in Italy today is an impatient corporativist', implying that at the height of the war against Bolshevism some of the Fascist leaders were still hoping to re-direct the movement to its Socialist/Communist origins, Italian style. Even well after the war, in 1957, Ugo Spirito, the main advocate of Fascist corporativism, wrote: 'Russian Communism is rooted in the reality of a people that conceives the values of the collectivity as constituent elements of its very life. Communion and faith are its principal characteristics.' Here we have complete confirmation of what Togliatti suspected in 1935—that the tacit assumptions behind Spirito's left-Fascism were not far removed from Communism. In the perceptive words of the American scholar, A. James Gregor, 'Soviet society has fulfilled ... the fascist dream of his [Spirito's] young manhood.'

I must at this juncture try to resist drawing you into a discussion of the astonishing revival, in the Social Republic of Salò, of some of the Fascist movement's early revolutionary inspiration, and the re-surfacing, in 1943-44, of some of Mussolini's early Socialist and Communist companions, for I have gone over this ground with Renzo de Felice in an earlier discussion. Let me, therefore, concentrate on only two aspects of Mussolini's short-lived Republic: the fact that men like the Communist Nicola Bombacci and the Socialist Corrado Bonfantini were alive at all, after 20 years of Fascism, to play a part, and that, under the Republic of Salò, an extensive social, and one might well say, Socialist legislation was put on the statute books which, after the collapse of Salò, the Communist-led Committee of National Liberation abrogated as one of its first acts.

Settembrini There is no question that repression under Italian Fascism was incomparably lighter than under Stalinism, and the beneficiaries of Italian Fascism included the Italian Communists. A story I have recently heard from an Italian Communist leader illustrates my point. In 1957 this man read a book by one of Togliatti's friends and collaborators (Renato Mieli), and, disturbed by what he had discovered about Togliatti's role in the Comintern, he went to see him and rebuked him to the effect that if Gramsci had been in the shoes of Togliatti, Gramsci would have behaved very differently. 'Oh, yes', Togliatti replied, 'Gramsci would have been among the first to be shot.' And, however repulsive it may be for us to weigh the relative merits of the intolerance of dictators, this opinion of Togliatti's certainly justifies Mussolini's words after the death of Gramsci: 'If the Communists had taken Gramsci, they would have put him to death at once. I let him live.' Gramsci, as you know, died after his release from prison.

Mussolini was not the bloodthirsty tyrant of the type of a Hitler or a Stalin. After Hitler's night of the long knives, in which Röhm and many others perished, Mussolini made a point of boasting that he was a moderate man. What Hitler has done, he said, was as monstrous a thing as if I had killed off the men who had helped me to power—the Bottais and Bianchis of our Party. Bianchi, he added, died in his bed in 1930—

Urban —and the assassination of Röhm and his SA followers was (to underline your point) also the turning point in Stalin's attitude to Hitler—a change from rabid hostility to a secret admiration of Hitler's ruthlessness culminating in an attempt, which was to succeed in 1939, to reach an understanding with him.

Settembrini Yes, Mussolini's ruthlessness was qualified. That Bombacci and Bonfantini (and there were many others) were able to play a part in Salò was due to the fact that they had been *allowed* to survive—in prison, out of prison, in *confino* and out of *confino*—but they stayed alive. And the Fascist *confino* was no Auschwitz and no Gulag. It usually meant banishment to some small island where the prisoners were allowed to lead their own lives. Once or twice a week a police launch would arrive from the mainland to check their numbers, but it took some ingenuity *not* to survive in *confino*—

Urban —Altiero Spinelli told me that he shared his *confino* with various other Communists, including Amendola, and that it was during this period, on the island of Ponza, that the local Party organisation expelled him on higher orders because he had refused to take the Party line on the Moscow show-trials. When I expressed surprise that such a party-cell could exist and function in what I thought was a concentration camp or prison, he described the political prisoners' life in *confino* more or less on the lines you have described.

Settembrini The compromises Mussolini had to make with the Monarchy and the Church robbed him of the possibility of becoming an absolute ruler of the totalitarian type. Whether he made these compromises because he was a kindlier man at base than Lenin or Stalin, or whether it was his opportunism that made him behave in a manner that made life under him incomparably more tolerable than it was under Lenin, not to say Stalin, is not a matter of great concern to me. There may be truth in both judgments.

Urban There was undoubtedly a streak of Leninist violence in his make-up which, as you say, he had to suppress. He told Ciano in 1940: 'If, when I was a Socialist, I had had a knowledge of the work of the Italian middle class, not purely theoretical as learned by the reading of Karl Marx, but practical, based on experience such as I have now, I would have launched a revolution so pitiless that, by comparison, the revolution of Comrade Lenin would have been child's play.'

At the same time Mussolini could be very indignant about atrocities committed by others—especially the Nazis. When he was shown, on 4 December 1939, a confidential report of German behaviour in freshly occupied Posen (as it then was), Ciano records in his *Diary*: 'With a simplicity which accentuates the horrors of the facts, he [the author of the report] describes all that the Germans are doing: unmentionable atrocities without reason. The Duce himself was indignant; he advised me to see to it that by indirect channels the American and French newspapers get the contents of the report. The world must know.'

Where I see Mussolini's character most clearly at variance with the textbook type of the totalitarian dictator is in his sense of self-mockery. For example, in his preface to Margherita Sarfatti's biography of him, Mussolini says:

> In this book my life is to be found recorded—at least, such part of it as can be made known, for every man has secrets and shady nooks that are not to be explored. . . . In essence, it is no great affair—my life. There is nothing extraordinary in it to capture the imagination. No victorious wars . . . No creations of new systems of thought. It is a life full of movement, certainly, but it is a less interesting life, for instance, than that of the late Mr Savage Landor, the great traveller.

But to return to those Communists and Socialists who gained a new lease of life under the Nazi/Fascist Republic of Salò—

Settembrini   —You have mentioned Ugo Spirito, and he is a good example. After a left-Fascist past under Mussolini, he became a Communist and Stalinist when the war was over. But many other leaders of the Italian Communist Party also hailed from left-Fascism. Some of them indeed had been publicly involved with the Republic of Salò. For example, David Laiolo, an important Communist and a former editor of *l'Unità*, wrote a book at the time of Salò in praise of the Republic of Salò (*The Mouth of the Woman–The Mouth of the Gun*). Alicata and Ingrao both came from Fascism, and as I have already indicated, most of the cultural politics of the Italian Communist Party in its Stalinist period were in the hands of ex-Fascists. I regard this as quite natural—to *them* the thing was familiar. Italian Fascism and Italian Communism are contained in a single circle: the Fascists came from the ranks of revolutionary Socialism and anarcho-syndicalism—the Communists issued from the ranks of Fascism.

Urban So, if the phrase 'social-Fascism' had not been rendered meaningless by both Stalin and Mao, it would make sense to speak of a single Italian 'Fascist-Socialist' movement, comprising an interchangeable personnel of Communists and Fascists?

Settembrini Indeed it would. Togliatti understood this very well. He realised that the Italian Communist Party stood no chance of becoming a mass party unless it associated itself with revolutionary Fascism and dissociated itself from the pre-Fascist liberal tradition. In the first few years after the war, the Italian Communist leaders consistently portrayed Fascism as a revolutionary movement which had betrayed its original pur-pose, and the Communist Party as the movement carrying out the *authentic* Fascist revolution. 'The enormous distance that appeared to separate us from the mass of young Fascists', Tog-liatti said in 1948, 'was due largely to a misunderstanding.'

It is here that we must look for the origins of de Felice's distinc-tion between 'Fascism as a movement' and 'Fascism as a régime'. And if today the Communists are hostile to this distinction, it is because their current policy is to present themselves as heirs to Italian liberalism, not Fascism. De Felice has committed the unpardonable indiscretion of reminding them that for 20 years they had been keeping embarrassing company.

Urban Why did the post-Fascist Committee of National Libera-tion abolish the Socialist legislation of Salò? This was, on the face of it, a self-defeating measure, for Salò envisaged the abolition of capitalism, industrial self-management, a struggle 'against the world plutocracies', radical land-reform, cooperative and state farming, and the socialisation of everything that 'in scope or function, goes beyond private interests'. Let me raise the ques-tion in the form in which A. James Gregor has raised it: 'All that woúld have been necessary to obviate the "anti-national objectives" of the legislation on socialisation would have been the election of representative Socialist or Communist factory collegia and committees. Instead, the laws themselves were abrogated and the control over Italy's productive enterprise was returned to its capitalist owners. Today that control remains securely in the hands of those same owners.'

Did the Committee fear that building on Mussolini's social legislation might imply recognition of the legitimacy of the Republic of Salò? Was it psychologically impossible for the victors to recognise constructive intent in anything done by the defeated? To this day, it is not widely known that in the puppet state of Salò near-revolutionary economic and social measures were written into 'law'.

Settembrini Your question contains the answer: why is so little known about the social legislation of the Salò Republic? Because at a time when the Communists were priding themselves on their anti-Fascism, they had no interest in revealing that this common element existed with the Mussolini of Salò. In any case, they could not have taken advantage of it because they had to reckon with American disapproval. Those opposing the Communists also preferred to keep silent because they were trying to match the Communists in their anti-Fascism.

One might argue that the anti-Communists stood to gain from pointing to the similarities between what Mussolini had been trying to do in Salò in 1943–44 and what the Communists were proposing to do in their programme in 1945 or 1947. But, in the climate prevailing at the time, any intimation that Communists and Fascists were birds of the same feather would have called down upon you the great anti-Fascist national sentiment, and robbed you, as a force opposing Communism, of all credibility. Such was the temper of politics in Italy after the war.

Urban Perhaps it is asking a little too much of human nature to build on the heritage of one's enemies. George Kennan asks at one point in his *Memoirs* whether the forcible unification of Europe by Hitler might not have been exploited by enlightened statesmanship as a basis on which to raise a united Europe directly after the war. Theoretically, of course, it should have been possible, but after a savage war and six years of savage propaganda no one in Europe was, or could be expected to be, enlightened enough to say: true, we have all been united by German occupation—but let us now forget the history of this involuntary unity and fill it out with democratic content in the spirit of Jean Monnet. People do not act like that, and I suspect the Italian Communists' failure to play the cards which history dealt them through the Republic of Salò has an equally simple explanation.

Settembrini   There were also certain hard, factual reasons why Kennan's idea was impracticable. What sort of political forces were still on their feet after the collapse of Nazism and the devastation of Europe? Nationalist forces—de Gaulle for example—and the Communists. The first had set their faces against European unification, the second were determined to destroy democracy as well as spoil any chance of a united Europe. The prospects of a democratic united Europe rising directly from the ashes of the Third Reich were poor. Europe had to wait.

Urban   We have been saying rather damaging things in this conversation about the origins and originators of the Italian Communist Party—damaging, that is, for a Party which has built its legitimacy and reputation on an unerring anti-Fascism. Aren't we in fact supplying Moscow with fresh ammunition at a time when Moscow is already darkly hinting through Bilak and Zhivkov as well as its own spokesmen that the Italian Communists are renegades and splitters? Aren't we making it easier for Moscow to claim: 'From Gramsci to this day the Italian Communist Party is honeycombed with Fascist tendencies and men taken over intact from the Fascists. Is this the kind of Eurocommunism', they would be warning Warsaw, Prague and Budapest, 'you want to follow?'

Settembrini   I don't think it is the Fascist past of some of the Italian Communists and the Fascist origins of parts of the Communist movement that will displease Moscow. What Moscow is really worried about is the possibility of the Italian Communist Party becoming genuinely *liberal*. In my opinion this is not at all what is happening, but Moscow's anxiety is concentrated on this point. Now if the Italian Communists *were* to go liberal, it is very much on the cards that the Russians would, in their propaganda, accuse a genuinely liberalised Communist Party of being 'Fascist', probably using, to reinforce their case, the kind of evidence we have here listed. But this is standard Soviet procedure—every Communist party that has tried to detach itself from the Kremlin has been anathematised as 'Fascist'. Let me say in parenthesis that the ready use the Soviet leaders make of the word 'Fascist' is implied proof that, for them, Fascism is a Socialist heresy. The application of 'Fascist' to Tito, for example, meant two things: first, that Tito had refused to toe Stalin's line and had therefore fallen into 'heresy' and, second, that 'Fascism' was an even more culpable heresy. But both were challenges, not to the basic tenets of Socialism, but to its interpretation.

Urban   Trotsky certainly admitted that 'Stalinism and Fascism, in spite of deep differences in social foundations, are symmetrical phenomena'.

Settembrini   He did. The purpose of our polemics in Italy is to *make* the Italian Communist Party decide between its Fascist origins *cum* Stalinist past, on the one hand, and a genuinely liberal Eurocommunism, on the other. Why do the Communists dislike our insistence? Because they do not want to choose. But, under pressure, it is just possible that the Party will eventually shed its Fascist/Stalinist antecedents and emerge as a genuinely liberal Socialist force. What Moscow would say to this is of secondary importance, because a secessionist Italian Party would be accused of Fascism, whatever the reasons for its unorthodoxy.

Now the links between Mussolini and Gramsci which we have analysed in this conversation—and they have, of course, been examined before by others—are undoubtedly embarrassing, but they are embarrassing for the Russians much more than for the Italian Communists. Why?—and here we walk into the thick of Communist theology; because if and when it comes to an open break between Moscow and Rome, the Russians would want to set the Gramscian and Togliattian tradition against the Party's 'deviant' liberalism. In order to be able to accuse a 'rebel' Italian leadership of the betrayal of its trust, Moscow must be in a position to argue that *before* the betrayal the Italian Communist Party was following the correct line. Therefore it is very much in Moscow's interest to suppress the fact that Gramsci was a close associate of Mussolini's. If the Russians admitted the link between Gramsci and Fascism, then the entire history of the Italian Communist Party would appear to have been a ghastly error, and those liberal Italian Communists now challenging Moscow would seem entirely justified in their claim that all they were doing was correcting this error.

I do not, therefore, share your fear that giving much-justified publicity to the Fascist/Communist nexus would damage the international usefulness of the Italian Eurocommunist model. The Russians know all about Gramsci's and Bordiga's association with Fascism, but, as I say, if they want to keep their hands free to split an 'heretical' Italian Party by appealing to the orthodox elements within it, then they must keep the image of Gramsci, Bordiga and Togliatti entirely untainted.

Urban   Can you foresee a complete break between the Italian Communists and Moscow, with the Italian Communists picking up where the Prague reformers left off? This would entail a claim that the Eurocommunists alone can authentically speak in the name of Marxism, and that the real heresy was perpetrated in 1917—by Lenin and Bolshevism. Santiago Carrillo and the Spanish Communist Party have come very close to saying just that and have been promptly ostracised for it by Moscow. Doctrinally the truth of such a claim is incontestable; would the Italian Communists make it?

Settembrini They would find it impossible while they are fighting to get their hands on the levers of power. The whole appeal of the Party, and especially its grip on most of the Italian Left, rests, and has always rested, on Soviet backing and the mythology of the Soviet example. The day that image is destroyed, the Party risks its own destruction. A pro-Soviet faction may survive such a holocaust, but the Party as a major political force would not. You can break with Moscow *after* you have come to power—witness the examples of Tito and Mao—but an open clash with the Kremlin while you are still battling your way to office is tantamount to declaring yourself no longer to be Communists and certainly inviting such a charge upon your heads by Moscow. Communist parties cannot exist outside the gravitational fields of one centre or another. If the Italian Communists were, nevertheless, to have a showdown with Moscow while still in opposition (and, as I say, the chances of that happening are very small), they would have to line up behind another Communist model that also serves as a power-centre. At the time of the Sino-Soviet break, there was a danger that part of the Italian Party would shift its allegiance from Moscow to Peking. Togliatti recognised this and lost no time in declaring himself and the Party to be rigidly pro-Soviet. An anti-Soviet Communism that is neither pro-Chinese nor pro-Tito is in practical terms no Communism at all. It would mean a complete break with the past, and the Italian Communist Party has never countenanced that.

Their line has always been that they wanted to renew themselves only in the spirit of absolute continuity with their past. Pajetta said it when talking of the crisis of Czechoslovakia; Lombardo Radice said it talking to you and earlier in *l'Unità*, and so have others. Pajetta in particular made it very clear that while the Italian leadership were critical of the present leaders of Czechoslovakia, their criticism ended there. Attempts to involve us in a general assault on the Soviet system, he warned, will not succeed.

Urban Lombardo Radice *has* gone further than that, though—both in talking to myself and in an interview he gave *La Stampa* (on 8 December 1976). In the latter he said: ' . . . it is inevitable that the Socialist opposition to Socialist governments in the East (for example, Havemann in the GDR and Medvedev in the USSR) should link themselves at least ideologically with Eurocommunism. . . . In his speeches Berlinguer is concerned with revolution in Italy and Western Europe. But these speeches would become voices of opposition if translated and diffused in Moscow, East Berlin, or Warsaw . . . . The truth is that there is a clash between two general perspectives', i.e. those of Eurocommunism and 'the official Marxism of the Socialist countries'.

I would myself take these observations to be tantamount to a general critique of the Soviet system.

Settembrini Ah, but you must clearly distinguish between what the Italian Communists say for purposes of propaganda in the *non*-Communist press, and what they say in *l'Unità*, for it is only the latter that gives us some clue to their real intentions. I have here another article by Lombardo Radice under the title 'I am a Eurocommunist and a Bolshevik', and he means what his title says: being a Eurocommunist does not mean that he is anti-Soviet. Talking to yourself, he made this even more abundantly clear, and I am glad to see that his remarks were picked up by the international press and in a lecture by David Owen, and used in a speech by Henry Kissinger.

But Lombardo Radice (and others of a similar persuasion) have been saying these things for quite some time. In 1971, for example, Lombardo Radice wrote in a non-Communist journal: 'If we call "ruling classes" those bosses and commanders of the economy who control the workers and decide their wages and production, then without a doubt the managers of state organisations in countries such as the Soviet Union are a "ruling class"— in fact they are often absolute bosses. . . .' Well, the day I see Lombardo Radice write this in *l'Unità*, I will concede that there is a definite break with the Italian Communist past, but not before.

Urban Is there any reason why Eurocommunism, and especially its Italian variant, should not become an alternative centre in its own right? Students of Communist history of the distinction of George Kennan feel that this is already happening, and that its capacity to cause damage to the cohesion (such as it is) of the Soviet camp is great and growing. If the anguished protests of certain Soviet and East European leaders are anything to go by, Eurocommunism is a danger to them, and my surmise is that they will subject it to the same kind of abuse as Rosa Luxemburg and Lenin and Stalin heaped on Social Democracy. The process has already started with Carrillo and the Spanish Communist Party.

Settembrini Abuse—yes; alternative centre—no, and I take my explanation from Marx: 'No human being can be expected to commit suicide—neither can a political party'. To repeat an earlier point: the Italian Communists, as long as they are Communists, can never concede that the Soviet system has been a failure from its inception, because that would be tantamount to admitting that the Italian Communist Party, too, has been an error from the ground up. We must remember that it was only through presenting the Soviet Union as a democratic, just, glorious and mighty society that the Italian Communists have become the powerful force they are. They cannot reverse themselves on this cardinal point without asking for great trouble. For example, during the last election campaign Berlinguer declared it was true that the Italian Communists criticised the Soviet Union for certain mistakes, but they also believed that only in the Soviet Union and the other Socialist countries had the foundations been laid for real freedom and democracy.

If the Communists admitted that they were in fact not much better than Social Democrats and that their history was flawed at its base, they would forfeit every chance of getting elected through the democratic process.

Urban   So Italian democracy requires the Party to stick to its Stalinist/Fascist antecedents in order to facilitate its access to power through the ballot box—

Settembrini   —paradoxically for us—yes. They—the Communists—will of course argue that they *are* democrats.

Once the Communists are in power—*that* is the time for revising the sacred books and perhaps closing the sacred books. *That* might be the time for the Dubcek line to come into its own, but this is far too uncertain a possibility for risks to be taken on it. Berlinguer might very well argue that he feels more secure behind the protective shield of NATO than he would outside it, but how many Berlinguers are there in the Italian Party? We know that he faces a powerful opposition both at the top and among the rank and file. To facilitate a Communist access to power in the hope that, once in power, the Party *will* act as the Czechoslovaks did in 1968 would be a foolhardy step to take. It is the kind of risk Giolitti ran when he enlisted Fascist support as a counterweight to the Socialists, hoping that Fascism would stabilise Italian democracy and then retire peacefully. It did not. The Fascists took power, ensconced themselves in power, and stabilisation was given a miss. The parallel with 1977 is extremely telling, for today, too, it is the Italian bourgeoisie and the Italian industrialists who clamour for stabilisation through the good offices of the Communist Party. At a recent meeting of Communist intellectuals Berlinguer raised the question: why does the bourgeoisie hope for a Communist victory? Because, he said, the solution of Italy's economic crisis requires great sacrifices from the workers, and the middle classes and industrialists believe that only the Communist Party can persuade the masses to make them. But this, in my view, is not the way in which the Party really conceives its role.

Berlinguer made it clear that a rescue operation by the Party
would never be allowed to serve the recovery and restoration of
Italy's present social and economic order. For the Communist
Party, he argued, Italy's crisis and the austerity it entails present
between them an opportunity for a radical alternative to capitalism. They are the means for bringing about a revolutionary transformation of society. In other words, history is repeating itself:
now, as after the first world war, the industrialists hope that the
chestnuts will be pulled out of the fire for them by an extremist
party. The Communists on their part hope to exploit this expectation in order to get their hands on the country's jugular. After
that—they will see.

Urban Berlinguer, as a Communist leader, could hardly be
expected to say that he was going to restore capitalism—

Settembrini   —but that is the very thing he and other Communist leaders did say in their propaganda addressed to the
general public during the election campaign! At a by now famous
briefing at the Foreign Press Club in Rome, the Party's economic
leaders assured the Italian industrialists that the latter were right
in putting their confidence in the Communist Party, for the Party
was aware of their needs and capable of protecting their interests
much more effectively than were the Christian Democrats.

Urban A fine display of the dialectic of which Soviet Party
history offers the most telling examples. In 1936, Stalin was
interviewed by the American journalist Roy Howard, and this is
what he said, according to *Pravda* (5 March 1936):

Howard: Do you not think that there may be genuine fear in
capitalist countries of an intention on the part of the
Soviet Union to force its political theories on other
nations?

Stalin: There is no justification for such fears . . .

Howard: Does this statement of yours mean that the Soviet
Union has to any degree abandoned its plans and
intentions to bring about a world revolution?

Stalin: We never had any such plans or intentions.

Howard: You appreciate, no doubt, Mr Stalin, that much of
the world has for long entertained a different impression.

Stalin: That is the product of misunderstanding.

Settembrini Well, in the smaller compass of Italian politics
Giorgio Napolitano and Luciano Barca went so far as to say that
the Party recognised the necessity of keeping the Stock Exchange
in good order, respecting the market economy, and securing

ample profit margins for private industry—and, they added, only the Communist Party was in a position to assure these. But where did they say all this? In the pages of *La Stampa*—not in *l'Unità*. In trying to prognosticate what the Italian Communists might or might not do in office we can, as pragmatists and students of history, only go by what their leading thinkers and activists *have* said and done, not what they would like us to think they might do.

Berlinguer, Pajetta, Lombardo Radice and other Communist leaders claim that there is no break in the Italian Communist tradition. If we take the trouble of probing into what the founding fathers of Italian Communism did in fact say about Communist tactics, we must concede that the claim is justified. Here, for example, is how the allegedly liberal Gramsci, writing from prison in 1930, wanted the Party to proceed from opposition to power:

> The revolutionary prospects in Italy today can be divided into two alternatives—the more and less probable. The more probable is ... a period of transition.... There will be no immediate dictatorship of the proletariat, but between revolution and the dictatorship of the proletariat there will be a period of transition. Therefore the Communists must ... first fight for the Constituent Assembly. The Party's tactics must, therefore, be directed toward this goal without fear of appearing unrevolutionary. In the struggle against Fascism, the Communists must call for the Constituent Assembly before any of the other parties do, not as an end in itself, but as a means. The Constituent Assembly is the form of organisation in which the Party's action can be developed, and must be seen as an instrument for discrediting all the various projects for peaceful reform, and for showing the Italian working class that the only possible solution to Italy's troubles is the proletarian revolution.

My comment is: democracy for Gramsci was a means to kill democracy. We have no reason to believe that Berlinguer and the Italian Communist Party think otherwise.

Urban   This may well be the hidden purpose of the Party, but outwardly at least the Party's deviations from orthodoxy are spectacular and convincing, so much so that I can well understand the feelings of those East European Communists who perceive in Eurocommunism a most tempting alternative to Moscow's oriental despotism. Here you have a party whose leading cadres do not shy away from demanding the substitution of individual liberty for repression in Russia, Poland, East Germany and Czechoslovakia; who actively support people like Mlynar, Patocka, Michnik, Kuron, Biermann, Havemann, Sakharov and the other civil rights fighters; and who come very close to offering a frontal critique of the Soviet system itself.

Fabio Mussi, Cultural Editor of *Rinascita*, said in an earlier talk in this series:

> The whole sense of our policy is to demonstrate that Socialism has within it the capacity to develop along a road different from the one it has taken in Russia, and I find it significant as well as gratifying that the signatories of Charter 77 have specifically referred to the example of the Italian Communist Party . . . in our recent criticisms of the suppression of dissent in the Soviet Union, Czechoslovakia and Poland we have plainly stated that the root of the problem was structural; it could be understood and put right . . . only as part of the malaise of the entire party/state system . . . I do not see Leninism as the legitimation of the Party.

Well, however Machiavellian the intent of the Italian Communists may be, when I hear sentences of this kind, spoken as these were at the Rome headquarters of the Italian Communist Party, I wonder for how much longer Moscow can tolerate the thin (and not so thin) end of the Eurocommunist wedge. Men of the persuasion of Mussi have done precisely what you said you hoped the Party as a whole could be pressed into doing: aligned themselves with the spirit of liberalism and repudiated both the Stalinist and Leninist past. The magnetism of this alternative for restive Communists in Prague, Warsaw, Budapest, Bucharest, and indeed in Moscow seems to me manifest.

Settembrini   I fear it would be a mistake for them to believe that Italian Communism can offer a realistic alternative. Of course, we must understand their feelings: they are pinning their hopes to Eurocommunism for want of anything better. Seeing how the Russians acted in Czechoslovakia in 1968, they are clutching at every straw. But the Communist Party of a small country can only break away from Soviet colonialism if it has external backing. Ideally, it should be linked to a ruling Communist Party in a powerful country such as China. Italy and the Italian Communists do not meet either condition. To defeat Soviet rule in Prague and Warsaw you would, in the last analysis, need the American Army—nothing less. Eurocommunism, in so far as it is a genuine thing, is a factor of undoubted magnetism for East European *apparatchiks*, but in the correlation of international forces it is most unlikely to become a decisive influence. If Titoism did not, and could not—why should Italian Communism?

Urban   There are two points here: Titoism did have a formative influence in preparing the climate of rebellion before both the 1956 Hungarian revolution and the 1968 Prague spring. Second, totalitarian régimes, unless they are destroyed in war, can only be brought to their knees if there is a schism in the ranks of their own élites. I would have thought Eurocommunism might, eventually, be strong enough to widen and deepen existing disaffections and perhaps to create fresh ones. When we recall the magnetism which the idea of a united Europe has always had for the people of East and Central Europe, I cannot see why Eurocommunism should not have a like effect on the East and Central European Communist establishments. Admittedly all this may happen under the impact of Eurocommunism *without*, however, Eurocommunism becoming an alternative power-centre. But in whatever form it happened, it would be enough to challenge the authority of Moscow and thus to confront the Soviet leaders with the painful alternative of tolerating or refusing to tolerate it. They would stand to lose if they did—they would stand to lose if they didn't.

Settembrini   I disagree with you. The support which the two great western Communist Parties—the Italian and the French—are being given on their march to power by Communist dissidents in Eastern Europe is much more effective than the assistance these dissidents receive from the Italian and French Parties in return, for what they get is usually given late and less than willingly. If and when the Italian and French Communists gain power thanks to the credibility which the opposition in Eastern Europe has bestowed on them, they will be finally forced to choose between Leninism and Social Democracy—there is no third alternative.

But suppose they opt for Social Democracy without reservations—where would that leave them? They would become outcasts of the Marxist/Communist world fraternity, and their ability to support opposition in Eastern Europe would be reduced to the level of the Swedish Socialists or the British Labour Party—sufficient to grant political asylum to the victims of Soviet suppression, but good for little else.

I am ready to concede that if, once they have risen to power, the Italian and French Communists were to choose national Communism without parliamentary democracy and without individual liberty—in other words a form of Titoism—then this revamped semi-totalitarian model might still, or again, exert a certain influence in feeding the spirit of disaffection in Eastern

Europe—in those countries at least where a seamless totalitarian-ism still exists. But if you think of Kadar's Hungary—*there* a Titoist type of Communism would hardly be regarded as holding out a promise of decisive improvements in social welfare or cultural liberty, although it would, of course, mean a sea-change in the all-important matter of national independence.

But what kind of gain would any of this represent for Italy? To exchange the existing régime for national Communism—and without this Eurocommunism can be of little help to the internal opposition in Eastern Europe—would be an awesome regression. Many dissidents who are now resident in Italy and sympathise with Eurocommunism make no bones about admitting that if the Italian Communist Party were to come to power before having gone the whole way to Social Democracy, they would pack their bags and seek refuge elsewhere. Ironically enough, what they cannot see is that, if this were to happen, the responsibility for having clothed Italian Communism in an aura of democratic respectability would have to be laid at their own doorstep.

To sum up: if Communism becomes truly 'Euro', then it can no longer be Communist, in which case Italy stands to gain, and the dissidents may remain safely within our borders, but the Party's leverage in Eastern Europe will be gone. If, however, the Party remains Communist, its regression to Leninism is a possibility—indeed, in the long run, a certainty.

We must, therefore, bring it home to the Party that cutting its umbilical cord with Moscow is a less painful and less punishing alternative than keeping it intact. If we want the social democrat-isation of Italian Communism, we must force the hand of the Berlinguers and Amendolas—this is our only way of helping them.

Altiero Spinelli

8 How European are the Italian Eurocommunists?

Urban One of the surprises of the last Italian elections was your candidacy for the Chamber of Deputies on the Communist platform. Your decision to run for election in support of Communist policies was received with a mixture of horror and disbelief, not least because you were one of Italy's two Commissioners on the Brussels Commission and a leading European Federalist. Those not familiar with the intricacies of Italian Communist politics had reason to be puzzled. Has the PCI sufficiently changed its attitude to Europe for Altiero Spinelli to embrace it, or has Altiero Spinelli changed his politics because the Italian Communists appeared to be set for victory? In either case, there were questions to be asked, both in respect of your attitude to the Communist Party and of the Party's attitude to the policies you represent. What made you decide to run on the Communist ticket?

Spinelli My mandate at the European Commission was about to expire when the elections were announced (it expired at the end of 1976); and as I was close to 70, I decided to return to Italy and retire from public life. In the meantime, I was keeping a close watch on the Italian situation, and expressed my views in a number of articles and interviews. The brunt of these was that Italy was drifting away from the European Community and that only a coalition of all political forces could stop the drift. I saw that the Communist Party had gone through a certain evolution in its internal policies, and I was persuaded that the Party's offer of a 'historical compromise' was both right and feasible. It was right not only from the European point of view, but it was also an essential step toward creating a consensus without which Italy could not overcome its economic crisis or restore the authority of law and orderly government. Without the Communists, I argued, no Italian government could be strong enough to make

179

democracy work. I also observed that the Communist attitude to Europe as displayed in the Council of Europe showed a certain progress towards accepting the idea of European unification.

When the elections were announced, the Communist Party and also the Christian Democrats felt that they ought to broaden the bases of their respective parties by obtaining the support of certain independent politicians who understood and were willing to support their programme, without, however, either becoming Party members or identifying themselves in every case with the line of the Party. The Christian Democrats 'co-opted' Umberto Agnelli, offering him a safe seat in Parliament, and on the Left I was one of several persons to whom the Communists made a similar offer. I accepted this on the understanding that I would not belong to the Communist group in Parliament, that I would vote independently, and speak with complete freedom on any issue I chose. There was a certain risk in all this for the Communists. But they felt confident that as we saw eye to eye with one another on most points of general policy, the risk was worth taking.

Urban What were these points of general agreement?

Spinelli That the Party was committed to democracy; that the idea of an 'historical compromise' was seriously meant and would be respected; that European unification was to be supported and the country's present position in the East-West equilibrium maintained.

On all these points we reached agreement. The result is that I am indeed outside the Communist parliamentary group, but by virtue of my support of the Communist platform I can influence the Party's policies in those areas which matter to me most—its policies on Europe. I do not think I am boasting when I say that the Party has, in fact, adopted the line which I had sought and supported for many years, especially the need to transcend economic unification and move towards a European political union. I put it to the Party leaders that political union could only be achieved if all political forces in Europe willingly agreed to work for it. For the European Left, however, political union was a divisive issue in most countries. If this could be overcome, the Left might take the lead in guiding Europe to political union and shape that union according to its own lights. I therefore urged the Party leaders that the Party should get out of the Communist ghetto and establish workable relations with the European Social Democrats so that political unification would bear the imprint of broadly Socialist policies.

Urban It was on this understanding that you ran for election and were in fact elected.

Spinelli   Yes, and our understanding on these points has so far not been disturbed.

But, of course, there is another point here. News of my decision to contest the elections from a Communist platform caused a minor sensation at the time. Many people were unwilling to believe it, others were profoundly scandalised, including some of my colleagues in the European Commission. I was subjected to a number of interviews in the press, on radio and television and, as one might expect, the recurrent theme of questioning was: could the Communists be trusted? Would they keep faith, seeing that the historical record showed them to be saying one thing before they were in office and quite another when they have attained office? I should imagine your own thoughts run along similar lines.

Urban   They do.

Spinelli   My answer to this is as follows. The Italian Communist Party has been part and parcel of our political life for more than half a century. It is an organic element of our political thinking and political culture. For good or for ill (and I will not prejudge the issue) it is physiologically and psychologically a large part of Italian reality. It may well be that it will be the death of us, but if so, it will destroy us in exactly the same sense as any other political force might—through ineptitude, poor leadership, corruption and so forth—but not because it is a Trojan horse that will disgorge Soviet warriors once it is within the walls of Rome.

Now, this Party was formed under the impact of the Bolshevik revolution. Its avowed objective was to seize power and turn Italy into a dictatorship of the proletariat. The Communist Party was to lead the revolution and head the dictatorship. This was Lenin's prescription and practice in Russia in 1917, and the Italian Communist Party was founded on this model. Moreover, the Italian Party, as a member of the Comintern, took its orders from Moscow, and behaved in its unquestioning obedience to Stalin as the Jesuits obey the orders of their Generals—*perinde ac cadaver* (with cadaver-like obedience). Togliatti was an important leader of the Comintern, so that the Party's obedience had an extra guarantee in the person of one of Stalin's cardinals. This was the ideological and organisational basis on which the Italian Party began to function.

But if you look at the record of the Italian Communist Party you will find that at no time did the Party actually pursue anti-democratic, anti-liberal policies. Mind you, this was not for any lack of trying. Our Communists owe their good record to the political conditions into which they happened to be born: from the very beginning they were forced into opposition to Fascism and had eventually to go underground—

Urban —Shouldn't we, at the same time, remember the Party's common roots with Fascism, both having sprung from the Socialist Party of which Mussolini was one of the leaders?

Spinelli This is certainly true. But the only historically significant connection between Fascism and Socialism is that Fascism was a degenerate form of Socialism; and so in fact was Hitler's National Socialism—

Urban —of which we have telling proof in the presence, in the late 1920s, of left-wing revolutionary groups in or on the fringes of the Nazi Party, such as Otto Strasser's Union of Revolutionary National Socialists and the National Bolsheviks. In the 1920s it was not always clear whether Nationalism or Socialism predominated in Hitler's thinking. Goebbels, who served his Nazi apprenticeship in Otto Strasser's Revolutionary National Socialist faction, demanded in 1925 that 'the petty bourgeois Adolf Hitler' be removed from the Party!

Spinelli The point that matters for the purposes of my argument is that the Italian Communists were forced into illegality and fought Fascism with more determination than any other party; and when the political parties were dissolved by Mussolini, the Communist Party became the centre of the entire Italian Resistance. Eighty per cent of all political prisoners were Communists—not unnaturally, I might add, because they were the ones who took most of the risks. In their rhetoric the Communists stuck to the line that their struggle was not only against Fascism, but against 'the rule of the bourgeoisie', of which, they claimed, Fascism was but one of the symptoms. But the fact was that they were in alliance with several other parties and individuals who were also opposed to the Fascist dictatorship but were determined not to be dragged into another dictatorship after the fall of Fascism. This inhibited the Communist Party's radicalism: the dictatorship of the proletariat never got off to a start. One of the first things Togliatti said after his return from Moscow—and it was a great surprise to all—was that the Italian Communists must work within the context of parliamentary democracy and cooperate with other political forces. We might as well, he said, start with Badoglio; and they did! After the first post-war elections, in which the Communists came third, the Party took full part in hammering out what was after all a bourgeois Constitution. Indeed the veteran Communist Umberto Terracini was at one stage President of the Constituent Assembly. Not only that, but the Communists also voted for Article 7 of the Constitution, retaining Mussolini's Concordat with the Vatican. For this they were bitterly attacked by the Socialist Party and other parties on the democratic Left. But I would say with the benefit of hindsight that the Communist vote was an act of great political wisdom. The Communists *could* have prevented the Concordat from being retained in the Constitution, because without them the Constitution would not have received the requisite majority. But this would have meant war between the incipient Republic and Italian Catholic opinion. The Communists rightly felt that the peace of the state was more important than a controversial decision on the merits and demerits of the Concordat. In time, they must have thought, they might change it, but their first priority was not to prejudice but to build up what was inevitably a bourgeois democratic republic.

Urban Mussolini, with his strongly anti-clerical background had reached *his* decision to make his peace with the Vatican on similarly 'pragmatic' grounds. And he, like the Communists in 1946, had been attacked for it by his own 'revolutionary' left.

Spinelli Yes—what one has to remember is that in Italy, unlike Poland for example, the Church has been a force against national unity. The unification of Italy was achieved in the teeth of the Pope's opposition. Rome had to be occupied before Italy could be united. At the same time, the Italian people's religious loyalties to Catholicism were, and are, strong, and the Church, on its part, has always known how to live in relative harmony with different régimes. It recognised Fascism, but exacted as a *quid pro quo* the Concordat from Mussolini. When the Republican Constitution was drawn up, the Church's attitude to the new state was unchanged: 'We'll respect your institutions if you honour the Concordat'. And the Communists were prudent enough to see that it was imperative under the given conditions to underwrite the Concordat—it was proof that they were not bent on disruption and revolution. Had they been so minded, they would have sabotaged the Constituent Assembly, wrecked the Constitution, and invested their energies in creating the maximum amount of tension and disorder.

Urban All this may be clear to us 30 years after the event, but at the time it was far from being obvious. 1945–48 were the years of the Stalinist take-over of the whole of East and Central Europe. Everywhere the arrival of 'the dictatorship of the proletariat' was preceded by honeyed words about the Communist Party's democratic parliamentary intentions.

The great national task facing our country cannot be solved by either the Communist Party or by any other party alone. The Communist Party holds that it does not have a monopoly, and it does not need a monopoly, to work among the masses for the reconstruction of the new nation. The Communist Party does not approve of the idea of a one-party system. Let the other parties operate and organise as well.

These words were spoken before the 1945 elections by Ernö Gerö—the same man who became one of Hungary's most ruthless and most hated leaders when the Communist Party took monopolistic power in 1947–48. In Czechoslovakia, at the time of the post-war coalition government, Gottwald spoke repeatedly of 'the specific Czechoslovak road to Socialism'. This, he said, would not be a road 'through the dictatorship of the proletariat'; it would be a 'régime of a peculiar, Czechoslovak type' embodying a Marxism 'under new conditions'—'not a Socialist revolution' (and Benes, let it be said, told Bruce Lockhart as late as May 1947 that 'Gottwald was a reasonable man who believed in parliamentary democracy').One could quote many other examples from every one of Stalin's satellites. Therefore the Italian Communists' prudent words in 1946 and 1947 were no convincing indication, in the perspective of those days, that their intentions were different from those of Rakosi, Gerö, Gottwald, Dimitrov or Gomulka, all of whom spoke of democracy, parliamentary government, independence from the Soviet model and the 'strictest guardianship' of the Constitution (Gottwald). What was different in Italy was the absence of the Red Army, but in 1945–47 even this offered insufficient reassurance because Italy had, in Tito's Yugoslavia, a particularly aggressive form of Stalinism sitting on its northeastern frontiers. Let us not forget that, until Yugoslavia's expulsion from the Cominform, Tito's brand of Communism was in successful competition for extremism and brutality with Stalinism itself.

Spinelli This is true. When, for example, the Marshall Plan was announced, Togliatti, like Gottwald in Czechoslovakia, was eager to accept the American offer. But Stalin vetoed participation and Togliatti obeyed. The Italian Communists then fell in with the Stalinist device of trying to take power by popular front tactics in the 1948 elections—but failed.

Urban What is the character of the political forces to which the Communists were, and are, opposed, and what alternative policies do they offer?

Spinelli The Communists are facing in the Christian Democratic Party a force which has been in power for so many years that it has come to be regarded as Italy's natural government party—what the Germans call a *Staatspartei*. This party has had an embarrassing past which it has taken pains to live down. Its long symbiosis with the Church made it both anti-liberal and opposed to the secular nation-state. Its support of the policies of the arch-reactionary Pope Pius XII, and its associations with Fascism, would have made the Christian Democratic Party a sinister force in post-war Italian politics had it not been for the reforming influence of genuine democrats such as de Gasperi, Scelba and others. It is their merit to have recognised, as the Communists also had to recognise, that the country's democratic reconstruction would be gravely prejudiced if the Party started life under the Republic with the ballast of an anti-democratic and anti-liberal ideology.

Urban The Church was their Stalin, in your reading—

Spinelli —Yes, and as the Communists cut their links with the Stalinist heritage, so the Christian Democrats shed their dependence on the Church without being in any way disloyal to Catholicism, much less to Christianity.

Urban It sounds like an appealingly symmetrical arrangement—a harbinger perhaps of the 'historical compromise'—with each side jettisoning embarrassing bits of ideological furniture and concentrating on what the traffic would bear. Luigi Barzini's image of the Italian *modus operandi* is not dissimilar from yours. Italy's capacity for good sense and bad policies never ceases to surprise.

Spinelli I fear the Christian Democrats' good sense had its strict limits. Their long years in government have confirmed Acton's tag: power corrupts—absolute power corrupts absolutely. While the Christian Democrats did not, and do not, have absolute power, they have entrenched themselves in every domain of Italy's life with the permanence of a dynasty. The result has been corruption, nepotism and mismanagement in all areas of public and private enterprise. This, I must hasten to add, was not so in the early years of Christian Democratic rule. Italy's phenomenal rise, in the 1950s and early 1960s, as an industrial power, as well as its very significant contribution to creating the European Communities (as they then were), was largely the work of Christian Democratic leaders. But, as I say, the Party's stock is now exhausted.

Under these conditions the Communists became the natural point of reference for the entire opposition. Every election brought them fresh votes. Today they are in charge of many of our best run municipalities, and their influence in the trade union movement is paramount. Their respect for the law and for the conventions of parliamentary democracy is scrupulous. Is this the same Party of revolution and dictatorship which Lenin and some of the early Leninist leaders of the Italian Communist Party thought they were building? I hardly think so. The Italian Communists are men and women whose principal concern is the welfare and general good of the Italian people, who want social reforms to that end, and who are perfectly prepared to ally themselves with others to that end. They are people of the stamp of the Austrian, Belgian and British Socialists—in fact, Social Democrats.

Urban   Social Democrats at the top of the Party as well as at its grass roots?

Spinelli   The votes the Communists attract are, ideologically speaking, Social Democratic votes. This is not a party of militants—it is a party of millions of ordinary, reform-hungry people, and the *apparat* at grass-root levels is also Social Democratic much more than Marxist or Leninist.

Urban   What about the *apparat* at the all-important middle level where vested interests and calcified minds are normally guarantees of orthodoxy?

Spinelli   The *apparatchiks* at the middle level—the Deputies, the men who run cooperatives, trade unions, municipal governments and so forth—are anything but *apparatchiks* in the Soviet, or any non-Italian, sense of the word. They are neither revolutionaries nor a self-perpetuating caste of bureaucrats. They are ordinary people *of* the people and of Italian culture. They are indistinguishable from the kind of men and women one finds running similar organisations for the Social Democrats.

In the upper crust of the Party there continues to exist a small number of leaders steeped in the Stalinist past. Their ranks are thinning out and their influence is small. They have come to recognise that the secret of the Party's spectacular success was, and is, the distance it has managed to put between itself and the Soviet model of Socialism. They know that, if the Party had preserved its original character as a Leninist vanguard of the elect, it would never have attained the influence it has. Facts have taught them that there is an inverse relationship between ideology, Leninism and Stalinism on the one hand, and popular success on the other.

In the Italian Communist Party, too, nothing succeeds like success. When the choice had to be made between loyalty to the purisms of the established faith, and the promise of power based on the Party's popular appeal, the ideology was promptly dropped and the promise of power embraced. This is the way in which every ideological party proceeds when faced with the choice—it has happened in Italy and it is happening in France.

Urban I am a little disturbed by the unanimity with which the French Party has erased 'the dictatorship of the proletariat' from its programme. Seventeen hundred votes were cast for repudiating it—none against. Earlier resolutions *endorsing* 'the dictatorship of the proletariat' were (as Kissinger recently observed) carried by the same 1,700 votes for, with none against. The French Communist leaders must be extraordinarily persuasive. . . .

Spinelli I share your disbelief. France is intellectually more liberal than Italy, yet the French Communist Party has, until quite recently, been a direct appendage of the Comintern and the Kremlin. Maurice Thorez was not a product of *French* Communism; he was directly appointed by Stalin. No such thing ever happened in Italy. From the very beginning, the Italian Party had Gramsci as its principal apostle, closely followed by Togliatti, Longo and others. There was no need to scour Lenin or Stalin for suitable quotations when such could be readily found in Gramsci. The Italian leaders were home-grown Communists; their intellectual habitat, their social and cultural terms of reference were Italian. Consequently the critique to which they subjected the entire philosophy and programme of Italian Communism was profound and grounded in the realities of Italian life. Nothing of the sort could be said of the French Party. The manner in which they repudiated the 'dictatorship of the proletariat' would be unimaginable under Italian conditions: they rejected dogma— dogmatically! I am inclined to take French protestations of change with a pinch of salt. After Khrushchev's secret speech at the 20th Party Congress the following story was doing the rounds in Moscow: An anthropologist visits a cannibal tribe in darkest Africa. 'I'm told', he says to the tribal chief, 'that you still practise the shameful habit of cannibalism around here.' 'Oh no', protests the chieftain, 'we consumed our last man yesterday'. . . .

Urban I am not quite clear how and why the 'dictatorship of the proletariat' vanished from the Italian Party's vocabulary. I can see that, in the Soviet Union, where 'Socialism' has been on the books for 60 years, the party theologians had grounds for saying that, after those 60 years of 'building Socialism', the dictatorship of the proletariat has been superseded by 'the all-peoples' state'. This is, in fact, what the draft of the new Soviet Constitution says. But on what doctrinal grounds have the Italian and French Parties neglected or dropped the 'dictatorship of the proletariat', seeing that they have not *begun* to take the first steps towards 'Socialism'? I can understand their fear that 'dictatorship' is no vote-catcher in Western Europe—but could there be a profounder challenge to the entire concept of Communism, or a more opportunistic and possibly self-defeating way of selling it?

Spinelli The 'dictatorship of the proletariat' has never been *officially* dropped from the programme of the Italian Party, but it was quietly buried a long time ago. Not only that, but at the first legally held Congress of the Party in 1946 Togliatti stated: No one in the Italian Communist Party is expected to be a Marxist!— which goes way beyond repudiating the dictatorship of the proletariat. Togliatti added that most members and supporters of the Party were, of course, Marxists, but he saw the Party as a rallying ground for a practical programme, not a catechism. And this is naturally the way in which practical matters are handled in politics. There *are* Christians who believe that Christ's second coming will mean the end of the world, and there are scriptural sources to support their expectation. But show me a Christian who bases his daily life on it—any more than any convinced Communist would expect a just society to emerge from the dictatorship of the proletariat! Such people no longer exist.

The Italian Communists had two great obstacles barring them from eligibility to power: the dead weight of ideology and their loyalty, or suspected loyalty, to Moscow as the ultimate defender of the faith. It has taken many years of free debate to overcome them, but overcome them they did. Incidentally: no one in the Italian Party is subject to party discipline or the 'whip' system. The Party's debates are entirely free—as free, shall we say, as those of the German Social Democrats.

Urban I am intrigued by your repeated reference to Social Democracy. In their Bad Godesberg programme (1959) the German Social Democrats renounced Marxism as their official philosophy, which the Italian Communists have never done— even though Togliatti opened the gates of the Party to non-Marxist supporters and Lombardo Radice tells us that the Party might repudiate Marxism at its next Congress. In fact, not many weeks ago, Giorgio Amendola said: 'We are not going to go to Godesberg'.

Spinelli The notion of 'the historical compromise' is in my judgment the Italian Communist Party's repudiation of Marxism. I can interpret it in no other way.

Urban Why doesn't the Party say so?

Spinelli No party can utterly disown the principles on which its entire past and entire mythology were built. No party can be expected to say: we have been misguided or ignorant or naive for the greatest part of our existence—but *now* we are going to start a fresh chapter. If you drive self-criticism that far, you destroy your *raison d'être*.

Urban But this refusal, and the lessons imprinted on us by the behaviour of the ruling Communist Parties, accounts for the suspicion which continues to surround the Italian Communist Party's policies. Given the history of the world Communist movement, the Italian Party can hardly hope to benefit from any presumption of innocence.

Spinelli   Well, it is a cardinal principle of law that men are judged by their deeds, not their intentions. On that principle, the Italian Communists have been democrats and are democrats. Whatever their occasional rhetoric, they have stuck to the rules of parliamentary democracy. You may well be right in saying that the onus of proof is on them. But, for that, they have to be given a chance to govern.

Urban   You have said the idea of 'an historical compromise' is the Italian equivalent of the Bad Godesberg programme of the German Social Democrats. What particular circumstances were responsible for this significant initiative?

Spinelli   As the economic crisis began to hit Italy and the mismanagement of the country became less and less tolerable—and I am now talking of the late 1960s—the example of a well-run party, with great managerial skills and incorruptible service to its credit, made the man in the street aware that the Communists might offer a solution to Italy's problems. At the same time, the Socialists, whose alliance with the Christian Democrats had at one stage brought them an ephemeral growth, were losing support and began to talk of the necessity of an alternative government of the Left. All this induced the Communist leadership and the Party intellectuals to believe that the time was ripe for a new policy that would pave their way to power.

But how were they to approach the problem most profitably? The Communists had before them the example of Allende: a government which had the majority of the national vote behind it* and which ought to have been able to govern, but in fact was not. Why? Because the great mass of non-electoral power—the police, the civil administration, the judiciary, the holders of economic power: in brief, the Establishment—was against the elected government. In other words, the constellation of forces outside parliament, which was conservative, was a challenge, and a successful challenge, to the political power vested in the government through its parliamentary mandate. It is almost a law of politics that if the Left enjoys only a small parliamentary

---

* In fact, Allende had no majority support. In the 1970 presidential elections he won 36 per cent of the vote, and in the 1973 legislative elections 43 per cent (ed).

majority, its power is precarious and its life is in constant danger because, when the power of the non-parliamentary establishment, which is habitually conservative, is added to the parliamentary strength of the Right, the Right proves stronger. By the same token, a small conservative majority is enough to secure safety of tenure for a conservative government because to *its* parliamentary strength is automatically added the support of the non-parliamentary 'vote'.

The Italian Communists recognised that the coup against Allende was the result of an alliance between Allende's parliamentary opponents and his enemies in the Chilean extra-parliamentary establishment. Pondering this example they came to the conclusion that a similar fate might befall an Italian Communist government. Even if the Communists and Socialists united, they would, so the Communists realised, still be too weak to govern and resist the combined opposition of the parliamentary Right and that large conglomeration of non-parliamentary power that would try to defeat a Communist-led government.

The next step in the Communist Party's reasoning was to say that, in order to come to power and exercise power with any chance of success, the Party must come to an understanding with the Christian Democrats. It was argued that, even though the Communists were critical of the Christian Democratic Party's policies, it had to be recognised that the Christian Democrats were a popular party with a strong and honourable democratic component. It was with this Party—it was now recalled—that the Communists had shared the writing of Italy's new Constitution and the creation of the Republic. On such foundations a consensus could once again be created.

Urban   A most un-Leninist way of going after power—

Spinelli   —Oh, highly un-Leninist and anti-Leninist! It is the way of men who have learnt to deal with the real world. Lenin was an irrelevance. The Communists as co-founders of post-war Italian democracy were aware that democracy was in deep trouble and that the sole way of rescuing it was through a broad consensus similar to the one that existed just after the war. The Communists' ambition was (and is) a modest one. They realised that the mistrust which their past inspired would take them many years to expunge from memory and that they could not rule single-handed for the reasons I have just stated. Hence they concentrated on trying to obtain a share of power in coalition with the Christian Democrats, and that continues to be their present policy. The Communists were, in fact, saying: 'You distrust us. Very well, you need not advance us your confidence. If you agree to share power with us in government, in some areas you will be watching us, in others we will be watching you. You will see for yourselves that we are not plotting a revolution—we have no Red Guards, no armed workers and no Soviet Army to foist us on an unwilling majority.'

This perspective made the Party re-examine its entire political programme. Very briefly: their platform continues to include the nationalisation of certain major enterprises and the abolition of the market economy. But they propose to do this in a way that would amount to *socialisation*, on the model of strongly motivated Socialist Parties such as the Swedish and Dutch (the Germans are not so motivated), and not on the model of Soviet state-Socialism. This is, broadly speaking, where the Party stands in 1977.

Urban My scepticism is unassuaged. One famous Communist poster before Hungary's first—and last—free elections after the war showed a protective hand extended in a gesture of benediction, with this (originally rhyming) couplet for a caption: 'The Communist Party's concern is the private wealth of the little man'.

Spinelli Well, this is the kind of past from which the Italian Communists have to detach themselves. But, as I say, they are conscious of their handicap and they are, I think, on their way to overcoming it. The Party's evolution in its external policies has been every bit as significant as the one mapped out by 'the historical compromise'. And, of course, the crucial problem was its relationship with the Soviet Union. More and more, the Italian Communists came to feel that their links with Moscow were a millstone round their neck. Luckily for them, their efforts to cut the umbilical cord coincided with a number of favourable developments—de-Stalinisation after Khrushchev's secret speech in 1956, the Sino-Soviet dispute, and the ensuing collapse of the monolithic character of the world Communist movement. When church unity no longer exists, everyone is much freer to think and act as he likes. Togliatti fully exploited these opportunities by adding the idea of polycentrism.

The Communists' evolution did not, of course, follow a straight line. The 1956 Hungarian Revolution found the Party still deeply mired in dogmatism. The uprising was branded a 'counter-revolution', the arrest and execution of Imre Nagy were strongly supported, and the Soviet reasons for suppressing Hungary were approved. But certain hesitations could already be observed. For example, Giolitti (my current successor as European Commissioner in Brussels) left the Party in demonstration of his disapproval of the Party's attitude to the Hungarian events, and so did others. But by the time Soviet troops marched on Prague in

August 1968, the Party leaders got the message. They realised
that sticking to the Soviet line would lay them open to the accusation that, whatever they might be saying in their propaganda, the
moment a decision had to be taken in a critical situation, they
would always come down on the side of the Soviet Union. They
therefore criticised the Soviet action and have sustained their
critique to this day. They are now manfully supporting Charter 77
in Czechoslovakia, the Polish Workers' Defence Committee, dissent in East Germany, and civil rights in the Soviet Union.

But this break with the mother church left the Party's foreign
policy in a state of disorientation. As you know, a Communist
Party's attitude to Moscow is the bench-mark of its general per-
ceptions and intentions. For much the greatest part of its history
the world Communist movement was governed by the idea that
the might and influence of the Soviet Union coincide with the
interests of mankind. Proletarian internationalism was the doctrinal umbrella under which gains made by the world Communist
movement were never given up and central discipline was
enforced. But with this monolithic conception broken up—where
was the Italian Party to go? A swing to America would have been
too drastic to be imaginable. There were attempts to learn from
the French Communists and invest in left-wing nationalism. But
while in France the coupling of Nationalism with Revolution had
a long tradition in the French Revolution and the revolutionary
and Napoleonic wars, no such tradition existed in Italy. I do not,
mind you, approve of the French Communists' nationalism, but I
can understand its rationale—

Urban   —'National-Socialism' with an anti-American and
anti-German face—

Spinelli   —That kind of thing. The German Socialists' nationalism under Kurt Schumacher was an equally poor model,
though for different reasons. In Italy, nationalism under the aegis
of the Communist Party would have entailed the country's rapid
detachment from Western Europe and its relegation, culturally
and politically, to the status of an increasingly off-centre Mediterranean nation. It would have put Italy in the company of half-
developed countries nursing their grievances without much hope
of putting them right. This might have been an acceptable prospect for a certain type of atavistic Fascism, but not for a modern
and progressive party.

Urban   There is, though, a highly respectable democratic *and*
nationalistic tradition in Mazzini and 'Young Italy'. Wouldn't
these have offered the necessary historical precedent?

Spinelli   Despite their fame and formative cultural influence,
Mazzini and the Republican Party have never been central to

Italian politics. The popular traditions have been Catholicism on the Right and Socialism on the Left. Both were rather indifferent to the *Risorgimento* which was compromised, especially through the misuse of the name of Garibaldi (always a hurrah-word), by the Fascist régime. True, the Communist Party too paid tribute in its rhetoric to the *Risorgimento*, and there was a time when the Party had its own 'Garibaldi brigades'. But this was merely pandering to popular emotions—the intolerant nationalism which comes so easily to the French, whether of the Right or the Left, was absent.

With all these roads closed to them, the Italian Communists had no choice but to adopt European unification as the central plank in their new foreign policy. This carried the promise of many advantages, the main one being that a united Europe would assert its independence from both Moscow and Washington. In the event, our Communists did, in fact, walk down the European road, and I have been able to follow their development from close quarters and in some ways to influence them.

Urban   Without wanting to interrupt your story, let me just say that Moscow is extremely hostile to any idea of an independent united Europe, especially as advanced in Santiago Carrillo's *Eurocommunism and the State*. This is, on the face of it, surprising—after all, an independent Europe would diminish Washington's influence. But this is not the way the Soviet leaders look at it. Carrillo may very well have put his finger on the real motives behind the Soviet criticism when he said with his customary frankness on 28 June 1977:

What I cannot understand is how the USSR can prefer a Western Europe in NATO, in a certain manner under the control of the United States, to an independent and autonomous Europe such as we propose. This forces me to think that the existence of a NATO Europe, controlled by the United States, justifies a second Europe on the other side, controlled by the Soviet Union.

Spinelli   I would not take issue with Carrillo's suspicion—it is probably well-founded.

You will no doubt know that I used to be a Communist. I broke with the Party while in detention because I refused to toe the line on the Moscow show-trials (more of which later). After my imprisonment, which lasted from 1927 right up to the fall of Mussolini in 1943, I was considered one of the Party's worst enemies, and I am certain that if the Party had taken power after the war, I would have been among the first to be liquidated.

Fortunately for me, it did not take power.

When the idea of European unification began to get into its stride and I was heavily involved in the campaign for European Federation, I was first wondering whether, as a man coming from the Left, I should not try to work for the acceptance of my policies through and with the European Left. But I soon realised that this would be taking too narrow a view, and I decided to count my allies and adversaries not in terms of Left or Right but according to their willingness or refusal to work for European unification.

Well, it so happened that the Christian Democrats were the first to support the idea of Europe, and I have been closely associated with them, not only with Alcide de Gasperi who led the Italian side of the movement, but also with Robert Schuman in France and Konrad Adenauer in Germany. We had, as European Federalists, a certain impact on them.

After the Hungarian Revolution, the Italian Socialists (who were then in electoral alliance with the Communists and shared the latter's Moscow-centric loyalties) decided to cut the Soviet tie and were, as the Communists were to be ten years later, in a quandary as to what they should do next. Pietro Nenni invited me to collaborate with him in working out a European programme for his Party. I was most willing to do so, but when asked to join the Socialist Party, I declined. Nenni eventually became Foreign Minister and appointed me as his special adviser on European affairs.

Urban It seems to me that in a sense the Socialists were joining *your* 'Party'—

Spinelli —They were, and so were the Communists, because after the occupation of Czechoslovakia, the Communists approached me with a similar problem: Would I help them to devise a Communist policy on Europe? They had some vague idea that Europe was the road they ought to be taking, but they were not sure how to go about it.

Urban Did the Communist leaders approach you directly?

Spinelli Oh, yes. I was at the time director of an Institute of International Affairs which I had founded, and it was there that Leonardi for example came to see me with this problem. A little later Amendola re-established contact with me (we had been friends and comrades in the Communist Party until my expulsion) and it was Amendola who then took the lion's share in working out a European programme for the Party.

I was watching his evolution with great interest. He first spoke in vague Gaullist terms—'Europe from the Atlantic to the Urals'—that kind of thing; but when he saw that this kinship with Gaullism put the Party in an equivocal position, he began to limit the scope of desirable unification to Western Europe. Next, he shifted his position to demanding a 'confederal' Europe—a Europe of nation-states—but this was, of course, still very far from what Federalists like myself were seeking. Amendola then let it be known that the Party ought to assume a more positive attitude to the European Community, but he used a curious reasoning. The European Community, he argued, has been created by the bourgeoisie. Once the Communist and other left-wing parties could work from within it, they might turn it to their own advantage—'exploit' it, to use his word, against the bourgeoisie.

Urban   Did you hear him say this?

Spinelli   Yes, but I did not leave it unanswered. I explained to him that any attempt at 'exploitation' would be a dangerous mistake. The European Community, I said, is far from resting on solid foundations. It is still very much in the making and may yet fail.

'You must realise', I told him, 'that if you do come into the Community, you are going to exploit nothing. We want you to come in on condition that you are determined to help us to develop it—not to kill it.'

Amendola, who did not have a closed mind on the problem, understood the difficulties the European Community was, and is, facing, and gradually began to talk in federalist terms. That is where the matter stands at the moment.

Urban   There are two questions here. Does Amendola mean what he says, and does he represent the thinking of the Party?

Spinelli   My answer is 'yes' to both questions, and my reasons for saying so are these. The idea of European unification has different echoes in different countries. In Britain and France, Europe is a divisive issue; in Germany, Holland, Belgium and Italy it makes for national unity. The Italian Communists are well aware of the popularity of the European idea throughout Italian society and they cultivate it as part of their quest for a consensus through the 'historical compromise'. Europe fits in with their internal policies.

There is, moreover, the fact that in Italy the most fervent supporters of European unification are the workers. This is intriguing because the sad thing we can observe in most European countries is that, with honourable exceptions, the working class has become the most parochial, provincial, and even jingoistic section of society. This is most obviously true in countries which have a large immigrant population—whether as temporary guest-workers or permanently settled. The French and British working class may well be internationalist in the minds of Socialist theoreticians. But in fact their experience of foreigners is limited to two types of encounter: at home, where the foreign worker is resented simply because he is a foreigner, and abroad, where foreigners are met with on the tourist circuit in the shape of waiters and taxi-drivers. This is as good as not meeting them at all and usually serves to reinforce existing prejudices rather than to abolish them. Germany in this respect is an exception. There foreign workers are pretty well treated at every level—but then Germany under Hitler abused the labour of foreigners so badly that Germany's present fairness is perhaps no more than a compensatory reaction to the past, although I tend to believe that it represents a genuine advance in social tolerance.

In Italy there is hardly a worker or peasant whose father or brother or son has not spent years in foreign countries as a guest-worker. When these people speak of the Germans or French or Dutch, they know exactly what they are talking about: they have lived among Germans and Frenchmen, and they liked what they saw. For them the foreigner is not an alien they cannot comprehend, but a friend and employer and a source of a higher standard of living. The Spanish people have the same attitude, and one can see why Carrillo has no difficulty in leading a strongly pro-European Communist Party.

To sum up: the Italian Communists are responding in their pro-European policies to the real feelings and interests of the Italian people. In designing their new economic profile, too, Europe is of considerable help to them. After much internal debate, the Party decided not to opt for a planned, much less a command, economy. As the European Community makes it mandatory for the Nine to keep their national economies open, it provides the Italian Communists with an excellent justification for declining to do certain things they would not want to do anyway.

Urban   What about the vexed question of the Party's attitude to NATO? In my conversation with Professor Lombardo Radice, he made a highly equivocal statement on what the Party would do in a war-like East-West emergency, notably that it might, with certain qualifications, come down on the Soviet side.

Spinelli   The Party's initial attitude was, of course, extremely hostile to NATO. Then came a period of discreet silence while new attitudes were being worked out. This in turn was followed by the full acceptance of NATO as one element in the world's existing balance of power which guarantees peace. The current Communist attitude is that if Italy rocked the Western boat either by neutrality or by coming out against the Western Alliance, the imbalance in favour of Soviet power would be unacceptable.

Urban The imbalance in favour of Moscow would hurt Italian Communist interests?

Spinelli Yes, for what would it mean for the Italian Communists in real terms? Italy's north-eastern neighbour, Yugoslavia, enjoys a position of non-alignment. This is partly due to the Yalta agreement which exempted Yugoslavia from both the Western and Eastern spheres of influence. But it is also due to Tito's and the Yugoslav Communists' firm guardianship of their independence.

Today Yugoslavia is one important element in the equilibrium between NATO and the Warsaw Pact. This was well demonstrated after the occupation of Czechoslovakia, when the Yugoslavs let it be known that, if Soviet intervention looked like becoming a reality, they would not hesitate to ask for NATO assistance. The Italian Communists are extremely conscious of two dangers: one is the danger they might be inviting on the heads of the Yugoslavs by toying with the idea of Italian neutrality or directly repudiating Italy's membership of NATO. This would mean the weakening or disappearance of NATO from Yugoslavia's Western frontier, and making it, in the uncertainties that are bound to follow Tito's death, much easier for the Soviet leaders to risk the subjugation of Yugoslavia. The presence of NATO on the Italian-Yugoslav boundary is one of the guarantees, and possibly *the* guarantee, of Yugoslav independence.

The second danger is connected with the first. For the Italian Communists, with their highly unorthodox, Eurocommunist ideas, nothing could be more unwelcome than the arrival of Soviet troops on their frontiers. Berlinguer made this absolutely clear during the last election campaign when he said that he felt much better protected behind the shield of NATO than he would outside it.

Urban What exactly did he mean by that?

Spinelli He and the other Italian Communist leaders know well enough that working in a Western bourgeois society certainly faces them with great obstacles. Kissinger was against them, the present US administration may also be against them, they are up against old prejudices and so forth. But they feel that in the West they are free to fight these obstacles, and to fail or to succeed on the merit of their case. If, however, they came under Soviet protection, Berlinguer and his colleagues would soon be going the way of Dubcek, or worse.

Urban Their fears are surely justified. When one reads the accounts of Stalin's treatment of the Communist survivors of the Spanish Civil War, the roots of Santiago Carrillo's distrust of the

Soviet system are at once revealed. The memoirs of El Campesino, for example, one of the Spanish Civil War's most famous
Communist generals, are proof enough that the horrors of Stalinism implanted in the minds of most Spanish Communists a
lasting aversion to the Soviet type of Communism and a determination to run any future Spanish Communist movement (as El
Campesino put it) 'outside Stalinist Communism, or even against
it'. Dolores Ibarruri was, of course, not one of them; she chose to
be one of Stalin's most willing and ruthless instruments.

But to come back to Berlinguer's famous statement on NATO:
how did the rank and file react to it?

Spinelli   My cooperation with the Communist Party started
with the 1976 election campaign. In fact it was the Party that
organised my meetings for me, therefore I had ample opportunity to gain first-hand experience of what the Italian voters, and
especially the Communist voters, thought. It was clear from the
beginning that Berlinguer's words on NATO produced no
adverse comment, much less active dissent, on the part of the
militants or anyone else. Interest focused on the state of the
economy and Italy's relations with Western Europe and the
United States. The question of the Party's loyalty or lack of loyalty
to the Kremlin was a non-problem. It did not once come up for
discussion.

All in all, then, I would say that the thinking of the Italian
Communist leadership and of the rank and file are in close harmony. Many people doubt that this is so, but I can tell you as an
old politician that deception in politics may work for six months
or a year, but you cannot fool all your party all the time. Hitler
said in 1932 that he would rise to power through the democratic
process, as he did, and then proceed to throttle democracy, as he
also did. But if he had committed himself to respect democracy
for a period of *ten* years, not *one*, I doubt whether he *could* have got
away with killing democracy as soon as he found himself in
office. The Italian Communists have been forced by the state of
Italian politics to play the game of parliamentary democracy for
more than 30 years, and the rules of the game have had a profound influence on them. I am enough of a democrat to believe
that if 30 years of democratic education cannot change the minds
of men, then democracy is dead and we ought to think of better
ways of ordering human affairs. But I am persuaded that it isn't.

Urban   Are you certain that this education in democracy has
been assimilated by most of the Party? I often feel that the Berlinguers and Amendolas constitute a liberal and highly educated
élite whose hold on the rank and file may not stand the strain of

another rise in unemployment or inflation. Also, isn't there a modicum of truth in what *Novoye Vremya* says in its first attack on Carrillo, quoting a passage from the resolution of the 25th Soviet Party Congress: 'A concession to opportunism may sometimes yield some temporary advantage, but will ultimately be damaging to the Party'? I would have thought a principled Italian Communist on the militant Left would have no difficulty in agreeing with that.

Spinelli   Views of this kind *can* be heard on the far left of the Party. The charge is sometimes made that the Communist leaders are betraying the idea of revolution, that they are too anxious to adjust, and so forth. I would myself not ascribe great importance to these views. The Party leadership is seriously committed to the rules of liberal democracy—they want to make a success of it. It isn't that they could simply turn the clock back if their present policies failed and start preaching revolution and the dictatorship of the proletariat all over again. Any attempt of this kind would generate a serious crisis and probably split the Party.

Urban   What exactly do the Italian Communists mean by *compromesso storico*? Let me take the two words separately in their English connotations and see whether the meaning I read into the phrase does in fact correspond with the one it carries in Italian. In the broadest sense 'historical' simply means 'pertaining to the nature of history', as in an historical novel. But the word 'historic' has a narrower meaning, implying a certain value-judgment: 'noted or celebrated in history', and my impression is that it is in this latter sense that *'Storico'* is being used here.

'Compromise' in my interpretation has a weak and a strong meaning. The first implies 'a partial surrender of one's position in order to come to terms with another party'. In the strong sense, however, it comes very close to meaning a 'settlement'— *Ausgleich* would be the German word for it. This, I would assume, is the meaning we should associate with it in 'historical compromise'. The phrase thus read would then give us the following: 'an agreement of lasting significance to settle with our erstwhile antagonists'.

Spinelli   When I said a little while ago that 'the historical compromise' is the Italian version of the Bad Godesberg programme and a break with revolutionary Marxism, this is broadly speaking what I meant.

Translated into the currency of practical politics, 'the historical compromise' is (as I have already said) a very straightforward thing. *Mutatis mutandis*, what the Communists have in mind is an Italian 'Grand Coalition' on the Bonn model. They cannot see why, given their electoral strength and administrative record, they should be any less eligible for a share in power than were the SPD. The *Grosse Koalition* worked because Germany's conditions demanded that it should, and so—the Italian Communists argue—would an Italian 'Grand Coalition' for broadly similar reasons.

Urban If Communists were Socialists, the world would be a very different place.

Spinelli The point I am arguing is that the Italian Communists *are* Social Democrats. I have already said that they in fact repudiated Marxism in 1946, much before the Bad Godesberg programme. But to that I must now add that the German Social Democrats' electoral handicap was not the survival of Marxism in their programme but their nationalism. Under Kurt Schumacher, the SPD's first foreign policy objective was the reunification of Germany. The German people found this a dangerous priority. The important thing that happened at Bad Godesberg was that the Party drew up an entirely new programme. In it nationalism was dropped and the idea of European unification adopted.

But the Austrian example is even more relevant. There, in 1934, the Christian Socialists and Social Democrats fought a civil war over the Vienna workers' uprising. The revolution was put down by Government forces under the Chancellorship of Dollfuss; and the Social Democratic Party was dissolved. After the war, the two parties discovered that the electoral vote was evenly divided between them; and they came to the prudent conclusion that the frightful legacy of the inter-war period must be done away with. For many years they then collaborated in Coalition governments, which worked extremely well, and showed both parties to be politically mature and acceptable to all sections of Austrian society. My argument is that the Italian Communists are similarly acceptable partners both to the Christian Democrats and to the Italian public.

Urban I would need a lot of convincing that a Party which has spent the greatest part of its history fighting and, literally, burying Social Democrats would now limit its ambitions to those of Social Democrats. The differences between Bruno Kreisky's Party and even the Italian or Spanish Communist Party remain formidable.

I was watching Berlinguer address a mass *Unità* festival in Naples the other day. Although Berlinguer said nothing one could describe as 'revolutionary', the experience was nevertheless unsettling. Here was a gathering of more than 100,000 people giving the clenched fist salute to the rhythmic chant of party-agitational songs. There were torch-light parades and fiery speeches against the misdeeds of American imperialism in Latin

America and the crimes of the multinational companies—but not a word of criticism of the Soviet Union.

And all this in a vast sports stadium which Mussolini had built for similar purposes. I am not sure whether a Bruno Kreisky would have felt at home in this environment.

Spinelli Social Democracy covers a wide range of political activities. For example, the German Social Democrats have become a very moderate, liberal—almost conservative—force. They have administered Germany rather well but have certainly done nothing to change the structure of German society. Therefore the Italian Communists do not like to be considered Social Democrats in the SPD's sense. But in Sweden you have a very different type of Social Democracy—one which is radical and has managed to change the face of Sweden in 20 years. Our Communists would hope to achieve something analogous to what the Swedish Socialists have done.

We must not indulge in abstract terminology—there are Social Democrats and Social Democrats. Only puritanic theorists would expect the Communist Party to sit down and announce *ex cathedra* that at 3 p.m. on Thursday, 12 June, the Party political line changed from *A* to *B*. They do not expect other parties to do so—but for some reason they think this is the way things should be ordered in the Italian Communist Party! Of course, they are not.

But (as I have already said) the principal anxiety surrounding Communist participation in government concerns the Party's relationship with Moscow. And I can readily understand this. The Soviet Union *is* an imperialist, expansionist power. Who knows (so runs the argument) whether the Italian Party has not retained a vestigial loyalty to it? *I* am personally convinced of the Party's genuine independence; but I can see what the critics mean.

Urban But isn't the Party's money still coming from Moscow through the well-established channels of Export-Import companies?

Spinelli This may have been so for a time after the war, but for many years now the Party has been receiving no funds from Russia. And why should the Russians support it? Could the Soviet leaders, whose outsize stupidity and short-sightedness in all matters concerning human liberty (as witnessed for example by their treatment of Bukovsky and his exchange for Corvalan) put them on a par with the Nazis—could these same Soviet leaders suddenly become so sophisticated as to finance a Party that does nothing but make life extremely uncomfortable for them, on the tacit assumption that these attacks on Moscow are merely a display of clever electoral tactics and that at the decisive moment the Italian Party would toe the line of its paymasters? I cannot attribute such Machiavellian sophistication to men whose stubborn obtuseness is one of the marvels of modern politics.

Urban   So you do not believe the Party enjoys Soviet financial support?

Spinelli   I believe it does not. In any case, the Italian Communist Party has the most open financial administration of all parties. It would be extremely difficult to cover up funds received from Moscow. We must not fall back on the ideas of the 'conspiracy theory of history'. The Italian Party is master in its own house. You can see this every day in all its actions. But I would say this: if the Party entered a Coalition with the Christian Democrats, I for one would be hesitant to see their leaders fill such posts as Minister of Defence or Minister of the Interior in charge of the police forces. I'd be a little worried if they did, and so would others.

Urban   But if you say that the Communists are externally independent and Social Democrats in their internal policies—why should you be worried?

Spinelli   Because I am a cautious animal—because they *have* the record they have, and because after all, my reading of them *may* be incorrect. Therefore I'd be happier if they were given other posts. If they are not put in control of the Police and the Army, they cannot do serious damage.

Urban   But you do want to see the Communist Party change the face of Italian society—how can the Party do that without having its hands on some of the important levers of power?

Spinelli   It can do a great deal by concentrating on economic planning, rebuilding the civil service and civil administration, reorganising higher education and so on. It is not true that you can do nothing unless you have the police at your beck and call.

But to come back to my main argument. The Communists accept that they have to work within the Atlantic context, the European context and the parliamentary democratic context, in coalition, as they hope, with other parties.

You have asked: Would the Italian Communists honour Italy's treaty obligations in a warlike East-West emergency? My answer is to answer your question with another question. Would all NATO governments honour *their* obligations in an East-West crisis or war? My estimate of the intentions of European governments would be that the Germans would fight because the war would be fought on their territory—but the French, and the British, and the Danes, and the Norwegians? I have my doubts. And if the conflict was limited to the Soviet take-over of Yugo-

slavia, would the French and British stand up to be counted? I
hardly think so. The Americans might, and the Italians would,
because they would *have* to. In other words, NATO is an unsure
thing, quite irrespective of what the Italian Communists might do
in government.

But, fortunately for the balance of power, the Warsaw Pact is an
equally unsure thing from the Soviet point of view. If war comes,
it would be a very unwise Soviet high command that entrusted
the defence of Soviet Socialism to Polish, Czech, Hungarian and
East German troops. The Soviet marshals' fear must be, if they
have taken the measure of their allies, that these troops would
either not fight, fight poorly, or indeed do an about-turn and join
the enemy.

Both systems, then, suffer from great internal uncertainties,
and because neither system really functions, the equilibrium
between them functions extremely well—as long as they do not
go to war. But this useful state of uncertainty is now beginning to
outlast its usefulness. It is tempting to prolong it because it *has*
worked. But this must not blind us to the fact that this balance
built on imbalance is fragile—not because the West is in any
danger of Soviet attack, but simply because, certainly on our side
of it, the balance rests on too many unpredictable elements which
erode confidence. The European powers are reluctant to take full
responsibility for their defence and indeed for their relationship
with the Soviet Union—they prefer to rely on the Americans for
both, *and* for footing most of the bill. Consequently, the Americans have been made to feel that their primary relationship must
be with the Soviet Union. Henry Kissinger pursued this primary
relationship with unflagging zeal, but we must admit in fairness
to him that he never failed to warn the European allies that the
United States would in the long run be neither able nor willing to
carry the Western defence and decision-making burden virtually
single-handed.

Now, Europe cannot assume its responsibilities unless it
moves towards some form of political union. If and when it does,
the question of common European defence will come up again
and will have to be dealt with. A European defence community
would make it much more difficult for the United States to go
over the heads of the EEC countries and deal with Moscow direct.
It would stabilise Western defence by making every partner's
commitments and rights of representation crystal clear. The
Atlantic alliance would become a genuine partnership of equals,
as President Kennedy envisaged it; and the political rationale of
Western defence would be reasserted in a new and more convincing framework. I am persuaded that the Carter administration is

anxious to encourage this kind of development. But if European faint-heartedness and dithering continue and no progress is made towards political unification, then we have no right to expect better than some future Kissinger who would treat us (as Kissinger was forced to treat us) as second-class citizens. In the meantime the absence of political confidence bites deeper and deeper into the Western alliance and may, by accident or political miscalculation, push us into war with the Soviet Union.

But, you may ask, can we be sure that the Italian Communists would go along with all this? No, we cannot be 100 per cent sure—can one ever in human affairs? But what our five senses tell us is that the Italian Communists are not in the business of engineering international tension so that they may, once a crisis has been created, go over to the other side. Much rather do they *fear* such a situation and hope to extend their influence under the protection of a balanced relationship beteen NATO and the Warsaw Pact.

Urban Lenin's famous slogan during the first world war was: 'Turn the war into international civil war'. Things have come to an interesting pass if the Italian Communists now feel that their best chance of pushing ahead with Communism is under conditions of peace secured by the military umbrella of NATO! The Italian Communist case has yet to be tested, but Lenin's formula has been borne out by history. After the lost war with Japan, Tsarist Russia was shaken by the 1905 revolution. The first world war produced the Bolshevik seizure of power. The second world war saw Communist rule expand to the whole of Eastern Europe, the Baltic states, and eventually China. The war in South-East Asia ended in the triumph of Marxism-Leninism, despite three American Presidents' solemn pledges to the contrary. 'We will stand in Vietnam', President Johnson said on 28 July 1965. America did not stand in Vietnam. 'We ... cannot now dishonour our word and abandon ... those who believed us and who trusted us to terror and repression and murder that would follow.' America did abandon its allies and genocide in Cambodia followed.

No Soviet leader worth his salt (or job) can ignore these lessons and expect less gratifying results to follow from yet another conflict. War is a Communist success story.

Spinelli This difference in Soviet and Italian Communist expectations is precisely what convinces me, for one, that Socialism in the Soviet perception and Socialism in the Italian perception are opposed and probably irreconcilable.

Urban   Could the Italian Communists be trusted with the military secrets of NATO?

In 1975–76, when the Portuguese Communists seemed close to seizing power, the Portuguese Government was denied access to NATO's secret documents and excluded from its inner councils. Admittedly, Cunhal's people are Moscow loyalists.

Spinelli   I would formulate the question differently: *Are* there military secrets in NATO? I remember asking a close friend and colleague, the Belgian Commissioner, Henri Simonet (now Foreign Minister), who is a leading Socialist and has also held posts in earlier Belgian governments: 'How many NATO military secrets came your way when you were a member of the Belgian Government?' 'None', he said. And this goes for NATO as well as every government. If military secrets were known to all or even several members of a government, they would be secrets no longer. NATO's military secrets have an extremely restricted circulation. Communist participation in an Italian government would not be tantamount to giving them away to Communists. To get at the real stuff, spies have to be used, as I suspect they are being used, by both sides.

The protection of military secrets is just one of many excuses for keeping the Italian Communists out of power. The real issue is different. The arrival of the Communists in power or partial power would upset the vested interests and privileges of a great many people, not only in Italy, but in France and Spain too. Southern Europe is in many ways a highly inequitable society. The Communists make no secret of their intention to change it. Those to be deprived of their privileges naturally do not like this prospect. For them the alleged unreliability of Communists in government is an excellent alibi for barring them from power.

Urban   But surely you would agree that Kissinger is right in saying (and the Carter administration is pretty close to saying it too) that the American public would not be able to understand why the United States should find untold billions of dollars and keep 200,000 of its troops in Europe in order to support one Communist government against another? NATO was built on the concept that the Soviet Union and the system it represents are inimical to the interests and institutions of Western democracy. Whatever the intentions of Berlinguer and Carrillo may be—and I am not questioning your judgment of them—the US public would be incapable of making the fine distinctions, much less acting on the fine distinctions, of your argument.

Only a few years ago I had great difficulty in telling American undergraduate audiences that Communism in Yugoslavia and Chinese Communism were very different both from one another and from the Soviet model. Nearly 30 years after Tito's break with Stalin, says George Kennan, writing in 1977, 'It seems incredible ... that one should find oneself still obliged to emphasise that that country [Yugoslavia] is not under Soviet domination ... that it does not belong to the Warsaw Pact ...' and so on.

Spinelli   Of course the facts of life in Europe would have to be explained to the American people, but I don't think the Kissingerian argument is a strong one. After all, Kissinger spent large sums of money giving the Soviet Union technologies it badly needed and, more spectacularly, grain at punishingly low prices. I did not see the American public make more than a momentary fuss. Indeed the farmers and grain-dealers would have made a great fuss if the deal had *not* gone through.

The American aversion to having Communists in government in Western Europe is rooted in the simple fact that in every alliance the dominating partner likes to have its own men in power. In Eastern Europe the Russians rely on *apparatchiks* and policemen who share their way of thinking and have a vested interest in the survival of the system. In Western Europe, the Americans would like to see the affairs of their allies run by directors of multinational enterprises, civil servants trained in the Harvard Business School, and men of generally conservative inclination.

There has never been any question that the post-war division of Europe was here to stay. Kissinger and Sonnenfeldt made it repeatedly clear that Europe *was* divided into two spheres of influence and that the name of the game continues to be no poaching in the other man's preserve. President Ford's Freudian slip to the contrary may have cost him the presidency.

Urban   It is widely expected that the image of a Communist Party that succeeds in combining Socialism with freedom will have a magnetic attraction for the East European parties and governments and weaken, or indeed destroy, the Soviet hold on them. I wonder whether the Soviet leaders would allow this to happen. But even if there were some 'give' in the Soviet grip on Eastern Europe—wouldn't the damage which Eurocommunism would inflict on NATO's entire justification be far greater than the one it might inflict on Soviet hegemony in Eastern Europe? Eastern Europe *could* be held down by the addition of another three or four Soviet divisions and a purge of leaderships; but NATO without full US participation would collapse.

Spinelli   Without any doubt, the Italian Communist Party has already had an immense influence on Eastern Europe. For one thing, it is so much easier for East European Communists to express dissent by pointing to Italian Communism as their model, than to say that they want to become liberal democrats on the Westminster pattern. If they modelled themselves on Solzhenitsyn, their protest would not have the slightest chance of getting off the ground, and probably they would stand genuinely discredited.

I have often told the Italian Communists: every time there is trouble in Eastern Europe you come out with disapproving comments five minutes *after* the event. Why don't you sit down and make a fundamental critique of the East European Soviet system and issue your warnings before trouble arises?

Urban You've told this to some of your friends in the Party leadership?

Spinelli Yes, I have told Amendola and other leaders I normally see. I said to them: once trouble in Eastern Europe has come out into the open, *everyone* condemns the Russians, and the Italian Communists may be plausibly accused—as indeed they have been accused—of being mere opportunists by clambering on the bandwagon. You *can* do this without being untrue to the Communist past. You *can* argue that the Russian revolution was the greatest hope mankind has ever had, but then degenerated into a despotism which must be surmounted. You do not even have to re-open the question whether Stalin was a necessity. All you have to see clearly is that the present generation of intelligentsia are Soviet to the bone—you can no longer say that their minds have been formed under Tsarist influence or in French universities—and *yet* they feel (and are) oppressed, alienated and rebellious. You must take a deep breath and denounce this publicly, in speech as in writing, before a really big upheaval engulfs Russia and Eastern Europe, for I am certain that within ten years, possibly within five, the pressure for fundamental change will become irresistible in these countries. There is no stability under Soviet suzerainty.

Urban *Will* the Italian Communists come forward with the principled critique you have suggested?

Spinelli They are hesitant. They have apparently made a negative decision: if there is another upheaval in Eastern Europe, they will not be on the side of the Soviet oppressors—they will support Sakharov and the Polish Workers' Defence Committee and Charter 77. But whether they will come up with something more positive than that, I do not know. The demand is there. One highly important Communist—Jacoviello—has recently written a series of articles in *l'Unità* in which he admits (to summarise him in a sentence): we haven't yet summoned up the courage to produce a thoroughgoing critique of the social and political system in Eastern Europe.

Urban How important is the East European nexus to the Italian Communists? That the Italians are important to Eastern Europe is obvious. Is a new centre being quietly formed in the birthplace of polycentrism?

Spinelli The Italian Communists are not constructing a centre of their own—certainly not by any act of conscious deliberation. But they undoubtedly derive a certain sense of satisfaction from the fact that their ideas have found a ready response in Eastern Europe. It is psychologically of great importance to them to be able to say: 'Well, we are receiving support even from within the Communist countries.'

Why is this so important? Because our Communists feel isolated. Apart from the vocal and by no means negligible support of Carrillo and the Spanish Party—the French are a very doubtful asset—they have, or may, with the death of Tito, very soon have no allies. Carrillo is, of course, a staunch friend and he has had the courage to take on Moscow with no holds barred. But the Spanish Communists are a small party, and the Italians feel that they have no satisfactory links with anyone else—not even the Chinese. For a party which is used to internationalism, isolation is exceptionally inhibiting.

If you look deeply into the politico-psychological motivation of Italian Communism, it boils down to one factor: the split which occurred in 1921 in the body of the Italian Socialist Party—the Communists going one way, the Socialists another. The Italian Communists now feel that the fratricidal war must be ended—Socialists and Communists must come together and sink their differences. I do not think they would want to hold up this reconciliation as a model to be followed by others, any more than Tito wanted to, or did, advertise his model after the break with Stalin. If the model attracts people in Eastern Europe and the Third World, well and good, but our Communists have far too much on their plate to turn their hands to the exhausting and open-ended game of fostering a new Communist centre—

Urban —which will, of course, not prevent Moscow from saying that that is precisely what they are, 'objectively speaking', doing. . . .

Spinelli Nothing will prevent Moscow from making that accusation.

Urban I am much interested in the conditions surrounding your expulsion from the Communist Party while in prison under Mussolini. It sounds almost incredible that conditions in a Fascist prison should have made an active Party life possible.

Spinelli As you know, the Communist Party is like the Church: wherever two Christians gather together, there is a congregation—wherever two or three Communists meet together, there is a Party cell. In prison, the Communists were organised—we had our cells and leaders and communication with the outside world.

But remember that Fascist prisons were not of the Nazi or Stalinist type. Nor were they anything like concentration or labour camps. They resembled more closely those old-fashioned Tsarist prisons where the prisoners read (and wrote) books, and educated themselves to be more effective revolutionaries. We, too, had all these facilities. For example, when we decided to write a book, we could, through permitted channels, obtain all the documentation and research materials we needed. The Communists in particular have always held that imprisonment is a period of intense revolutionary education which the bourgeoisie bestows on them in order to make them better revolutionaries! I began studying philosophy, history, economics and sociology, and my education in prison turned out to be revolutionary indeed—because I soon discovered that there are more things in heaven and earth than Marx and Lenin suspected.

For many years, therefore, my comrades and I were involved in sharp discussions, but as we were in prison, we agreed that the decision whether I should remain in the Party or leave it should be deferred until we were set free. In the meantime, however, along came the Moscow show trials, and word reached us from the Central Committee that all Communists were expected to give written testimony of their condemnation of Zinoviev, Kamenev, Evdokimov and all the others condemned at the time as spies and saboteurs. The procedure was the usual one: first a resolution by the Central Committee, then one in the sections, and finally a resolution by each Party cell. So, one day news reached our little Communist community on the island of Ponza, in the Bay of Naples, that we had been ordered to sign a statement of loyalty to the Stalinist line.

Urban Was Ponza your place of imprisonment?

Spinelli No. In 1937 I was transferred from prison to *confino* on the island of Ponza together with 300–400 other Communists. But the Soviet order would have reached us in prison, too, for our clandestine channels were working perfectly. As political meetings were not permitted in *confino*, we had to reach our decisions in small groups of three. Groups like these were allowed to walk together over the island without anyone discovering what they were discussing.

One day I was taking a walk with Amendola and a woman comrade [the companion of another Party member]. Amendola told us he had received documentation about the Moscow trials, that we had to take a position, and he suggested that we declare our loyalty to Stalin and condemn the wreckers, spies and saboteurs. This was the hurdle I could not clear. I told my two comrades that Stalin's action represented in my opinion a degeneration of revolutionary thinking; that the Soviet Union was clearly in the grips of a serious crisis which Stalin was cynically turning into spy fiction. Amendola replied that my recalcitrance would cost me my membership of the Party, and he added that perhaps this was what I really wanted. I had no further meetings with the Party cell. About a week later Amendola formally told me that I had been expelled from the Party for petty-bourgeois deviation and ideological degeneration. (Two years later the same fate befell Umberto Terracini, one of the Party's oldest and most respected leaders, who objected to the Ribbentrop-Molotov pact and was booted out by Togliatti.) After my expulsion I spent six more years in *confino* on the island of Ponza. But from the moment of my refusal to sign, I became an un-person in the eyes of my former friends and comrades. They ignored me when they saw me—for them, I ceased to exist.

Urban   Giorgio Amendola has come a long way since Ponza.

Spinelli   He has. I remember chatting to him not so long ago, after he had made a fine speech in the European Assembly in support of European unification. 'Amendola', I said, 'you expelled me from the Party more than 38 years ago, and now—what do I see but that you and your comrades are Spinelli-ites to a man!' Amendola smiled: 'Well, we have changed.'

Luigi Barzini

9 The Italians and the Communist Party

Urban Is Communist rule compatible with the sentiments of a people as profoundly conscious of the novelty and precariousness of its national identity as the Italian?

The struggle for Italian unity and independence from foreign influence, which started in 1513 with Machiavelli's famous 'Exhortation to Liberate Italy from the Barbarians' and culminated, after many reversals and periods of quiescence, in the *Risorgimento* and the unification of Italy in 1861, was a bitterly contested and chaotic affair. The story need not be told here, for no part of the world identified its own hopes more fervently with the progress of the *Risorgimento* than the nations of Central and Eastern Europe.

The point that needs stressing is that the nineteenth century idea of revolutionary nationalism was both democratic and religious—in some cases, indeed, mystical. Nowhere was this more manifest than in the philosophy of the father of Italian nationalism, Mazzini. For Mazzini, the Italian people was the 'Messiah people'. 'To Italy', he wrote, 'belongs the high office of solemnly proclaiming European emancipation.... We cannot have Rome without giving Europe a new faith and without freeing Humanity from the incubus of the past. The destiny of Italy is that of the world.'

Mazzini's idea of 'democracy', too, is steeped in the mystic conception of nationhood. Democracy for him means the harmonious coexistence of nations—all equally necessary and equally accomplished in the eyes of God, with Italy just a little ahead of others in 'spiritual authority'—rather than any democracy of the people, which he suspected of standing for rebellion and thus subversive of the perfect harmony he was seeking. It is a

211

notion that is, of course, especially incompatible with the Socialism of his time and ours.

In Fourier's system, for example, it is not the economic theories
Mazzini criticises; with these he is largely in agreement. But he
asks:

> Do you believe that for man it is only a question of regulating
> his existence and setting his house in order? That the void that
> consumes his heart is merely caused by the absence of control-
> led production . . . and a lack of economic equilibrium? Do you
> believe that great revolutions are simply the outcome of a bad
> industrial order? . . . Disabuse your mind of such ideas. The
> void is far deeper, the needs of human nature and of the epoch
> in which we live are far more numerous and more spiritual
> than you think. Man is a being that goes ever in search of the
> key to a great mystery. . . . Our faith has failed us. We feel the
> need to love and to believe; because loving and believing
> constitute life. To believe in what? To love what? . . . Every
> doctrine that does not begin by giving an answer to such
> questions, is false. . . .

The very notion of conflict between social classes is, for Mazzini, a
characteristic of a backward stage in civilisation which decreases
and eventually disappears as mankind advances, according to a
divine plan, to moral perfection. Class warfare, therefore, is not
only unjust but in fact the worst crime against society.

Such, then, were some of the ideas that ministered at the birth
of the united Italian nation-state: a high conception of the mission
of the Italian nation as the 'Messiah people', the 'initiator people',
running side by side with a conception of democracy that is in
some ways very modern, because it takes issue with the narrow
materialism of the Socialist-Communist doctrine for its failure to
do justice to 'the uneasiness, the anxieties, the febrile agitation by
which men's minds are troubled today'—alienation, in fact, as it
would be called in the 1970s.

If Mazzini's nationalism were the whole story of Italian nationalism it would, on the face of it, be difficult to explain the arrival of
the Communist Party at the gates, and perhaps indeed in the
corridors of power, for Communist doctrine denies the primacy
of nationhood even though Communist propaganda exploits
nationalism. Could a people which has suffered so much to attain
its sovereignty as a nation sacrifice it for the sake of a social
philosophy which regards the nation as a reactionary and transitional phenomenon? In other words, how is one to explain the
acceptance by the people of Italy of the Communist Party as a

national party and a parliamentary party?

Barzini   The first thing we must remember is that the idea of Italy—the idea that there is a country called Italy inhabited by people called Italians—is an aristocratic one. Since the end of the Roman Empire it was more or less confined to the idea of an Italian language which was kept alive by poets, artists, historians and philosophers rather than the people. To this day, Italy is divided into many provinces, each with its distinct dialect, and when I say 'dialect' I am less than accurate, for these vernaculars are Romance languages in their own right, many of them unrelated to one another, and the regions where they are spoken have traditions and a character of their own. The Italian language, which is the acorn from which the nation grew, was invented by one man, Dante Alighieri, who did not call 'Italian' the language in which his *Divina Commedia* was written, but *vulgare*—the common tongue, the language of the people—and he admitted that he coined it out of a basic Tuscan dialect, on which he superimposed expressions borrowed from Lombardy, Sicily and Provence.

It was the existence of Dante's national poem that first endowed Italy with a sense of unity—spiritual unity—of its own. For many centuries the language of Italian law, government, the church and the universities had, of course, been Latin. From Dante's poem, from the idea that an Italian language existed, many centuries later the Italian nation came into being.

But, as I say, Italian unity was an aristocratic idea. If we had had universal suffrage in the nineteenth century and a referendum had been held on the unification of Italy, I don't think the 'unifiers', the 'Italians', would have run to more than 5 per cent, and, as a matter of fact, when Italy was finally unified, the number of people who spoke Italian was about 5 per cent. A hundred years ago, spoken Italian, which is the language you hear everywhere in Italy today, was an artificial language, not unlike the Hebrew spoken in Israel today or the Erse taught in the schools in Ireland.

Some of the fathers of Italian unity could not even speak Italian. Cavour spoke French; he had three French aunts, his cousins lived in Geneva, he was in and out of London, Paris and Geneva but he never set foot in Rome. He acquired a strange Italian based on a French-Piedmontese dialect; his Italian was almost non-existent. Garibaldi was born in Nice and spoke Niçoise. From Latin America he had brought back Spanish; his Italian was primitive. He wrote some very bad books in bad Italian.

Italian was, therefore, a minority language which had been

invented and preserved down the centuries more for moral and political purposes than for anything else.

Urban   'We have made Italy; now we have to make Italians', Massimo d'Azeglio (Prime Minister of Piedmont) said in 1871.

Barzini   That's right. Italy, like Germany, was not born out of the matrix which had given birth to older nations such as the Spanish, the French and the English—feudalism giving way to absolute monarchy and then to constitutional government.

The idea of nationhood, that is, loyalty to one's own people, language, culture and national boundaries rather than to the Prince, was a new thing, imported into Italy and Germany in the wake of the Napoleonic armies. It was in the turmoil of the Napoleonic era that the Italians generated the ideology and found allies for their political struggle from which national unity eventually emerged, in large part, as you say, under the influence of Mazzini.

But national unity in Italy has always been a fragile thing. There are (to name only the most obvious) the differences between Northerners and Southerners—the former solid Alpine burghers in the Austrian and Bavarian mould, while the Southerners have the features and manners of Greeks, often with Saracen blood in their veins. Their respective ways of life are also different. The burgher in the North is a Middle-European who believes in the solution of his problems through industrious effort and the wealth it produces (the word for money in the Milanese dialect is *gei*—borrowed from the German *Geld*). In Southern Italy, on the other hand, the focus of man's concerns is not money but power. Hence politics and intrigue are the special art of the Southern Italians, while the North Italians are the founders of industry and the managers of large business organisations. What we have here are in effect two nations.

Italy's great fragility is well expressed in the popular phrase that it is a country of 'a hundred cities'. This is a meaningful expression when you consider that France has always been equated with Paris, and the first thing the Germans did after the unification of Germany was to enlarge and heap the insignia of a great capital on Berlin. The diffused character of Italy, the patchwork quality of its background and life-style, profoundly affected the solidity of its government.

But there were other influences, no less serious. We have one problem which no other country has: the existence within our boundaries of one of the oldest and morally most powerful institutions in the world—the Roman Catholic Church. It is bigger and more influential than any combination of multinational companies, if you will excuse a vulgar comparison. How could

Italy become strong, how could a unified Italian government ask for the unreserved loyalty of the people, when stronger than the very government was the Church within its borders, a Church which had fought the unification of Italy, a Church which made it necessary for the Italian army to conquer Rome in 1870—or, to be precise, to go through the motions of conquering it, because there was no armed resistance and there were few casualties? Consider for a moment the abnormality of this state of affairs: to have this monstrous thing, this great, holy, centuries-old institution within Italy, with its ancient claim on the bulk of the citizen's loyalties, leaving only a secondary type of loyalty—one of recent origin, more rational and artificial than the one the Church claims—to support the Italian nation-state! The fragility of Italy is written into its structure and history.

Coming to the problem of Italian Communism, I invite you to consider that while in Northern and North-Western Europe the industrial revolution was generated and maintained in a Protestant environment—even in France some of the leading industrialists were Protestant—in Italy industrialisation was wholly imported and gave rise to none of that coherent social philosophy which made industrial civilisation a less turbulent and less irresponsible affair in Northern Europe than it was in our country.

Urban   I assume you go along with Max Weber's thesis that there is a correlation between Protestantism and the spirit of thrift and capitalism?

Barzini   Not entirely; in fact, I should like not to believe what Weber says, but when I look around and see that the Irish are not noted for their business acumen or wealth, whereas the Scots are; that the Protestant cantons of Switzerland are more highly developed and richer than the Catholic ones, I have to assume that there is something to Weber's theory.

Industrialisation in Italy was a transplant: the Italians imported know-how, the art of money-making and the rest, but all this was unaccompanied by that moral fermentation which produced, in England for example, not only capitalism, but, at the same time, a sense of middle-class moral responsibility which permitted widespread social legislation, early trade unionism and the rise of the Labour Party. The connection between Protestantism, capitalism and Socialism is really well established.

In Italy (as I say) we received industrialisation late and badly. We exploited the proletariat and did nothing comparable to what the English and the Germans did to temper the effects of exploitation. Thus Italian Socialism was a form of revolt against this brutal variant of capitalism. It was inevitable that it should come, and it was right that it did come.

The Italian Communist Party is a descendant of nineteenth-century Italian Socialism, and although in 1921 it split off from the main body of the Socialist Party, the history of the Italian Communist Party is coextensive with the Italian workers' movement itself, so that our Communists can rightly claim that they are heirs to its heritage. This, of course, makes them uncomfortably Italian for Soviet tutelage.

Moreover, the Italian Communist Party has more paid-up members per capita than the Soviet Party; it is the largest party in the Western world. It could not be that if it were not a genuinely Italian party. Undoubtedly, until a few years ago the Party was a tool of Soviet power although, of course, this has always been denied. Whether it still is, or will be once again, I do not know, but I would hazard the view that the Party has only been able to be a highly effective ally of Soviet imperialism, as it has, because it *was* a native-born political force, fully integrated into Italian reality. The Soviet Union and her allies have, in turn, given the Party a great deal of moral and financial support, although the latter is, again, denied.

So what we have here is a very large and powerful party but one that lacks ideological unity. Very few Party members have read or care about Marx and Lenin. Even among the leadership the fathers of Communism are more often quoted as a concession to the pieties of ideology than as practical guides to action. Very few Italian comrades go around with manual in hand trying to do what the book says they should. They are much too sophisticated for any such thing.

Urban   Is the Party genuinely felt to be an Italian party, not only by those who have joined it and vote for it, but the country as a whole?

Barzini   Yes; I would say the Communists are the best Socialist Party we have. This is, in the circumstances, not very difficult, because in any competition for the title of worst Socialist Party in the world the Italian Socialists would be certain winners.

But there is also another and more profound reason. The concept of liberty—individual liberty—is a predominantly North European and Protestant, and only partly a French, notion. We have, of course, our own concept of liberty: Machiavelli and Guicciardini talk of liberty; there was a famous polemic on liberty between the Republic of Venice and the Papal authorities, and so on. But the Italian concept of freedom is not that of the individual facing the state; it is, rather, restricted in its meaning to the liberty or autonomy of the city or the republic, or what used to be called the 'universities', that is, any organised group which has won for itself certain corporate freedoms and privileges. The freedom of

the individual, the freedom of life, and the pursuit of happiness
are not native Italian notions.

And because personal liberty does not strike a chord in the
Italian mind, its absence is not regarded as a tragedy. Therefore
the Communist Party, with its lack of emphasis on the freedom of
the individual, does not provoke the same sense of abhorrence
and rejection as it does in some other countries. 'Why,' (the
Italian will say to himself), 'we have always had oppressors and
tyrants, and we have always managed to beat them at their game
by making friends in the right places, weaving connections and
intrigues to outwit them.' The Italian will accept the tyrant and he
will put a good face on unjust laws, but secretly he will set about
making a mockery of the law and put down the tyrant. That is
what has happened throughout the centuries, and that is how
Fascism was paralysed. Followed to its monstrous consequences,
this attitude has also produced the Mafia, which is, if you like, a
rather special organisation for the defence of group privileges.

Urban I might add that the art of outwitting unpleasant gov-
ernments is not an exclusively Italian characteristic. Czechs,
Poles and Hungarians are past masters at this game. I don't think
Josef Schweik was in need of lessons from Guicciardini.

Barzini Of course not, but in Italy the game has a much
longer history than it has in Central Europe and has become
second nature, not only to the little man of the type of Schweik,
but throughout society, very much including its upper reaches.

Well, we are facing in the world today some terrifying problems which are unsettling countries more advanced than ours:
how to organise mass-industrial production without reducing
man to slavery; how to maintain authority and discipline in
society; how to produce wealth without destroying the environment; and so forth. One enticing method of solving these problems is by authoritarian rule, and that was the way it was done in
Italy under Fascism. It was not a very efficient way of doing
things, it didn't even industrialise the country properly, but it did
give the Italians the verisimilitude of success and a show they
could enjoy. Most Italians today would not be truthful if they told
you they *wanted* Communism, any more than they did Fascism,
but many of them are, for the reasons I have just mentioned, not
as reluctant to accept a Communist type of régime as other people
might be.

Urban The Fascists drained marshes and injected order into a
chaotic society; the Communists might do the same—so would
run their reasoning.

Barzini Yes, but (they would add) the individual can always
find his way through by having friends in the right places and

giving free play to the Italian's native bag of tricks.

But I would not be so simple-minded as to say that Fascism and Communism are the same thing. The two are vastly different—they have different philosophies, different concepts of human nature, they come from different points of the historical compass and so on. All this is well known.

But from the practical point of view, from the point of view of the citizen who has to decide whether the man sitting on top of him with the power to lock him up if he says the wrong thing wears a black shirt or a red shirt, the difference is not very important.

There is yet another important factor. The Italian Communists did produce a great thinker—one of the best Marxist scholars of the contemporary world: Antonio Gramsci. I must confess to having a great weakness for him. Let me explain.

I am an Italian *liberale*, that is to say, I hail intellectually from Hegel and Benedetto Croce. My ancestors fought in the wars of the *Risorgimento*; two of them landed with Garibaldi at Marsala, one from my mother's and one from my father's side. One of my maternal grandmother's cousins was Daniele Manin, the last head of the ancient republic of Venice at the time of its restoration in 1849. My brother was killed in the Resistance during the last war, and I was myself imprisoned by the Fascists. I am saying all these things merely to show that no one could accuse me of having a great liking for authoritarian régimes, either in terms of family history or the record of my own life. But I have great respect for Gramsci.

Gramsci was a disciple of both Marx and Croce, and to some extent a legatee of nineteenth-century liberalism with an instinctive understanding for individual liberty. He is, among Communist scholars (Lukács was much less concerned with the political policies of Marxism-Leninism), the only one who tried to find non-authoritarian and non-totalitarian answers to the questions asked by Communists of history and society. Whether or not his solutions would work, no one knows, but we must admit that Gramsci has written convincingly and eloquently on these problems. Also, Gramsci was a great student of Machiavelli, and one of Gramsci's handles to popular fame was, as you know, his theory that the modern 'Prince', *The New Prince*, that is, the seat of all power and self-conscious political organisation, is the Communist Party.

Gramsci's analogy with the Prince has more than symbolic significance. Consider the machinery for succession in the Italian Communist Party. It is a strictly élitist affair which has proved highly successful. The disorder, the contradictions and doubts of the democratic process have all been eliminated. If you have ambitions of becoming a Communist leader you cultivate the friendship of the current leaders. You serve them loyally because you want to convince them that you are worthy of being made a member of the *apparat*, from where you may eventually emerge to become a leader. But you do not try to be clever in *opposition* to existing leaders or policies. A smart man does not join factions.

What I am trying to say is that the Italian Communist leadership works by co-option, and the Party is, therefore, headed by a self-perpetuating priesthood. Gramsci chose Togliatti, and Togliatti chose some of the best brains in the Party to succeed him. Many of these people, and *their* chosen successors, are still in office, so that you may well say that Plato's idea that the philosophers should be kings, and the kings philosophers, has here been put into effect. Italian Communism is therefore run by an aristocracy— that is the secret of its power. It is the secret of Communist parties everywhere, but in Italy, thanks to the seminal policies of Gramsci, this new aristocracy has perpetuated itself more successfully than elsewhere. Some of the Italian Communist leaders are brilliant men.

Urban Would their public acceptance perhaps be precisely due to the fact that they rose to prominence undemocratically?

Barzini It depends on what you mean by the word 'democratic'. The Catholic Church has a strikingly similar machinery for selecting cardinals and electing the Pope. The upper reaches of the Church's hierarchy are not at all unlike the Central Committee and the Politburo of the Communist Party or, if you will, vice versa (we must give it to the Church that it has been much longer in business). At the same time isn't the Catholic Church a very democratic organisation, where John XXIII, a simple peasant, could rise to be Pontiff?

I am saying all these things to show that the Italian Communist Party is not alien corn in Italy; it is not an artificial creation; it is, by the standards of the Italian political parties, not of recent origin. Its successes at the polls are in good part due to its own merits, but partly also, as in a game of tennis, to the fact that its opponents have made too many mistakes.

Urban In your celebrated book *The Italians* you depict the character of the Italian people in terms of three main symbols: Casanova, Cagliostro and Guicciardini.

The life of Casanova is too well known to need rehearsing. Cagliostro was a cross between a superior confidence trickster, magician, freemason and adventurer who claimed to be thousands of years old, remembered everything he had seen in his long life, would reminisce about the building of the pyramids and relate what Jesus had told him. He was a manufacturer of love potions, he turned lead into gold and foretold the future. In short, he was the perfect showman of the eighteenth century, a creator of make-believe where the present was too disappointing to bear. The Cagliostro streak in Italian nature is, if I may quote your own description of it, 'a retaliation *all'Italiana* against a world that had made ... [the Italians] poor, powerless, despised. ... They live among *papier-mâché* reproductions of reality to avenge themselves on an unjust fate.'

Guicciardini is, by contrast, a sixteenth-century symbol of the art of the possible. He is the man who knows how to cut corners, trim his sails to the prevailing winds, survive in a world of wars, revolution, foreign occupation, under the reign of tyrants and lacking protection by the law. 'In the ordinary circumstances of life', Guicciardini wrote, 'use truthfulness in such a way as to gain the reputation of a guileless man. ... Deceit is the more fruitful and successful the more you enjoy the reputation of an honest and truthful man; you are more easily believed.'

What are the chances that a party as austere and theoretical as even the Italian Communist Party tends to be would prosper in an environment in which the lover, the trickster and the trimmer or, if you like, sex, illusion and low cunning are the principal landmarks? I would have thought the joyless rationalism and indigestibilia of Communist doctrine might agree with the tastes of Prussian intellectuals and Cartesian Frenchmen, but would not go down well in Italy.

Barzini The answer, of course, is that they don't. Italians don't read Hegel, they don't read Marx, and they don't follow nineteenth-century precedents. More important, the Casanovas, Cagliostros and Guicciardinis are within the Communist Party as well as outside it. The presence of the Casanova principle is exemplified by the fact that Communist Party supporters are practically in control of all Italian film-making, radio and television. Many of the best-known directors, writers, poets and conductors are Communists. They have embraced something that they think is Communism, not because they have read Marx or perhaps any other Communist literature, nor because they know what happened in Petrograd in 1917, nor because they want to nationalise the means of production. They are, rather, gripped, as Majakovsky was gripped, by a vague and pleasing feeling that the dawn of a new era has arrived.

What the new era is going to look like, they don't know. You and I know what it is going to look like if it does come about, but these people don't. They are elated by the notion that the world is theirs, tomorrow will be a better, or, at any rate, a different, day, and that is enough. That they will end up killing each other, as you and I know, or if they don't someone else will remember to do the killing for them, does not enter their calculations. Mind you, their political leaders do not, of course, go about proclaiming that the future is dedicated to concentration camps and mass executions. As a matter of fact, if you ask an Italian Communist: What about the concentration camps?—he will himself give you a very qualified answer. That, he would say, does not at all depend on us; it depends on what sort of resistance the reactionaries will put up. If they resist us, we'll be forced to do certain unpleasant things we'd be happier not to have to do, and so on.

Urban I have always found it puzzling that men and women who fancy themselves as 'intellectuals'—your academics, writers, journalists, film directors—should display such an appalling lack of intelligence when it comes to judging the character and record of Communism. Have these 'intellectuals' heard of the name of Stalin? Have they heard of the revelations of Khrushchev's speech at the 20th Party Congress? Of Hungary in 1956, of Czechoslovakia in 1968, of Gulag?

Barzini This is a complicated question. Part of the answer is that many of them are simply stupid. A poet who can write a great poem but can't buy himself a railway ticket, catch the right plane, or check his bank account is a commonplace example. He may possess intuitive intelligence, which is not at all the kind of intelligence you are required to have in practical commerce with the world. The other day I talked to Antonioni, who thinks of himself as a Communist of sorts, and asked him about his political views. The consummate nonsense that poured out of his mouth was amazing. He said he was a 'revolutionary' Communist, so I probed a little into his idea of liberty. Freedom, he pontificated, was the panoramic moment on the barricades—the moment of truth, the moment of life. There was, he opined, no freedom before the barricades or after the barricades. This half-baked philosophy, which wouldn't make a sixth-former proud, was the best I could get from one of our most admired film directors. A great artist is not usually a thinker. If he were, he would not be a great artist.

Urban I realise that painters and musicians may be unworldly people, but most of the people we are talking about are writers, historians, economists—the literate and numerate estate of society—whose business it *is* to be intelligent. Or was Eugène Ionesco right in saying: 'It is not his fault if he doesn't understand. He's an intellectual'?

Barzini Let me offer some explanations. Many of these

people joined the Party when they were very young. Now they are middle-aged; they have a position, a career behind them, and an established place in the left-wing *costellazione* of Italian society—all built on their association with the Party. Can they resign at this stage of their life because they no longer share the utopian vision of their youth? It is as if you joined the army as a young fellow because you felt military service was the greatest thing on earth, but when you reached the rank of colonel you discovered that you were a pacifist at heart. What do you do? Do you give up your career and your pension because you have changed your mind? It is a serious predicament, but you don't resign, because you have really no choice.

Another explanation I would suggest is this: there is an old tradition of the court artist in Italy. Dante went from court to court, so did Ariosto, so did Torquato Tasso. Every great painter you care to mention in the history of Italian art was supported by the Pope, the Medicis, an Este or a Gonzaga, so that the habit of acquiring one's security and privacy to do one's work by joining the court of a powerful personage is second nature in Italy. The phenomenon we are examining fits in with this tradition. Why should an able philologist, or biologist, or whatever, not join the Communist Party if that leaves him absolutely free from all worries? The Party will see that he advances respectably in his career; he will become a full professor; he will have just about everything he could wish for professionally and socially *and* the time and peace of mind to do his own work.

Urban   A man at the court of the 'New Prince', in fact.

Barzini   A new prince, yes.

Urban   But your court artist is only free to pursue his fancies because his patron is not in power. As soon as the prince has attained power, the courtier will not be so free. Has this occurred to the Italian Communist intellectuals?

Barzini   If you are not a fool, when the prince mounts the throne you dedicate yourself to Byzantine studies, which is risk-free. Even the Russians are managing to get away with that. The Italians say: 'Only a madman thinks of politics. The smart fellow "navigates." '

Urban   I think you still owe me an answer: have these Communist intellectuals bothered to read the evidence—Lenin's orders on the use of terror (cleanse 'the Russian land of all noxious insects, scoundrel fleas, bedbug rich'); the record of Stalin's show trials; the cultural tyranny of Zhdanov; and Khrushchev's speech at the 20th Congress?

Barzini   I have myself often brought this up with friends of mine in the Party. They have no real answer.

I was once trapped into a public debate with some left-wing Christian Democrats. It soon transpired that the audience was, in fact, solidly working-class Communist. I saw that I was the only one on the platform to defend the non-Communist record, therefore I got up and said that I had fought very hard to defeat the Communists in the 1948 elections, but I didn't fight for myself alone; I also fought for you Communists, because in 1948 Stalin was alive and the sort of Communism he would have forced upon you if you had won those elections would not have been to your liking. They seemed to be in agreement.

You mentioned the Cagliostro side of the Italian character, and I said Cagliostro was inside the Communist Party. Well, what could be more Cagliostran than the design of the Communists to take power in Italy and at the same time to use NATO and the European Community, not only to protect themselves from Soviet control but, in fact, to make it possible for them to tell the Russians exactly where they get off? You first use the West to enable you to claim that you are both Italians and Communists, you then tell Moscow that you are in no essentials erring from the faith, and you finally persuade the West that you do not belong to the bloodthirsty breed of Slavo-Communists. This is surely Cagliostro's prestidigitation at its best.

But let me also point to another element in the clever design of the Italian Communists: they are out to bring back the Pope alive. If they succeeded in creating a pro-Communist régime, which would obviously have to be content with implementing a less than fully Communist ideological programme and thus tolerate the Church, they would be showing the world that the Catholic Church can survive in symbiosis with a Communist or para-Communist régime. The moment this was demonstrated, the Communists would inherit the earth. They would conquer South America within a decade, capture Spain within a few years, and swing the next French elections.

Urban This is what Kissinger suspected would happen and was trying to discourage. What you are describing is a European variant of the domino theory.

Barzini Domino theory or no, the fact is that many of the world's Catholic masses are so bewildered by the problems facing them that they can easily be bought by Communist flattery. Remember we are not talking about sophisticated people but poor and uneducated peasants and labourers. All you need is a small percentage of the Catholic vote going left, and the Communists have it. There are highly vulnerable Catholic masses in Latin America where Marxism has already made inroads via both the Communist parties and the left-wing Catholic clergy, and you have Catholic rebels in France and Spain and Portugal. A swing is very much on the cards, and the key to it all is in Italy.

Urban It has been argued by people like George Kennan and Olaf Palme, the [former] Swedish Prime Minister, that a free-wheeling Italian or French Communist Party attaining power, or even a share in power, would harbour greater dangers for Moscow than it would for us, because the magnetism of alternative West European centres of Communism would destroy Moscow's tenuous hold on its satellites in Eastern Europe.

I do not myself think this is a reasonable supposition, because it takes no account of what we know of Soviet power and Moscow's willingness to use it. Yugoslavia has been, for Eastern Europe, a more powerful and more relevant alternative centre of attraction for over a quarter of a century than Italy could ever be, and although it is true that the Yugoslav heresy has had a powerful influence in Eastern Europe, every time it showed signs of leading to active defection, it was stopped short by Russian tanks. Is America, or NATO or the SPD going to support the spread of Eurocommunism?

The West cannot prevent any Western Communist Party from attaining power if the electors decide to vote it into power, but the Soviet Union can, and does, use *its* power to suppress any unwanted internal development in its empire, including, and especially, alternative conceptions of Communism.

Barzini The Soviet leaders are perfectly aware that Eurocommunism represents a danger for them. To mention a trivial example, until a few years ago you could find all the Italian Communist publications at the Moscow news stalls; you can no longer. If you demand to read *l'Unità* in your hotel, they will produce a copy for you, but it is not on sale. The Russians understand perfectly well that the Italian, or shall we say Western, variety of Communism offers the only up-to-date and intelligent Communist programme. It is, in fact, so intelligent that, in order to gain the voters' confidence, the Western Communists have to show themselves to be something that is no longer Communist.

Urban But the basic problem seems to me this: Communist participation in West European governments is very likely to destroy or weaken NATO, and absolutely certain to undermine its *raison d'être* no matter how shrewdly the Italian Communists navigate between trying to undo American hegemony in Europe and enjoying its protection. But the parallel disintegration of the Soviet system as a result of the magnetism of Eurocommunism is no more than a hope—ill-founded, as I see it, for all the evidence suggests that it cannot happen. In other words, we would be exchanging almost certain disaster for the possibility of a most unlikely gain. I don't think Machiavelli would approve.

Barzini   At this point we have to get down to fundamentals. Why do we call a development a 'disaster'? What do we stand for? What is the kind of policy I'm ready to defend with my life? Is it the private ownership of public utilities? The private ownership of the banks? Clearly, no. The market economy? Perhaps, up to a point, because it has by and large provided a good self-adjusting mechanism for the conduct of our economic affairs. But most things we normally subsume under the word 'disaster' or 'dangerous' are of very secondary importance to me. I am a man, a writer, a student of human nature; the only thing I deeply care about is my personal liberty—the liberty of writing, of reading, of meeting people, of exchanging ideas. It is perhaps a minor, egotistic preoccupation which only a very small percentage of the world's population—0.00001 per cent—appreciates, but without this freedom, without the protection of the law, I could not live.

I remember talking about these matters to some American friends in New York lately. They asked me: But why are you so much against a Communist take-over in Italy when Berlinguer says he will respect this, that and the other thing?

But, of course, Berlinguer never mentions the word liberty; he talks of *pluralism* which would mean a return to the kind of polity that existed under feudalism where power rested with the barons, and social stability was determined by the equilibrium of power among them. That is pluralism, not liberty, and we can all envisage a modern version of it being installed in Italy via the unions and other corporate organisations. What *I* want is my liberty guaranteed by the law and lawful institutions, and not by the good will of a Sardinian gentleman [Berlinguer]. I don't want to entrust my liberty to him, no matter how well-meaning he may personally be.

This is what I'm fighting for, I suppose you are fighting for, and many of the people listening to us are ready to fight for. We are not fighting for the Gross National product, for consumerism, or higher productivity. Those things can be taken care of better and faster by authoritarian and totalitarian régimes than by a libertarian society.

Consider the Brazilian experiment. Here is an authoritarian régime producing more and more and giving the people a higher standard of living year after year. Is that what I want? Is that what you want? Is that what we're ready to make great sacrifices for? It isn't. Perhaps we are Don Quixotes fighting for something nobody else feels is desirable. . . .

Therefore my definition of what is 'disastrous' becomes a very

limited and a very personal one. It is *my* definition and that of
some of the people I most respect. But are we enough? Are our
preoccupations vital enough? In my heart of hearts I know that
they are, because the future depends on our liberty and the ideas
that can only emerge from liberty. But do millions of people
understand our concern? Do they care? Or do they think of us as
the ordinary Russians think of their dissident intellectuals—as
gadflies, *Schoengeister*, or latter-day aristocrats?

Urban Let me come back to Cagliostro and Guicciardini—
symbols of Italian showmanship and the high art of deceit. You
have said the Cagliostros and Guicciardinis are thoroughly integrated in the Communist Party and to some extent determine its
policies. But what about the Cagliostros and Guicciardinis outside the Communist Party? Would they not thwart and frustrate
and make nonsense of the Communists' designs in the first place?

Barzini Not in the first place, because the Cagliostros and
Guicciardinis are never purposeful and strong enough to prevent
any serious thing from happening, let alone the serious purpose
of a large political party. But later on, the Italians will know how
to outwit the Party, disobey the tyrants, frustrate their plans, and
disorganise their lives. This happened under Fascism and it has
always been the way in Italy. But it is no solution to the problems
of Italian society. The Italians need what Machiavelli calls
virtù—which is a little more than virtue—manly courage to defend their liberties. They haven't got it.

Urban Do you really feel that the Italian Communists, handicapped as they are by all those factors of restraint and debilitation
which you have described, would in the longer run nevertheless
make a serious attack on individual liberty?

Barzini I can't give you an answer to that question. Personally, if the Communists came to power, I would get out of this
country and watch from the outside whether they would keep
their promises. My guess is that they might keep them to a
considerable extent provided there was no international crisis.
But if, after Tito's death, there was grave tension around Yugoslavia and Soviet troops arrived on the Italian border, or if there
was a crisis in the Mediterranean, which is not inconceivable, I
am not so sure that the Italian Party would live up to its present
commitments. I am not even sure that the Party would be led by
its present leaders. They might be discarded on the principle that
they were good enough to conquer power in Italy, to win friends
and influence voters, but useless, and indeed a hindrance, *in*
power. This is, incidentally, one of the reasons why the Italian
Communists do not want to take power single-handed. The kind
of policies they follow, the kind of ideas they bandy about, and

the sort of party they have constructed are all made for use in opposition or in a coalition government where the Party need not keep faith with doctrinal commitments.

Urban I heard Giorgio Napolitano make the point recently in London that the Party was fundamentally opposed to single-party rule because it feared that a purely Communist government would unleash overwhelming and probably violent public reaction. But this is not your interpretation of the Communists' reluctance to go it alone?

Barzini This fear may play a part, but I believe the other fear is greater. I was talking about this to a Communist the other day, and I underlined my puzzlement at seeing the Communists so anxious not to take power all by themselves. After all, this wasn't exactly Lenin's way. 'You are vampires', I said to him. 'You know that when the clock strikes 12 you will go around trying to suck people's blood. Therefore, to protect yourselves from yourselves, you want an ally to keep you on a leash.'

The Italian Communists know well enough that left to themselves the concentration camp is inevitable. Why is it inevitable? Because their basic programme to revolutionise society, to change the economy and the ways of men, takes no account of human nature. There is no country where it has yet worked, and the Communists are never allowed to admit it for fear of destroying the myth they stand for. The faults, the breakdowns in the economy, the repressions are variously attributed to the class enemy, surviving bourgeois attitudes, traitors within the ranks, foreign agitation, psychological warfare, nationalism, whatever—never to the doctrine itself. Therefore, when the discontent of the people can no longer be contained by ordinary repression, a scapegoat has to be found, and that scapegoat cannot, of course, be the massive wrong of Marxism itself, but this or that group— an ever-widening group—of people, who are then put into the camps. The more poorly the Communist system works, the more concentration camps the Communist system needs.

Urban There would, then, appear to be in Italy an intriguing coincidence of two evils: the inability of the Communists to run an efficient civil society, and the inability of the Italians to run an efficient civil society, and perhaps the two are two sides of the same coin. In the last five years or so the idea of an efficient Communist Party, as opposed to a corrupt Christian Democratic administration, has been the hope on which many Italians liked to fall back as one way out of Italy's troubles. But if the Communists are propelled into power and begin to tangle with Italy's national (as distinct from its much less daunting municipal) problems, disillusionment with the Communists will set in as surely as it did with the Christian Democrats, and the country will run out of political alternatives—with the exception of the extreme Right. From the point of view of the survival of Italian democracy, it would, paradoxically, almost be better to allow the Communists to govern single-handed, and keep an iron reserve of uncommitted constitutional alternatives, than to have them in a coalition. But, of course, we are far from being sure that, once in office, the Communists would allow alternatives to exist.

Barzini Whichever way one looks at it, we are entering dangerous country. What will the Communists do as partners in government? How will the Italian people react? My impression is that no party can last long in alliance with the Communists. It has never yet happened, nor, I think, is it likely to happen in future. The Italian Communists would destroy their allies, and therefore an underground opposition to Communist rule would be created as soon as the Party gained access to power as part of a coalition government. Remember that during the last few years of Fascist rule, Italian Fascism no longer really existed. It was a laughing matter; nobody believed in it. But it took a world war to get rid of something that had in fact already destroyed itself from within. If we are going to have the Communists in power, it might take a third world war to liberate us even from a weak Communist régime.

Urban Why should the Italians develop so strong a passion for orderly government, an efficient civil society, propriety and organisation in their public affairs at a time when the fashionable thing throughout the world is to encourage decentralisation, regional decision-making, co-determination in industry and a general loosening-up of all rigid structures, bureaucracies and regulations? The Western world has chosen to move towards the kind of good-natured ungovernability which is, as you say, Italy's natural contribution to man's happiness: we are all aspiring to the state of Italy. Why should Italy now of all times aspire to the state of Prussia?

Barzini Well, an expert ethologist, industrial psychologist, or demographer might agree with you that Italy's sweet disorder is a more humane and less alienating condition to live in than the work ethic of Switzerland. The pleasantness of life in England, too, may be due to a similar, though I think less sweet, disorganisation. The trouble is that the man in the street takes a different view; he complains if the trains are late, if there is no fresh bread in the shops, if telegrams are delivered three days late, and so forth. Everybody in this country wants to live like an Italian—to be as pleasantly independent, disorganised and disorderly as Italians are—but at the same time to live in Switzerland. And that is a little difficult.

But, of course, the decentralisers are really right; one of the facets of liberty is a certain disorder. Confronted with powerful modern organisations which depersonalise and regiment the individual, one of the few ways in which he can resist is to live as the Italians do. The Italians talk a great deal of getting efficient through the medium of the Communist Party, of acquiring method and a new integrity, but I very much doubt that they will ever succeed in ruling themselves as Prussians. So if the world is, as you assume, aspiring to the state of Italy, I can assure the world that the Italian model is here to stay.

Urban   But there is, according to your reading of the Italian character, also another trait in the Italian mind which does not, on the face of it, sort well with the good-natured inefficiency of Italian society. You have written some very eloquent pages in *The Italians* on the Italian flair for systematisation—the urge for cut-and-dried solutions, for elaborate laws and directives, for visual form as a way of overcoming the rank vegetation of nature and conquering the fear of the meaninglessness of life. By *sistemazione* the Italians reduce a hostile and contingent world to familiarity and manageable proportions. Isn't there a contradiction between this passion for orderly arrangements and the triad Casanova-Cagliostro-Guicciardini?

Barzini   Before answering this question, let me elaborate a little on the extent to which *sistemazione* is part of the Italian mind. I must refer you again to Dante's *Commedia* because without it Italy would not be Italy.

Before you even start reading the *Commedia* you are given enormous maps showing the precise layout of the scene of action. There is a cross-section of Hell where the Unbaptised occupy the First Terrace, those guilty of Lust the Second, of Gluttony the Third, and so on, each of the Seven Deadly Sins being given an exact geographical reference point. You have a map of the Ptolemaic conception of the universe where Paradise is divided into nine concentric heavens which rotate round the earth, and Jerusalem, for example, is shown just north of Hell, Mount Purgatory is just south of it between the Hemisphere of Water and the Hemisphere of Land, and so on. So, before you start becoming an Italian by reading the *Commedia*, you are exposed to the punctilious *sistemazione* of our national poet.

Urban   This side of the Italian character would, then, accord well with the, by now, old-fashioned mechanistic scientism of Communist doctrine?

Barzini   Yes. But your paradox isn't real. The love of system and the love of chaos can go well together. Many years ago, on my way back from America as a young man of 21, I was up for military service. Someone came to my father and told him that I should look up a friend, General XYZ, not because it was thought that I should try to evade military service, but because we felt that I should serve in Milan to be trained as an officer in one corps rather than another. I went to the War Ministry (this must have been in 1930) and got into the elevator to go up to the floor where I had been told the General had his office. In the elevator there was a *regolamento*, about two feet long, in which it was laid down what category of person was allowed to use the lift going up, and who could use it both going up and coming down. Now, going up *and* down was a privileged thing reserved for the highest officers of state in the Kingdom of Italy. The common people had to walk down. But there was a paragraph stating that those who had certain disablements, lost a 'lower limb' in the first world war, etc., were also entitled to ride both up and down, and there were several other qualifications permitting or restricting the use of the elevator.

Well, anyone who sat down and wrote ten pages of rules and regulations on how the lift was to be used must have been mad. But the point is that nobody paid the slightest attention to these rules—people rode up and down in the elevator; there was no one to enforce the *regolamento*.

But, clearly, this fine table of rules, with its neat divisions and sub-divisions, satisfied the Italian's inner urge to believe that there was somewhere in the world a superior order which could be imposed on chaos, even if it was done only on paper.

Urban   The Italians are, in fact, playing and outplaying the system, much as the East Europeans have learned to with theirs.

Barzini   They are not always outplaying it, because the rules are there and cannot be totally ignored. The law can be brought out from retirement, dusted down and used against one's enemies at the right moment. You can always yank a man out of the elevator going down, and point to the rules forbidding him to do so if you think it is opportune to put him in the wrong. That the rules are ignored at all other times does not concern you if you think this is the time to catch your man out and get him into trouble. I suppose the East Europeans' fortunes in playing their system alternate similarly between success and failure.

Urban   I am still not quite clear whether, in your view, the access to power or partial power of the Italian Communist Party would harm us more than it would harm the Soviet Union.

Barzini   A Neapolitan friend of mine, who was once a leading member of the Communist Party but is no longer a Communist, was sent to an important meeting of Communist Party functionaries in Prague in 1948 or thereabouts. The main discussion was (according to his account which I have every reason to trust) devoted to the question: What would the various Communist parties do in case of a third world war? My friend made a speech spiced, as he thought, with a sense of irony and cynicism, in which he said that the best thing the Italian Communists could do would be to exert their talents as allies of the enemies of the Soviet Union because that was the surest way of undermining the Western side and helping the Soviets. Nobody thought this was a joke; the idea was given approval.

And I rather believe these Communist functionaries were expressing a realistic appreciation of what it means to have Italian Communists as your allies. Suppose they joined the opposite side: could there be a worse punishment for the Soviet Union? The Italians would play havoc with Soviet Communism.

Urban What you are saying is that the Italian Communists would wreck whichever side they decided to support, and this sounds neat and entertaining. But I'm a little worried about your earlier remark that in an international crisis the Berlinguers and Amendolas and Napolitanos of the Party would at once be jettisoned and the Muscovites elevated to leadership. In that case the music-hall quality of the Italian Party would quickly turn into tragedy—for the West and for non-Communist Italy.

Barzini Yes, the moment there is severe tension in international affairs, Moscow will have to tighten up in Italy. It will need absolute loyalty from the Italian Communists.

Urban Would a radical change of this sort be supported or resisted by the Communist rank and file?

Barzini It would be supported, because the rank and file are on the whole much more Stalinist than Dubcekian. In 1956, when many Party intellectuals revolted against what the Soviets had done in Budapest, the rank and file were firmly on the side of Soviet action: that is how you treat the class enemy (they said), that is the way to show strength, that is the way to destroy your opponents. And they are Stalinists to this day. Therefore the Italian Communist leaders have to think not only of the American point of view and the Soviet point of view, but also of these dyed-in-the-wool Stalinists at the grass roots of the Party, as well as the extra-Parliamentary extreme Left who are in many ways very influential. Veering too much towards Social Democracy, moderation, and ideological concessions would be playing into the hands of this bloodthirsty Left. I should not like to be one of the Italian Communist leaders—they are walking a tightrope.

Urban The more I listen to you the more I am confirmed in my opinion (and I have already briefly hinted at this) that Kissinger has correctly appreciated the danger-signals in the Italian situation. The only question is—and this has been much debated— whether Kissinger, as US Secretary of State, was right in telling the Italians (and French) what sort of repercussions a Communist participation in government would have on American opinion and American policies. He has been accused of interference and of using threats which would prove counter-productive. Would they?

Barzini Not at all. Italy has, down the centuries, always had to play the game dictated by the interests of outside powers. There is a very old Italian proverb reflecting the wisdom the Italians have gleaned from the wars which the French and the Germans and the Austrians have fought on Italian soil since time immemorial: 'We are the friends of both French and Germans as long as we have enough to eat.' While it is shocking for the French to discover that the American ambassador has said something that might sound as if he was trying to influence French internal politics, in Italy this kind of thing is taken for granted. Take the history of Italy during the last century. Look at the months preceding Italy's entry into the first world war: there was intrigue and pressure from the Germans, the Austrians, the English, the French to get Italy into the war on their side. Mussolini himself started *Il Popolo d'Italia*, a Socialist paper, in favour of Italian intervention on the side of the Entente powers with money given him by the French ambassador. This sort of thing has always been considered quite normal in Italy. What would be considered abnormal would be if the Americans, with all their wealth and power, kept their mouths shut and did *not* tell the Italians what they ought to do. Even if the Americans put their message badly, it is expected of them to come forward and speak the lines which their rôle on the international scene has given them.

Urban I notice Admiral Azevedo, the Portuguese ex-Premier, has taken a similar attitude to American advice. It is up to the Americans, he said, to decide whether Communists could have a place in Portuguese government. 'As long as the United States remains intransigently opposed, I don't see how it's possible for the Communist Party to have a share in government.'

Barzini The trouble with American interference is not that it is too much but that it is too little. The Americans want results; they want the settlement of international problems according to their lights and interests, but all they want to do is talk about it. I was in the Far East when the Japanese took Manchuria. All the Americans thought fit to undertake was to remind all parties to the conflict of the Open Doors Policy and the treaties signed at the beginning of the century. That was not good enough. Yet today again that seems all the Americans are able to offer. I am not decrying proclamations and the expressions of noble sentiments—they can be effective within limits—but they are no substitute for a policy. As I say, nobody in Italy is shocked that Kissinger has said the lines which his part on the world stage required him to speak. But nobody is going to be shocked either if his words prove entirely ineffective.

Urban   Are you saying that America's image in Italy is that of a giant with fine words but feet of clay?

Barzini   Without wanting to be unkind to America, that is what the ordinary Italian thinks of the US today. The public feel the Americans can always lend you some money—and that is undoubtedly what they are going to do in the coming weeks*— but that is about the only thing they seem to be able and willing to do. Where they did take a different kind of action, as in Vietnam, they did it in the wrong place and in the wrong manner.

Urban   No opprobrium would attach to American monetary intervention in the Italian elections?

Barzini   None. This is, again, accepted practice, and the reasons for it are clear and simple—though not so clear and simple if you are in the grips of the American puritan conscience.

The practice was started by the Italian Communist Party after the war when it was entirely financed by the Soviet Union. We, the non-Communist parties, did not have the funds to organise ourselves to resist this threat, and the only way in which we could counter it was by accepting help from outside sources, both foreign and Italian. The early financing was done mainly through ENI, the Italian state oil monopoly, and the custom gradually established itself whereby one asked the big concerns for a percentage of their turnover. This is how the Christian Democrats and the other non-Communist parties were to some extent able to ward off Soviet interference. None of this was illegal at the time; the legislation making it illegal is only a few months old. Of course, the illegality comes in when you give money to a man who does not account for what he has received. But I cannot, in the light of the circumstances in which it came about, condemn the practice itself. It is easier to preach morality from Capitol Hill in Washington than to practise it on the Capitoline Hill in Rome.

Urban   We started this dialogue with my wordy introduction on those lofty, universalistic sentiments, especially as expressed

---

* I.e. preceding the 1976 general elections [ed].

by Mazzini, which ministered at the cradle of Italian nationhood in the nineteenth century. And I was wondering how those sentiments, which invested Italy with a Messianic role among nations, and repudiated Socialism and Communism in the domestic life of the nation-state, would accord with the rise of Communism in Italy in the 1970s.

Barzini Mazzini, Cavour, Garibaldi and the other, less well-known leaders of Italy in the nineteenth century and the beginning of the twentieth century, worked,in a world which was very limited. These men were the *optimati*—the élite—of their time, and their thinking appealed to a limited, though very influential, audience. Today we live in an age of universal suffrage and rapid emancipation in which the only ideas that matter are those that can inflame the passions of the masses. Fascism had this appeal, though it rested on an invented, unauthentic ideology, but, nevertheless, the slogans of Fascism made people feel that they were marching forward to a better future and equipped them with a sense of pride and self-respect. The appeal of Communism springs from similar sources.

I am, as you well know, an admirer and student of Benedetto Croce. But Croce's idea that progress can only mean the progress of man's freedom, that man is responsible for his history, for his fate, that 'all history is contemporary history'—who is conscious of any of this? Who cares? Such ideas interest a very small number of Italians, perhaps 3 per cent of the electorate. We all suffer from a certain *déformation professionelle* when we imagine that history in our time is made by men of intellectual distinction and moral responsibility.

Urban So when the chips are down, the Italian public will vote for whichever extremist party, whether Communist or Fascist, has the most catchy slogans to offer and the bread to go with them?

Barzini The Fascist Party is out, of course; they have played their card and lost the game. The battle is between the Church and the Communist Party, two symmetrical, irrational constructions which have the key to the psychology of the Italian masses. They are both alien to me; I don't understand either.

I don't believe the blood of St Januarius liquefies every April on the anniversary of his beheading. You are, as a matter of fact, not required by the Church to believe this for it is no more than a pious Neapolitan legend, but millions of Italians fervently go along with it, as they also believe in Communism, the coming of a classless society and the workers' paradise. The duel is between myth A and myth B. It is all very strange and depressing.

I simply watch and think and try to understand. But I'm not

sure that I do. I feel as Dante did as he was approaching the gate of Hell (*Inferno*, III, 16–18):

> We've reached the place I told thee to expect,
> Where thou should'st see the miserable race,
> Those who have lost the good of intellect.

Andrei Amalrik

10 Russia and the Perplexing Prospects of Liberty

Urban With the emergence of an apparently new breed of Communism in Western Europe and Japan, the question must be asked: has the Soviet Union the capacity to reform *its* brand of Communism? If so, does our experience of the Russian collective psyche and of the Russian past tell us how far any opening up of the Soviet system—indeed, of any Russian system—is likely to go?

On the face of it, the evidence is not encouraging. To cite random examples of how famous witnesses of the Russian scene saw the balance between despotism and freedom in the Russia of their time, let me start with an extract from the very first authentic description of Muscovy—Baron von Herberstein's *Rerum Moscoviticarum Commentarii*, of 1571: 'This people', Herberstein observes, 'enjoy slavery more than freedom; for persons on the point of death very often manumit some of their serfs, but they immediately sell themselves for money to other families.' And in another context, discussing the power of Wassili III, Herberstein says: 'It is not clear whether the Prince has to be a tyrant because the people are brutish and uncultured or whether they are made as uncultured, harsh and cruel as they are because the Prince is such a tyrant.'

Three centuries later, an eagle-eyed French traveller's experiences give us little more cause for comfort. Writing in 1831, the Marquis de Custine observed:

> Other nations have tolerated oppression; the Russian nation has loved it; she still loves it. Is not this fanaticism of obedience characteristic? ... To look at the Kremlin does not create pleasure but creates fear. It is not beautiful; it is terrible, terrible like the reign of Ivan IV.

Such a reign blinds for ever the human soul in a nation which has patiently submitted to it to the end. The last descendants of these men, branded by the hangman, will suffer from their fathers' betrayal of trust—treason against humanity degrades peoples unto their remotest posterity. This crime does not consist just in administering injustice, but in tolerating it.

Even Alexander Herzen, the liberal Westerniser, remarked with some bitterness of the Russian people's passive obedience: 'A long servitude cannot be an accident, it must correspond to some national trait'.

Finally, we have your own eloquent testimony. *It*, more than any of the earlier ones, makes me wonder if the liberalisation of Russian political culture and of the Russian body politic—whether under the Soviet or any other system—could go beyond certain narrow limits. In *Will the USSR Survive Until 1984?* you wrote (in 1969):

... the ideas of self-government, of equality under the law for all and of personal freedom—and the responsibility that goes with these—are almost completely incomprehensible to the Russian people.... The very word 'freedom' is understood by most people as a synonym of the word 'disorder'.... As for respecting the rights of the individual as such, such an idea simply evokes bewilderment. One can feel respect for force, authority even, ultimately, intelligence or education, but that human personality of itself should represent any kind of value—this is a preposterous idea in the popular mind.

Amalrik Yes—the general trend in Russian history has been undoubtedly tyrannical, but running side by side with this mainstream in our past you will also find rivulets of incipient liberalism. Herberstein was writing about the oriental despotism of Muscovy, but Novgorod was ruled by a government which was democratic by the yardsticks of the time. There have been peasant insurrections in Russia—Bolotnikov's uprising during the Time of Troubles (1606–7); revolts in the towns (1646); a revolution led by the Cossack, Stenko Razin (1667–71), and one later (1773–75) by Pugachev. While it would be absurd to describe these savage, and savagely suppressed, rebellions as 'liberal'—they were attempts to enthrone the 'true tsar' as head of an organic, holy civilisation rather than to 'liberalise', much less to destroy, the system—they showed, nevertheless, that the Russian peasant was, under certain circumstances, prepared to challenge his oppressors—whether the oppressor was Tzar Alexei, or the boyars.

Having said that, one must admit in all candour that it is impossible to imagine that a Western type of democracy could readily, or perhaps ever, take natural roots in Russia. The country is too vast, too heterogeneous, it contains too many nationalities, customs, cultures and historical traditions to be effectively held together by anything but an authoritarian régime. Count Witte once said: No one should be surprised that Russia is badly governed—the astonishing thing is that she is governed at all.

None of this means, however, that there is no room in Russia for a great deal more freedom than there is now, but we must, as I say, be conscious of its limits.

Now if the Soviet Union were to fall apart under the pressure of war or revolution, undoubtedly on its ruins would arise a number of sovereign states. What would these be like? Any state arising in Central Asia, for example, would certainly not be modelled on American democracy—it would be authoritarian or worse. The Baltic states and Georgia, on the other hand, would be much more likely to resemble liberal democracies of the West European type. What would happen in Russia itself I have great difficulty in saying.

Herberstein's observations of the Muscovy of his time provide pointers of a limited kind. The cruelty of the ruler and the beastliness of the people *were* mutually supportive—I would, like Herberstein, not wish to say which came first. The sad fact about Muscovy was that the Prince ruled over a patrimonial state: he *owned* his subjects as well as the land they lived on in much the same way as a farmer owns and can dispose of his pigs. This was in stark contrast with European feudalism, where certain hierarchical but agreed rules bound all members of society into a vast network of duties and obligations. But what 'agreement' can there be between the farmer and his pigs? The savagery of the Russian people is rooted in the savagery of this relationship.

Also, the first Russian state was in Kiev, in the south-west of Russia, but under the pressure of a variety of invasions (I will not attempt to list them) the Russian state was gradually pushed eastwards—from the more cultured to the less cultured parts of Europe. The price the state had to pay for its independence was isolation and an ever greater loss of culture. These facts have left an indelible mark on the Russian character and Russian history.

Custine's claim, however, that, while other nations tolerate oppression, the Russian people love it, is a little exaggerated. They don't love it—but they can conceive of no other way in which life could be ordered. Hence they regard and tolerate oppression as a necessity—even as a duty. I remember talking to a Russian worker some weeks before the 1968 occupation of Czechoslovakia. He was utterly confused and perplexed by the sight of a free press, free radio and television. 'What sort of a government is it that tolerates so much disorder?' he asked. 'Power must be such that *I* live in fear of it—not that *it* lives in fear of me!'

Urban In his excellent book on Custine, George Kennan argues that Custine's reading of Russia may not be very accurate on Russia in the 1830s, but it is accurate enough as a prescient analysis on Russia under Stalin.

Amalrik I would say Custine was right about both.

Urban What about Custine's remarkable observation: 'Russia sees Europe as a prey which our dissensions will sooner or later deliver up to her; she foments anarchy among us in the hope of profiting by a corruption she promotes because it is favourable to her views'?

Amalrik I have nothing to add—if we look at Soviet ambitions and the state of Western Europe in 1977, we can see that Custine was prophetically right. What he feared in 1831 has been gradually happening since 1945, and is increasingly successful in the 1970s.

Urban Elsewhere Custine argues that the suppressed energies of the Russian people are easily externalised and harnessed to the aggressive ambitions of expansionist rulers. Is there, in fact, a connection between frustration at home and aggression abroad?

Amalrik There is indeed, but the connection has many facets. One is simply that, whereas in a free society the energies of the individual find many outlets, in an authoritarian society they can go in one direction only—national aggrandisement and expansionism. In the Soviet case, this means pressure, under the fig-leaf of Communist ideology, on Western Europe. I have no doubt at all that the ultimate Soviet intention is the seizure of Western Europe through a variety of military and political measures, of which Eurocommunism may or may not be one. I can't, incidentally, see how it could *harm* Soviet interests.

Another facet of the problem is the Messianic trait in the Russian character. Deep down in their hearts the Russian people believe that there ought to be only one state in the world—a state of perfect justice and righteousness. Two Romes have fallen—the third Rome is Moscow, and there will not be a fourth.

There is, moreover, a good deal of plain jealousy in the Russian soul: life is hard—why shouldn't everyone else suffer if we do? Here, too, Czechoslovakia acted as a litmus paper. When I tried to explain to Russian workers in 1968 that all the Czechoslovaks were trying to do was to live a decent life, their reaction was invariably: 'If we can't, why should they?'

Urban But the mirror-image of this attitude is also part of Russian reality: 'They flog the muzhik, let them flog us' was a typical cry of populist intellectuals in the 1870s and 1880s. Russian Messianism is, of course, well documented in Russian history and literature. It is pre-Communist and, as some argue, it is also heavily intertwined with utopian Communism. 'A certain otherworldliness', Sergei Bulgakov wrote in 1909, 'an eschatological dream of the City of God (under various Socialist pseudonyms), and a striving for a salvation of mankind . . . are . . . the immutable . . . peculiarities of the Russian intelligentsia.' The question is: would Russian Messianism prove to be a *post-*Communist phenomenon as well? Suppose the USSR collapsed by 1984, would the dream of the City of God, perhaps in the form of rampant Russian nationalism, survive? Or might it take a genuinely religious form to expel the demons that are corrupting the body of the Russian people—as an Orthodox revivalist might put it?

Amalrik Communism as a Messianic creed had, as we all know, a very great attraction for the Russian intelligentsia. It offered a single key to the world's problems; moreover one that called itself scientific but engaged, at the same time, all the religious energies its followers could muster. If the Soviet Union fell apart and several states emerged in its wake, my impression is that Messianism would disappear with it, at least in its concentrated, and therefore politically dangerous, form. One peculiar kind of Messianism might, however, survive and probably prosper, rather in the way in which Russia took over from the dying Byzantium: Central-Asian Turkic nationalism. The Pan-Turkic movement is the world's most rapidly growing ideology, and in Soviet Central Asia we can see it stirring vigorously. Not so long ago a book appeared by a Kazakh in which no less a claim was made than that everything that has been done of any value in the Soviet Union is of Turkic origin. The author was, of course, heavily taken to task for his views in the local press, but it strikes me as significant that a book of this kind should have appeared in Kazakhstan in the first place.

Urban But a Pan-Turkic nationalism could hardly claim to have a universal appeal—even coupled with Islam, its catchment area would stand no comparison with that of Marxism. The first trick of any workable ideology is that it must speak in the name of mankind.

Amalrik Well, I could personally never see the attraction of

Communism as an international movement; its universal appeal, to the extent that it really exists, has always been a mystery to me. But as Communism has undoubtedly had some international appeal, I cannot exclude the possibility that Pan-Turkic nationalism, too, will have some. After all, National Socialism as an international ideology was, strictly speaking, also a contradiction in terms, yet it prospered outside Germany—

Urban —it was indeed 'international' enough to inspire the infamous Reinhard Heydrich to say (whether in jest or by way of a macabre paradox): 'As a National Socialist, I am also a Zionist', and the Soviet attitude to Zionism is based on the same logic.

Now Russian Messianism is limpidly expressed in Dostoevsky's phrase: 'this people is a Godbearer'—a Slavophile notion, which I suppose has its origins in God's message to the children of Israel: 'ye shall be a peculiar treasure unto me above all people ... an holy nation'.

Amalrik It is the same kind of idea—consciously or unconsciously, the Russian people consider themselves a chosen race. They believe that Russia is destined to embody a divine kingdom on earth. This may be a religious kingdom or one in the guise of Communism. In either case, the kingdom requires an empire, and an empire imperialism.

Urban How widespread is this consciousness of a Messianic mission in the 1970s? It was certainly strong a hundred years ago, when Dostoevsky's Slavophile contemporary, Nicolai Danilevsky, wrote with a flourish of unconscious Marxism/Fascism: 'It is as impossible to fight the historical cause of events as it is impossible to fight superior force. From these general considerations we gain the certitude that the Russian and Slav cause, which is in truth the universal and pan-human cause, cannot fail.'

Amalrik As an undercurrent of feeling, Russian Messianism is universal. Of course, the language expressing it is not part of the ordinary man's vocabulary, but the intellectuals and writers are aware of it and speak it; for others it is hidden in the deeper recesses of their consciousness. There are times when it breaks surface—others when it retires to the depths again. It is, in Russia certainly, a mark of good breeding to believe that man does not live by bread alone—that it is all very well to care for your family and have satisfactory personal relations, but over and above these there must be something else to give meaning to your life. This may be a religious idea, a utopian ideology or blind faith in your nation—but whatever it is, it demands service and self-sacrifice, and these are the things the Russian psyche covets above everything else.

Urban The idea that the Russians are the world's 'natural Christians' is not limited to Slavophiles. A formative experience of my own youth was Walter Schubart's then famous book *Europa und die Seele des Ostens*. Schubart's message went way beyond the claims of Slavophiles, for he perceived in the Russian people a people of archetypal, pre-Christian Christianity.

In contrast to Promethean man [Schubart wrote], the Russian people have Christian virtues as an indwelling national characteristic. It is no exaggeration to speak of the inborn Christianity of the Russian ... soul. The Russians were Christians before they were received into Christianity—Christians without Christ.... What we can see in Russia today [1938] ... is the rebirth of Christianity from the Slavic East.... In the Soviet Republics things stand where they stood at the beginning: Antichrist is raging, the churchbells are silent ... but there are people who, after a day's work, ... preach their faith privately at night.... These are the people called to fulfil Russia's world mission: to reconvert Europe to Christianity.

We can, with the benefit of hindsight, discount some of Schubart's wilder claims (he was fiercely anti-Nazi and anti-Western, as well as anti-Soviet) but if we think of that profound moral questioning that runs through virtually everything Pasternak and Solzhenitsyn, for example, have written, then I would hazard the claim that today the only part of the world where the moral climate of Christianity is seriously at home *is* Russia. Perhaps one should, in the light of the tradition established by Turgenev, Dostoevsky and Tolstoy, expect nothing less; perhaps the tragic nature of the Russian past, and present, warrants nothing else; but as a contrast to the secularism and moral decay of the West, Russia's continuing preoccupation with problems of the true and good life under some secular or non-secular dispensation strikes me as surprising—and wholesome. Concern about the state of one's soul and the future of mankind, even if it involves no particular kindness to individual men and women, seems to me a better way of spending time than buying and selling 'futures' on the stock market.

Amalrik I have a suspicion that if the Russian people could play the stock market, the exorbitant amount of time and attention they devote to the state of their souls would appreciably decrease.

Some of the Russians' 'natural' Christianity has, as we know, been taken up by Communism—the link between the two is well established. The feeling that life is short, of doubtful meaning, studded with corruption, imperfection and frustration—that the sins of man and of nature are the principal characteristics of human existence—has led some to Christianity, others to Communism as its bastard substitute. But this search for religiosity is not entirely a Russian peculiarity. The ability of so primitive and dated a philosophy as that of Marx and Engels to survive and even to prosper in the Western countries is surprising, and I can put it down to one thing only: the need of that class of men who would, in earlier times, have furnished the priestly caste of society, to surround their existence with the certainties of a secular creed. In Russia, to this thirst for a single satisfactory explanation of all the world's ills is added the need to balance one's pedestrian deprivations with a sense of moral superiority—'we have frightful housing and not enough meat, but our minds dwell on higher things!' In sum: if the ordinary Russian is a natural Christian, he is also a natural hypocrite who knows how to make a virtue of dire necessity. His Messianism is not all of a piece.

Urban   I'm glad you have said that. It reminds me of Herzen's extremely perceptive account of his experiences with captured Russian troops at the time of the Crimean War. Herzen was surprised to see that the Tsar's men, as soon as they were taken prisoner by the English and French, repudiated loyalty to their sovereign and were quite prepared to fight against their former master:

> Will it be believed? The only fear which these unhappy men entertain, is to be obliged to return to their former life. Their captivity under the English flag they look upon as a deliverance.... 'Why do not the English and French ... enrol us among their troops?' 'Is it possible', I observed in reply, 'you would fight against the Emperor Nicholas, your Sovereign?'
> 'He would no longer be our Sovereign, and his quarrel would no longer be ours.'
> These words ... proved to me what I have always thought, that we must not expect to find feelings of patriotism in the hearts of slaves.

In other words, one type of Messianism in any case—the tyrannical rule of Nicholas I—proved fragile, even counterproductive, although Nicholas supposedly enjoyed, in the eyes of his subjects, both secular and divine authority.

Amalrik   Yes—we could see similar things happening in the second world war when large numbers of Soviet troops set up house on the German side under General Vlasov. Hundreds of thousands of Russians fought on the German side despite the extraordinary cruelty with which the Nazis behaved on Russian territory. If the Germans had proceeded more reasonably, if they had offered the Ukrainians and White Russians, for example, some kind of autonomy, they could have augmented their forces with a huge and reliable Russian army. Russian Messianism has its reverse side—a lightning disappointment with the god that failed and a savage determination to take revenge on him. If you believe in the Hegelian dialectic, this is an example of it.

In the Crimean War the Messianism deserted the Tsar's troops as soon as they discovered that life under the English—even a war prisoner's life—was much better than their lives had been as 'free' soldiers under a despotic and cruel emperor.

Urban   Would Soviet troops behave in a like manner in a conventional war between East and West?

Amalrik   That would depend. If the Russians managed to take NATO by surprise and then advanced rapidly and got through most of Western Europe without meeting much resistance, my guess would be that the Russian troops would stay loyal. They would have no immediate cause to waver (victory has its own momentum) and no time to do so. (I am naturally assuming that the Soviet leaders would be wise enough to involve no satellite armies in any such enterprise.) But if the war became a long-drawn-out affair, and Russian troops were bogged down on foreign soil where their performance is traditionally weak, and the home front began to get restive because supplies were running short, and the legitimation of the war were undermined because it could no longer be presented as 'defensive', and if— most important—the Western powers gave timely and effective support to those elements in the Soviet state who oppose the Soviet system—then I would not vouch for the reliability of Soviet troops. Their indoctrination would turn into a furious anti-Sovietism with all the latter's imaginable consequences.

But let me add that I rate the possibility of war between the Soviet Union and the West very low at present.

Urban   In *Will the USSR Survive Until 1984?* your hypothesis was that Soviet rule would collapse under the combined pressures of internal disaffection and a long conventional war with China. How would Soviet troops behave if they were confronted with another ideologically motivated force? Your forecast was that the war would start between 1975 and 1980—this gives us another two years.

Amalrik   I don't think the Russian troops would have cause to be tempted by anything the Chinese might have to offer. To be a war prisoner in English hands in the Crimea was a great change for the better after army life under Nicholas I, but to be a prisoner of war in China would be a very different matter. A Sino-Soviet war would be, as you say, a conflict of two highly intolerant Messianisms which have been abusing and challenging each other for many years. It would be a cruel conflict fought over both ideology, race and territory. One could hardly think of a more lethal combination. Scores would be settled over a whole range of issues with fearful consequences.

Urban Do you still think the war will take place as announced?

Amalrik I still think a Sino-Soviet war is extremely likely, and so do the Chinese, but it might not take place until the Chinese have improved their military potential, and we don't know how long that will take.

Urban Do you regard your 'education' in exile in Siberia and the other hardships you suffered at the hands of the Soviet system as Gorky regarded his 'universities'—a retrospectively welcome encounter with Russian life as it really was, and a stimulus to change it?

Amalrik Conditions of suffering and unfreedom have different effects on different people. One can react passively—'that's how it has to be'—and endure the hardships. One can attempt opportunistically to accept the system, rise as far towards the top of it as one can, and join the oppressors. Alternatively, and this is the exception more than the rule, one's sense of justice and dignity is outraged, which in turn leads one to demand the reform or destruction of the system. People take what they want from their experiences.

What Gorky learned in Kazan from his 'universities' was that ignorance was the prime cause of the misery of the Russian people, and he came away from Kazan firmly convinced that the agents of spreading knowledge, that is, the cultured intelligentsia, had to be preserved and encouraged. He thought one could take culture and education as a self-contained compartment, separate it off from questions of politics and morality, and *give* it to the people. If ignorance ceased to exist, men would become better. This is what made him join the Bolsheviks. He thought they were the force that could tame anarchy and preserve culture, even if they made culture serve their own ends. He was sorely misguided.

Urban In what sense, then, would you regard Siberia as your 'universities'? More generally, is everyone's 'Siberia' a precondition for certain truths to emerge? My own experiences in the second world war led me to no such conclusion. I was once ordered, as a member of an Hungarian Army unit, to witness the execution of a deserter. The beastliness and brutalisation of *everyone* after the event was as horrifying as it was lasting.

Amalrik I may well say that Siberia was part of my 'universities'. The trouble is that a vast number of people suffer, just suffer, with no sign that suffering makes them any better or wiser. The majority haven't the ability to turn their misfortune to good account. The majority are inarticulate. Those who do not perish in the process have only one thought in their minds: how to get out quickest. Millions of people have been through Stalin's camps before and after the war, yet only one man and three women set pen to paper to warn the world of what they had seen.

Urban Doesn't this prove Herzen's point that Russia's long servitude *does* correspond to some natural trait? One knows, of course, that most people find it harder to give a coherent account of their sufferings than to endure them. I was made especially conscious of this by the very first sentence in Djilas' book *Wartime*: 'It is a much more difficult and formidable task to relate a historical tragedy than to take part in it'.

Amalrik I would not want to pass categorical judgment on the Russian people or on Russian traditions: side by side with a long tale of despotism, there exists (as I've said) also a weak but detectable Russian voice of liberalism, illustrated, for example, by Herzen. My own family was part of it, and I suppose my own questioning of Soviet rule goes back to it.

The naked facts about man's reaction to privation and suffering do not make pleasant reading. Most people succumb to hardship and die. Of those who survive, all but a very small number want to put their experience as far behind them as they can. But there *are* exceptional individuals who are not destroyed by suffering but actually profit from it. These are, of course, usually not the polite and accommodating types, and some of them prove very difficult when at liberty again—Solzhenitsyn, for example.

The problem of 'useful' hardship is a tricky one. Too much of it destroys, but if you have none, your muscles waste away through lack of exercise. Ideally, one should have a nice balance—enough to stimulate but not enough to kill. The difficulties you run into must be difficulties that can be theoretically overcome. Under the Nazi system (and that is our only valid comparison with Stalinism) those inmates of the concentration camps who were not sent to the gas chambers or executed in other ways could hope for an achievable alternative—a free, prosperous, liberal and democratic Germany, and, in fact, that alternative has amply materialised. Stalin's prisoners had no such hope; for them the defeat of Nazism meant the perpetuation of their enslavement. The incentive to fight back, because there was light at the end of the tunnel, was absent. It is still absent. Taking this question on a wider ground, I would say that the achievement of a Western type of free society will elude Russian liberals for the foreseeable future. It is simply not in the cards history has dealt the Russian people, but a less iniquitous system than the one that exists should be possible.

Urban I am still curious to know what accounts for the fact that nowadays the clear calls for liberty reach us from Solzhenitsyn, Sakharov, Bukovsky and yourself—men born and entirely brought up in a Soviet environment. Is a brutal and omnipresent lie perhaps a necessary catalyst for the clarification of one's thinking, for simplifying the chaos in one's soul, for telling good from evil? In the psychologically overcrowded climate of the Western world we seem to have become incapable of making similarly straightforward distinctions. Perhaps the authentic call for freedom must necessarily come from those parts of the world where freedom is in jeopardy or has ceased to exist. This was certainly so after Hitler had taken over in Germany. Thomas Mann, writing from his self-imposed exile in America in 1938, observed: 'A period of lawlessness and anarchy reigns over public opinion. But for that reason, paradoxical as it may be, the spirit has entered upon a moral epoch, let us say an epoch of simplification and of humble-minded distinctions between good and evil.' Is this confirmed by your experience?

Amalrik Total lack of freedom is tyranny—a free-for-all freedom carries within it the possibility of licence. Some forms of unfreedom certainly help us to make clearer distinctions. Our daily life is surrounded by inessential accretions: when these are removed, the bare bones of what is essential stand out in better relief. Only we must make sure that the bones are not those of a skeleton—lack of freedom can go too far, in which case it becomes a killer.

When a man goes on beating against a door which is for ever closed to him, his situation is tragic, but if he goes on beating against it not realising that the door has been open all the time, he is a tragi-comic figure. The best things in Russian, including Soviet, intellectual life happened in periods when the harshest tyranny had lost its edge; many difficulties remained, but the difficulties were such that one could overcome them. The fuss in the Western world about the alleged tyranny of the Western 'system' strikes me as arrant nonsense: the doors have been wide open all the time. The pampered offspring of the Western middle class are 'alienated' because they have had it too good for too long. In no other way can I explain Jean Genet's grotesque view that society owes a debt to the West German terrorists 'for making' us understand ... by their acts, outside prison and within prison, that only violence can put an end to the brutality' which M. Genet claims to see all around him in Western society.

Urban But you would agree, wouldn't you, that some of the intellectual leadership of the Western world has passed to a number of Russian émigrés?

Amalrik You flatter us by saying that—I think we are having *some* impact. What does it mean? My hope is that Russian *libertarian* Messianism will be a vaccination against the disease of *Soviet* Messianism. The British, for example, ought to bear in mind that when Solzhenitsyn shakes his fist at them on the television screen and accuses them of double-dealing, flabbiness and cowardice, they are only experiencing the mild shock of vaccination. The real thing—the arrival of the Soviets on their soil—would be much harder to bear.

Urban Ah, but you have got that one wrong. The British loved Solzhenitsyn's strictures. His interview proved one of the most popular and most discussed telecasts in years. Nothing is more masochistically embraced by the British than reminders of their immorality and decadence—even reminders coming from a foreigner if the foreigner has moral authority and if his message has an aura of Old Testament prophecy about it. And, to be frank, the British have a lot to be abused about.

Amalrik Well, if Britain enjoyed Solzhenitsyn, perhaps she will enjoy Soviet occupation too. It is a guaranteed way of satisfying the finest dreams of masochists. But once you have the Russians in Trafalgar Square, it will be too late to change your minds. The Soviet Union is a little insensitive to the kind of considerations that made the British abandon, in a matter of less than 20 years, the largest empire the world has yet seen. The Soviets *will* carry the white man's burden—against other white men as well as blacks.

But let me add that the Russian émigrés do not regard it as their main duty to warn the West—they act in their own interests. At the same time, the West could do worse than listen to what these men have to say and draw the necessary conclusions. If the West simply shrugs its shoulders and turns its back on the Russian émigrés, saying that these are excessively excitable Slavs with an axe to grind, then the West will be, psychologically and in its foreign relations, very poorly prepared for dealing with the Soviet Union. To put it at its lowest, the Russian émigrés have brought to the West a storehouse of experience which the West would neglect at its peril.

Urban At the risk of sounding cynical: the purely Western interest would, I think, be better served if heavy irritants such as

Solzhenitsyn and yourself stayed in the Soviet Union and did your stuff from within the system. By expelling you, the Soviet leaders rightly (as I see it) expected that, after the first excitement was over, your novelty in the West would wear off and you would, politically speaking, be a force of rapidly diminishing importance. And the evidence *is* pointing that way: Kuznetsov had an enormous press when he defected; Sinyavsky's name stood for the first known *samizdat*; Pavel Litvinov was a byword for demonstration on Red Square—but could any of them claim the attention of the Western public *today*? Sakharov matters as long as he is in the Soviet Union, but once out, he too will be picked up by the Barnum Circus of American public opinion and dropped when he is spent.

Now, looking at all this from a purely Russian but long-term point of view, one comes to the same conclusion, for it is at least strongly arguable that the liberalising, rebellious element *inside* the Soviet Union serves the Russian people's future more effectively than it can, and does, from the West.

I know that Solzhenitsyn, for example, fully realised all this but was physically forced out of Russia by the KGB. Also, it is perhaps less than fair to offer gratuitous advice of this kind from the safety of Western Europe; we all tend to be brave with other people's lives.

Amalrik You have already referred to the fact that most of us have been physically or psychologically *forced* out of Russia. The differences between death in a camp and death by KGB-inspired thuggery in the streets of Moscow or in a psychiatric institution are not very important if you think you ought to live. In any case, the democratic movement is not running out of steam, no matter how often Yuri Andropov may threaten us (as he did at the grotesque celebration of the hundredth anniversary of the birth of Felix Dzerzhinski, founder of the Cheka) that we are the paid agents of imperialism and will be treated as such.

First, not all critics of the system leave Russia, and, conversely, not everyone who has left the Soviet Union was a critic of the system—whatever they may now say to improve their image in Western eyes. Second, Russia is, as it always has been, the scene of a constant turmoil of thinking, and sufferingly thinking, people. The spirit of resistance is replenished every day. Can you imagine a country populated with figures of the kind that fill the pages of *The Brothers Karamazov* cowering under the whip of any system, much less permanently accepting defeat? I am not (to repeat) saying that Russia is the natural home of liberty, but it is the home of a turbulent refusal to accept injustice.

The duty, as I see it, of the Russian emigration is threefold: it must offer its experience to the West in the hope that the West will learn from it, but it must also extract what is relevant from the Western experience and use it to correct Russia's picture of itself and of the world. Third, the Russian émigré must then speak his mind in books and broadcasts that are heard in the Soviet Union so that his usefulness as an outpost of the Russian people is not wasted. After all, we all hope to return one day.

Urban You mentioned *The Brothers Karamazov*—doesn't the Soviet Communist Party, *mutatis mutandis*, play the same kind of role in relieving the Russian people of the fearful burden of freedom of choice as the sixteenth-century Catholic Church did in Dostoevsky's reconstruction of the Grand Inquisitor? And shouldn't we give it good marks for that?

Very briefly: the Grand Inquisitor argues that man is unable to make sense of the inner freedom bestowed on him by Christ's teaching—'... a tranquil mind and even death is dearer to man than the free choice in the knowledge of good and evil'. Liberty breeds confusion, and confusion unhappiness. Seeing, then, that man is unable to cope with his liberty because he is a child and a slave by nature, the Church revised Christ's work and based its rule on three forces that alone are capable of conquering man's confusions and setting his conscience at ease: miracle, mystery and authority: 'And men rejoiced that they were once more led like sheep and that the terrible gift which had brought them so much suffering had at last been lifted from their hearts'. Was this culpable revisionism? Not at all. The 'correction' of Christ's teaching (says the Grand Inquisitor), was an act of the Christian love of mankind for the Church had done no more than charitably relieve the burden by allowing weak human nature even to sin 'so long as it was with our permission'. But a price had to be paid for the Church's 'corrections'. The happiness of millions, who could now live and die peacefully because the Church had given them an unambiguous line on Christianity, was a function of the assumption of man's sins, and thus of the reinterpretation of Christian teaching, by the Church itself. A few thousand men, sole guardians of the mystery, keepers of the secret of 'revisionism', would now carry the burden and the responsibility. But they would bear their sins with an easy conscience because men are pitiable children whose happiness must be the Church's first concern. 'They will marvel at us and be terrified of us and be proud that we are so mighty and so wise as to be able to tame such a turbulent flock of thousands of millions. . . . Yes, we shall force them to work, but in their leisure hours we shall make their life like a children's game, with children's songs, in chorus, and with innocent dances. Oh, we shall permit them to sin, too.... We shall tell them that every sin can be expiated,' says the Grand Inquisitor.

Not to labour my analogy unduly—all this is very Russian and amazingly prescient. Suppose we read Communist Party for Catholic Church, and Marx for Christ, an encapsulated version of Dostoevsky's chapter would then run along these lines: Marx's reading of history and his prescription for the classless society were too vague and libertarian, and took too little account of human nature, to be applicable to the real affairs of men. Along, therefore, had to come the Leninist Party, which took upon itself the sin of revising Marx by superimposing on his gospel firm rules for action. Lenin and his disciples were perfectly aware that they were doing violence to Marx's vision, but, realising the weakness of the human element, they were persuaded that Marx's ends justified Leninist means. The happiness of humanity depended on the ability of the few at the top of the Party to direct the revolution in the name of Marx but with the instruments, if need be, of the Inquisition. All this, however, could be said only in the secrecy of the innermost core of the Party, if indeed it could be said at all. Hence the inquisitions within the Inquisition, and ultimately the rule of one Grand Inquisitor. Thus the Party became the fountainhead of 'miracle, mystery and authority' and the Grand Inquisitor their keeper and interpreter.

Does this make any sense to you?

Amalrik In broad outline your parallel is correct. I happened to have re-read the 'Grand Inquisitor' chapter shortly before I left the Soviet Union, and I was very conscious that man's ability to use and enjoy his freedom is limited. Freedom of choice easily becomes a burden, and to have decisions made for you, almost any decision, becomes a blessing. This is not my ideal of human maturity, but it is a fact. In one respect, however, the Grand Inquisitor is a little wide of the mark. It is true, as I say, that people like to have decisions handed down to them, but they also want the possibility of rejecting those decisions, or of taking different decisions, to be left open. They may not want to use that possibility once in their lifetime, but the fact that it exists—that their autonomy is safeguarded—is important to them. And this is as it should be. The spiritual health of society absolutely demands the existence of this emergency exit.

Now—was Leninism as complete a distortion of Marx as you have hinted? I don't think Lenin so much distorted Marx as narrowed his message. Marx can lead you to all sorts of conclusions. When I came to read Marx for myself, having had experience of Marxism in action in the Soviet system, I soon discovered that everything the Soviet Union did, and does, could be found in Marx if one cared to look for it. If I had been born and raised in the West, I might quite possibly have found very different things in Marx's writings. I can, incidentally, add to your parallel: for many centuries the Roman Church was opposed to people reading the Bible by themselves, unaided, as it were, by authority. By the same token, in the Soviet Union, the reading of Marx by isolated individuals is strongly frowned upon. When I was in prison in Magadan, a certain Colonel Tarazov often warned me when he saw Marx's volumes in my hands: 'Ah, but you won't understand Marx as he should be understood!'

Urban The Russian Orthodox Church, too, was every bit as concerned about the 'correct' reading of the Bible as the Catholic Church; until late in the nineteenth century only expurgated editions of the Bible were printed for public use and, as Custine observed: 'They never preach in the Russian churches. The Gospels would reveal liberty to the Slavs'. So I should imagine your colonel's remark reflected a native tradition.

But (to come back to the question in hand) would you not say that the idea of the Leninist Party—the idea of a disciplined, conspiratorial vanguard—is a highly un-Marxist idea?

Amalrik Yes, that is actually a very *Russian* idea. It cannot be found in Marx. Nevertheless, when you take Marx in the round, you find that, despite contradictions and inconsistencies both in substance and in detail, the two fit together remarkably well. Lenin may have forced Marx, but the responsibility for Leninism and Stalinism is intellectually rooted in Marx. Marx's vehemence, his vitriolic language, his white-hot hatred for his opponents, his Prussianism were the ground on which Lenin and Stalin built their monstrous rule. They could no more disown Marx than Marx could disown them. I have little time for Western fads of the young Marx—'good'—and the old Marx—'bad'. The *whole* Marx leads, directly or indirectly, to Lenin. And if it does, your parallel with the Catholic Church is not entirely convincing because the New Testament contains no clue to, or justification for, the sixteenth-century Church or the Inquisition. It militates strongly *against* the spirit of both.

Urban What about the lonely unhappiness and sin of the leaders of the Church or the Party—the burden they have assumed for the greater good of the people? Would it be totally wrong to think that even a monster like Stalin suffered from this? A leader of that kind may not believe in God or Marx, but, in Dostoevsky's words:

is that not suffering ...? In his last remaining years he comes to the clear conviction that it is only the advice of the great and terrible spirit that could bring some sort of supportable order into the life of the feeble rebels, 'the unfinished experimental creatures created as a mockery' ...He therefore accepts lies and deceptions and leads men consciously to death and destruction. Keeps deceiving them all the way, so that they should not notice where they are being led, for he is anxious that those miserable, blind creatures should at least on the way think themselves happy. And the deception is in the name of him in whose ideal the old man believed so passionately all his life! Is not that a calamity?

Amalrik   My grief when I hear of the sufferings of Stalin is very limited. His crimes are not such as could be forgiven. He was (as I have just said) not being untrue to the original ideology—he was only developing and perfecting, with devilish cunning and cruelty, certain aspects of it. No, neither Stalin nor his accomplices in crime were 'unhappy'. The unhappy ones were those they destroyed. Even of the Grand Inquisitor it would be quite wrong to say that *he* was the unhappiest, as Dostoevsky intimates—after all, he lived to the ripe old age of 90; the unhappiest were the heretics he had burned at the stake.

Urban   But at least the heretics died in God, whereas Bukharin died in Marx. The first could expect resurrection—Bukharin only rehabilitation.

Amalrik   Bukharin was unjustly treated, but to some extent he had his own guilt to answer for.

No, the psychology of Stalin and the men who fawned on him and served him was much simpler than your analogy with the Grand Inquisitor would suggest: these men came to power because they were desperately hungry for power. They wanted to rule and they used the machinery of Communism as a convenient escalator to power. But once in office, the verbiage about ideology and making the Soviet Union safe for 'Socialism' was cast off and tyranny alone remained. It was in this congenial milieu that pathological cruelties, repressed ambitions and personal feuds could be given free play and caused the death of millions.

Now there may have been the odd individual among the Soviet leaders who realised in his old age that he had betrayed the Covenant and was trying to make amends. Khrushchev may have been one of these, but he had to be removed from his position before he could become 'unhappy'. While in office, these men were charmed by the intoxication of arbitrary power—they carried their 'sins' lightly. We must make no excuses for them. That they have saved the ordinary citizen from the agonies of freedom sounds like a neat thing to say, and there is a modicum of truth in it. But at the end of the day—can we say that the burden of freedom is unsupportable? After all, the Western world has carried it for centuries without finding it impossible to cope with its consequences. At some point the Russians, too, must break out of their self-enclosing circle of unfreedom. One will, of course, always find Party functionaries who rationalise the Party's rule in terms reminiscent of the rationalisations of the Grand Inquisitor. 'It is very hard to govern people', they will tell you, 'we have taken a dreadful burden upon ourselves'—but these are lies. They love their power and are extremely reluctant to part with it. The type of corruption and self-debasement they will not stoop to, if that is the price they have to pay to stay in power, has yet to be invented.

Urban 'Power is also a fatherland', Djilas remarks of the wartime Yugoslav Communists' refusal to relinquish power to anyone, anywhere.

Amalrik Yes, and he ought to know, having been one of the first and most uncompromising guerrilla (as they then were) leaders in Montenegro.

The Soviet Party has by now become an apparently inexhaustible provider of secure parishes for a self-perpetuating Communist clergy. But these priests do not believe in God—they believe in the preservation of their privileges. The divine right of kings has been replaced by the divine right of a pensionable *apparat*. Faith in any form of Communism is dead in the Soviet Union—and it is dead because the Russian people have experienced it. The world's remaining supporters of Communism are to be found in Western Europe—and they support it because they have not seen it in action. Perhaps they ought to.

Bartolomeo Sorge, S.J.

11 Will Eurocommunists and Eurocatholics Converge?

Urban Much has been made of the similarities—alleged or real—between the Roman Catholic Church and the Communist Parties—similarities in structure, 'ideology', and the enforcement of ideology. Communism has been called a secular faith; education at the Comintern school is said to have been modelled on Jesuit examples (Ignatius's *Spiritual Exercises*, so Wolfgang Leonhard tells us, were required reading); the expulsion of Tito from the Cominform and the split between Moscow and Peking have been likened to doctrinal quarrels in ecclesiastic history, to schisms in the Church, and rival papacies. Some of these analogies will no doubt strike you as overdrawn or non-existent. Certainly the Roman Catholic Church has been unwavering in its condemnation of Communism, and it is only in the last few years that it appears to be moving towards a subtle reassessment of Marxism, without, however, conceding that Christianity as a religious faith and Marxism as a materialistic ideology are in any way comparable.

However this may be, the Church and the Communist Parties in the form in which they exist today in Russia and East and Central Europe have at least one thing in common: both are conservators of social order, stability and tradition. Their shared hostility to liberalism in the nineteenth century is a matter of record. Today, Church and Party are equally suspicious of all looseners of the fabric of society: of disintegrating counter-cultures, and the disseminators of new social mores. Church and Party are, in this respect, closer to one another than is either to the Left Bank in Paris or the East Coast intelligentsia of the United States. One can see evidence of this involuntary convergence in the subtle understanding that exists between Church and State in

Poland; one can infer it from the observations of Archbishop Franic of Spalato, who remarked at the recent synod of Bishops that the principal danger to Catholics in a Communist country was not Communist atheism but the influx from the West of 'moral permissiveness', eroticism and the like; and one can also see it from the articulations of the Communist leaders themselves. Berlinguer put it clearly: 'Values such as justice, fraternity, peace in a democratic order, the renewal of the family, human dignity are not to be found only in those texts from which the Catholic conscience draws its inspiration, but also in our programme. . . .'

Father Sorge   Undoubtedly Marxism, or what popularly passes for Marxism, appeals to many people in the world today as the greatest promise of man's liberation by his own efforts alone. But precisely because this hope relies on the fragility of man's unaided works, it is bound to be disappointed. The tragedy is that millions of men and women believe in good faith that Marxism can do what it cannot. Christians must recognise that the hope of liberation which Marxism has stimulated is in itself good—that man's hunger for justice, brotherhood, humanity and hope are legitimate expectations. At the same time Marxism's vision of man and history is flawed *ab ovo*. The materialist doctrine on which it is built takes account of only one part of human experience—man as a producer and consumer—and thus falls into the familiar error of *pars pro toto*. Man's need of a transcendental vision is as elementary and, if you like, as 'material' a need as his need to work and find satisfaction in his labour—and Christians believe it is a need superior to all others. In *Populorum progressio* Pope Paul VI reminds us of the danger of elevating a godless doctrine to the status of an idol: 'Man can, of course, organise the world without God, but without God he will inevitably organise it against man. Exclusive humanism is inhumane humanism. Man can only realise himself by transcending himself.'

In other words, the hope of a society in which all men participate on the basis of justice, and which rejects the concept of bourgeois liberalism and individualism, is in itself right and legitimate, but Christians cannot hold, indeed they emphatically reject, the idea that a change in the organisation and ownership of production and the elimination of 'antagonistic' classes can bring about the brotherhood of men.

Marxists have never been able to do justice to the fundamental questions of human life. What has Marxism to say to the mother whose child has been run over by a car? To the handicapped and incurably ill? To those who suffer from simple loneliness; unrequited affection; the inability to match knowledge of the right thing with doing the right thing; the loosening of the bonds of love between parents and children, husbands and wives? What does it say to those who have lost faith in their work, their vocation, their country, themselves? And, above all, what does it say to those who fear the meaninglessness of the whole human enterprise and tremble at the thought of the pain and apparent finality of death? If death is the end of human existence and man's dignity is based on his role as a producer, what hope can sustain the disabled, the unbright, the economically weak and unproductive in a Marxist society?

On all these points Marxism is silent, and cannot but be silent. Surely this is proof enough that any analogy between it and true religion is most superficial, resting as it does on the similarity of hierarchically organised human institutions and the impact of Russian tradition on most of the world's Communist Parties. This has induced them to surround their philosophy with an entirely un-Marxist aura of fideism and, indeed, revelation.

That said, one need not question your point that in matters such as the peace of the community, the stability of family life, social justice and a certain reluctance to sanction precipitate change, the Church and the Communist régimes in Eastern Europe do tacitly share a number of assumptions. But this is not saying very much. The orderly condition of society and the cultivation of a web of mutually satisfactory human relations must be the ambition of every secular state, and Christians have no reason to protest if that order is secured under a Marxist dispensation provided that the conception of what a well-ordered society stands for does not end there. But I agree that the East European spirit of public puritanism is not objectionable to the Church.

Urban Would you, then, also agree that the Church stands for a conservative order?

Father Sorge No, I would not. In one sense Christianity stands for the most modern, democratic, and indeed egalitarian order. While Marxism can assign no value to a human being not involved in the production process, in the Christian view useless lives do not exist because we are all the sons of God. The handicapped, the mentally retarded, and sufferers of every kind are equal in the eyes of God, and of every Christian, with those strong and healthy in body and mind. Indeed, the former perform a uniquely significant task by inspiring their more fortunate brothers and sisters to remember that the human condition is perennially contingent. The revolutionary message of Christianity is as fresh and relevant *vis-à-vis* the Marxist conception of man and society as it was in relation to earlier despotisms. When

Christians speak of the combined godhood and manhood of Christ, they mean two things: that all men are born equal because they are the sons of one father and, secondly, that there is, through the god-manhood of Christ, an unobstructed circuit of communication between man and God: every one of us can rightfully aspire to rise above his fallible self because we have all received an element of a superior self—God—from our common father.

Urban A Marxist would probably remind you that this revolutionary and libertarian component of Christianity did not emerge until the challenge of nineteenth-century liberalism and Marxism forced it to do so. It was only after that that various Popes began to notice and address themselves to the miserable condition of the workers and tried to formulate a Christian social teaching. But until that point, the Church spoke with a different voice. To the infidels impaled during the Crusades, the heretics burnt at the stake, to Protestants and Jews massacred under one formula or another drawn from Christian doctrine, the brotherhood of man and his freedom to use his open circuit to God were not always manifest. I have great respect for your metaphor for it equips Aristotle's 'featherless biped' with the spiritual ability to rise a little above his earth-bound condition, but I would not know how to answer the objections of those who claim that Christianity, as expressed at various points in its history by the institutions and practices of the Church, has been mired in the same sins and prejudices as have other institutions of the time. And if the interpretation of the Christian message was so often governed by human error, then—so a non-believer might argue—God's signal to man may not have been all-powerful.

Father Sorge The Church is composed of human beings, and human beings are prone to error. We do not, from the vantage point of the twentieth century, consider that the human element in the transmission of the word of the Gospel has always acted in the spirit of the Gospel. Time and place have imposed their particular contexts on the servants of the Church, too.

When thinking of the challenge of Marxism in our own time, Christians must remember that the Church, as the transmitter of Christ's work, does not have enemies, it is not 'against' anyone—it is for God and man. The Church has no hatred for anyone and cannot have any. There is no reason why Catholics should feel bitter towards those who think differently from themselves, including Marxists. Ideological animus is not in keeping with the true spirit of the Gospel which distinguishes between error and erring human beings. The Gospel invites us to challenge the Communist view of the world in the framework of peaceful engagement, not a self-paralysing and sterile anti-Communism. At the same time, Christians realise that, although Marxists may be fighting for significant human ideals, their philosophy is seriously flawed because it is merely the latest in a long line of idols which man has constructed in recent centuries, only to see them shattered. One of these was the myth, during the period of the Enlightenment, that reason was capable of solving all human problems. Then there was the mirage of unlimited human progress, first fed and then contradicted by the industrial revolution, followed by twentieth-century nationalism with its grotesque claim of self-sufficiency. To these were added the régimes born of the Bolshevik revolution—régimes of inequality, fear, concentration camps and mental asylums.

But precisely because so many idols have fallen, there is now a real possibility that men will once again look to Christianity for an answer to their problems. They will often do so with scepticism or in terms of harsh dispute, but there is no doubt that the ideals of freedom and human solidarity which the world is seeking, and which the young generation feel especially keenly, bring with them an exceptional openness towards Christian hope.

This hope has its specific character which makes it different from other human promises. It is not based on a philosophy, or an ideology, nor on human forces alone, nor on one social class. Its defining characteristic is its transcendental dimension. All attempts to belittle this dimension in order to reduce Christianity to a programme of social or political reform must be resisted. We are not Christians because we hope for the end of the capitalist system of production or the collapse of totalitarian régimes in Eastern Europe, but we hope for the end of all forms of injustice because we are Christians.

Urban Your challenge to Marxism strikes me as a distinctly mild one. When I remember the militant articulations of every Pope since Pius IX to John XXIII, I wonder whether your view couldn't be appropriately described as a form of Eurocatholicism, the implication being that it, like the Italian Communists' attitude to Muscovite orthodoxy, is a deviation from the established teaching of the Church.

In 1846 Pius IX condemned, in his encyclical *Qui pluribus*, 'the execrable doctrine called Communism'. In *Quanta cura* the warning against 'the most fatal errors of Socialism and Communism' was reiterated. Other Popes acted likewise, comparing Socialism and Communism to various secret and anarchic societies of the nineteenth century. In 1937 Pius XI declared in *Divini redemptoris*: 'Communism is intrinsically wrong, and no one who would save Christian civilisation may collaborate with it in any undertaking'.

In 1949 Pius XII warned in a decree of the Holy Office: 'All believers who profess the Communist, materialist and anti-Christian doctrine, and all those who defend and propagandise this doctrine, will be *ipso facto* excommunicated by the Apostolic See as apostates of the catholic Faith'. In *Mater et magistra* John XXIII reaffirmed what had been said in *Quadragesimo anno*: '. . . the opposition between Communism and Christianity is radical. . . . Catholics may not adhere in any way to . . . Socialism, first, because it is a temporal concept of life which maintains that welfare is the prime objective of society; secondly, because it advocates an organisation of society whose only scope is production to the prejudice of human freedom. . . .' The Vatican Council once again condemned Marxism without, however, mentioning it by name.

The Church's voice was, then, consistently critical and, indeed, hostile to Communism. Its condemnation antedates the *Communist Manifesto* by two years, the Bolshevik revolution by 71 years, and stretches in direct line to the reign of John XXIII. How do you reconcile with all this the Church's current attitude to Communism, seeing that there has been no change in Communist dogma, any more than there has been in that of the Catholic Church? It is surprising to see representatives of the Church engage in systematic dialogue with men whom Pius XI declared unfit for any form of cooperation. To quote one example, after the 1976 elections the Bishop of Ivrea, Monsignor Bettazzi, wrote a letter to Berlinguer which was published in *Il Tempo*. In it he argued that although Communism as an atheistic ideology cannot be compatible with Christianity, Christians should distinguish between theory and practice. There could be no ban on a dialogue which aims at practical cooperation since the Party's record in the humanitarian and social fields was meritorious. The Bishop justified the action of those Catholics who voted Communist by saying that 'they hoped in this way to achieve a more just and therefore more Christian society'. He also congratulated Berlinguer on having included militant Catholics in his list of candidates.

Is Bishop Bettazzi *ipso facto* excommunicated on the strength of Pius XII's decree of 1949? Are all Catholics who voted Communist?

Father Sorge Your anxiety is shared by many Christians; let me therefore try to explain. The Catholic Church is in the world but not of the world. However, to the extent that it is in the world, it has to deal with human affairs in an ever-changing context. Up to the Vatican Council the debate about the relationship between Christianity and Marxism was rather theoretical. The monolithic philosophy of Marxism-Leninism expressed itself, between 1917 and 1956, in the imposition of the Soviet model both on the world Communist movement and on individual countries under Soviet rule. To this rigidity of ideological commitment and concentration of power, all the more dramatic during the rule of Stalin, the Church reacted by denouncing the whole Communist phenomenon, emphasising that it was impossible for Christians to collaborate with it in selected practical areas, much less to embrace it as an overall philosophy.

In the 1960s, however, the ideological and political unity of the Communist bloc began to weaken. In 1956 the 20th Party Congress, with its revelations of the crimes of Stalin, set the scene for fissiparous change. In the early 1960s the conflict between China and the Soviet Union broke surface, Yugoslavia's independent model of Communism was gaining credibility and, in 1968, in Czechoslovakia, we saw an explicit search for 'Socialism with a human face', paralleled in different forms by 'humane Socialism' in Cuba, and Allende's 'parliamentary Marxism' in Chile—all of which failed.

At the same time, some important Social Democratic parties in Northern Europe, notably the German at Bad Godesberg, repudiated their traditional commitment to Marxism as their official philosophy. None of this went unnoticed by the Church. Rome maintained its rigorous theoretical opposition to Communism as an ideology, but began to take a fresh look at the socio-political context in which Communism operated. In 1963, in *Pacem in terris*, John XXIII made a distinction between ideology and its application in concrete situations. This proved fundamental for what was to follow:

> False philosophical doctrines of the nature, origin and destiny of the universe and man cannot be identified with historically determined, economic, social, cultural and political movements, even if these movements have their origin in such doctrines, and have been, and continue to be, inspired by them. Once elaborated and defined, doctrines do not change, whereas ... movements, working in constantly changing historical situations, will inevitably be ... modified. . . . Furthermore, who can deny that these movements, to the extent that they conform with the dictates of reason, and express the legitimate aspirations of human beings, contain positive elements worthy of approval?

This distinction of Pope John's led to the abandonment by the Church of a purely negative view of Socialism as a practical social phenomenon. A significant step had been taken toward preparing the ground for a Christian-Marxist dialogue while making no concession on the theoretical level. Thus, Paul VI wrote in *Octogesima adveniens* (1971): 'The Christian who wishes to act out his faith in political work seen as service cannot adhere to, without contradicting himself, ideological systems which are radically or even partially opposed to his faith and concept of man; he can adhere neither to the Marxist ideology, its atheistic materialism, its violence, the manner in which it absorbs individual freedom in the collectivity . . ., nor to the liberal ideology. . . .'

At the same time *Octogesima adveniens* reinforced John XXIII's observation that there are social movements which, although they have their origins in Marxism, have broken away from it in practice. Social movements, Pope Paul VI said, which guarantee the fundamental values of man—liberty, responsibility and spirituality—and which ensure his integrated development, are acceptable to the Church.

Urban   I am impressed by the Italian Communists' readiness to adopt (for whatever reason) the Church's formula on this point. Recently you have yourself authentically challenged (in *Civiltà Cattolica*) the Italian Communists to say whether they were prepared to repudiate Marxism as part of the cultural encounter between Catholics and Communists.

The challenge was taken up by Lucio Lombardo Radice in *La Stampa* on 16 September 1977. He said: 'Article Five of our Constitution, which requires members to adhere to Marxist-Leninist principles, is like a dead branch. It is necessary to cut it off to avoid misunderstandings. I agree with Father Sorge.'

Asked whether the Italian Communists could still be considered a Marxist party if members were no longer required to follow Marxist principles, he said: 'I understand the objection. I would prefer to say it is a Party which has its origins in Marx. Where is the difference? It lies in the fact that the PCI does not want to be a Party that possesses the established truth for all time. . . .'

Now this repudiation of Marxism—together with that of the dictatorship of the proletariat, which (so Lombardo Radice tells us) has already died a quiet death in Italian Communist usage—is almost too radical a turn in Communist thinking to command credibility. I am sure you would agree that the Church would never concede that the Holy Trinity has ceased to be an article of faith for Catholics—yet such is the concession the Italian Communists have been asked, and are apparently willing, to make. Once the Party has purged itself of Marxism and Leninism, by what right can it go on calling itself Communist? I admire Lombardo Radice's courage—or tactical shrewdness—but I cannot quite believe that the PCI *could* do as he suggests without inviting upon itself a complete loss of legitimacy (a partial and very damaging loss of legitimacy has already occurred).

My question, then, is: is the kind of assurance which Lombardo Radice has given a genuine concession to Pope Paul's words in *Octogesima adveniens?* Is it enough? More generally: are other important sections of the world Communist movement also cutting themselves loose from their Marxist-Leninist roots and thus making themselves more acceptable to the Church as a non-ideological social movement in search of justice and brotherhood?

Father Sorge We cannot deny that twenty years after the 20th Congress of the Soviet Party many things are in a flux on the Marxist-Leninist front, so much so that there are people who wonder whether some of the Communist parties aren't undergoing the same kind of change as the Western Socialists did some years ago, and whether, therefore, it would not be right to apply to them the same crucial distinction between 'ideology' and 'historically determined movement' as John XXIII and Paul VI applied to the Socialist parties. And, in fact, many Catholics justify their allegiance to Marxism by giving an affirmative answer to this question.

But this is a view which the Church cannot share. As you have referred to the Italian Party's response to our challenge, let me look at the extent to which the Italian Communists have, in fact, departed as a practical social movement from their Marxist ideological inspiration.

The relationship between Communist inspiration and reality is, of course, highly complex. Yet even a cursory glance at the Italian Communists' record leaves one with the firm impression that the demands of practical life have landed the Party in a crisis of ideology. Although the theoretical validity of Marxism is consistently affirmed, the Party is paying scant attention to the 'laws' and rules of Marx. The resulting tension between what is and what ought to be has set off a debate which is of wide public interest. It centres on the relationship between Socialism, democracy, pluralism, liberty, and the replacement of the 'dictatorship of the proletariat' by Gramsci's 'hegemony'. The question is: does the current cult of Gramsci represent the beginning of a repudiation of Marxism-Leninism?

I would hesitate to say it does. Gramsci is firmly within the framework of the Leninist vision. Where Gramsci differs from classical Marxism-Leninism is in the emphasis he places on the socio-cultural aspects of society: while Marxism-Leninism stresses economic structure and production relationships, Gramsci sees society as a complex, interdependent whole. Driven by the exigencies of practical politics, some Italian Marxist intellectuals (Bobbio, Collette, Salvadori) have, indeed, gone beyond Gramsci. They argue that in an advanced capitalist society 'hegemony' can be meaningful only if it is based not on brute force but on *cultural* hegemony—that political power must rest on consensus, and consensus must be deserved by proved moral superiority. Hence the Gramsci-Communists' attempt to revive the ethical component of Marxism and relinquish or play down its economic determinism.

Is all this enough? you ask. No, it isn't. We follow the Communists' evolution with great interest, but we are aware that they are as yet a long way from repudiating their original ideology. It may well be that it is, as you suggest, asking for too much to expect them to turn their backs on Marxism in explicit terms. If so, that, too, would be an answer. At the same time, the best we can do is to go on encouraging them to respond to our challenge in positive terms.

Urban But would it not be possible to say—as some Italian Catholics do—that the acceptance of Marxism as an economic analysis is legitimate and need not entail any identification with Marxist ideology?

Father Sorge This is for us a very real problem. The debate on it began with the publication, in the 1930s, of Marx's *Economic and Philosophical Manuscripts* of 1844. It was broadly inferred that the 'mature' Marx of *Das Kapital*—Marx the economist—was not the same man as had toyed with an all-encompassing ideology in his 1844 *Manuscripts*. Hence it was said that Marx the economist— that is to say, Marx as he has come down to us—carries nothing more lethal in his knapsack than a 'scientific' analysis of capitalist society. And in fact, many people thought, and think, that Marx the economist could be separated from Marx the ideologist. For example, Fidel Castro, addressing a group of Chilean priests in 1971, said: 'The strictly philosophical issues are not a fundamental problem in that when we speak of Marxism we are speaking of economics. It is therefore possible to be a Christian [in faith] and a Marxist in economics and politics ... without entering into philosophical questions.'

Urban Two brief interjections. First, the 1844 *Manuscripts* have usually been read as evidence of the liberal young Marx, as distinct from the mature revolutionary Marx of the later years, and I am a little surprised to hear you say that Catholic opinion should feel more threatened by Marx the liberal humanist than by Marx the father of scientific Communism. Second, I am not sure if I would attach much weight to Fidel Castro's Catholic witness.

Father Sorge   There is room for legitimate disagreement on both points. What we have to bear in mind is that Marxist practice is neither 'scientific' nor can it be divorced from ideology. Marxists hold that the economic activities of man have a formative influence on his cultural environment, the kind of society he lives in, and so on. We need not quarrel with this observation. But then Marxists go on turning this empirically verifiable influence into an absolute to the point where they ascribe the whole development and character of society to it. This is manifestly unscientific. It is the result of wishful thinking—ideology—rather than observation and analysis.

Take another example: Marxism sees a conflict of classes in capitalist society. Undoubtedly conflicts exist, but to carry the idea of the class struggle to the point where it becomes the sole motor of history and the only criterion of the morality (or otherwise) of human activity, is lacking in all scientific evidence. It is, again, an extrapolation from ideology—not a description of what is, but what Marxists think there ought to be.

Nor has the record of Marxist prognostication done much to endorse the 'scientific' claims of Marxist analysis: the pauperisation of the proletariat in the capitalist world has not taken place— the proletariat has become affluent, and is still becoming more and more affluent. Capitalism has not erupted in revolution, not even in the wake of the collapse of imperialism—on the contrary, it was 'Socialism' that erupted in revolution, as witnessed by Poland and Hungary in 1956 and Czechoslovakia in 1968. It is not a broken-down *capitalist* America or Germany that is lining up for *Soviet* shipments of grain, sophisticated technology and 40 billion roubles' worth of Soviet credits to stave off revolution, but a congenitally enfeebled, corrupt and impoverished *Soviet* world that is daily applying for Western *capitalist* help to stave off economic disaster. And why have the Marxist hopes gone so badly wrong? Take a brief look at Marx's labour theory of value. It runs roughly like this.

All value originates in work and time invested by human beings: *therefore* all capitalist profits are unpaid human work/ time—*therefore* the machine, by diminishing the use of human labour, diminishes the profits of capitalists—*therefore* the capitalist compensates for the decline in his profits by increasing the exploitation of the workers—*therefore* the misery of the workers, i.e. of practically the whole population, becomes unendurable— *therefore* the capitalist system erupts in revolution. You will notice that not a single element in Marx's chain of reasoning comes from the real world. If only one stone in his structure were to crumble in the light of facts, it would be enough to destroy the whole building. The truth is that every one of his stones crumbles in the light of evidence. Of all the critiques of capitalism we have seen presented to the world in the last 150 years, Marx's alone is entirely untenable. Marx's forecasts have come unstuck because they are based on ideology. Nothing could be less scientific than Marx's social analysis; nothing could be less inevitable than the inevitability of Marx's 'laws' of history.

You have challenged me to say: why could a Christian not lift the acceptable, that is, the economic, aspects of Marxism out of the woolly whole of Marxism as a life-philosophy, and use those alone as a tool? My answer (already implicit) is: Marxism is not only a critical interpretation of the capitalist system but also a blueprint for an alternative society. Therefore, even though there may be a case for saying that the Marxist method of analysis is ideologically neutral, it cannot be considered in isolation from Marxist ideology as a whole. We *all* want man's liberation from exploitation, including, where it exists, capitalist exploitation. But what kind of liberation do we want? What is the nature of the society we want to build? What are our moral priorities? It is on these questions that Christians and Marxists part company. Marxism as an all-embracing secular creed has made it impossible for us to separate Marxist method from Marxist ideology. It is, therefore, not admissible for Christians to use Marxism as an economic and political tool, thinking that they can adopt it in isolation from its ideological context.

Urban   But there are, aren't there, many Christians, especially in Italy, who do just that—'Christians for Socialism' and others, both organised and unorganised. Are they in error?

Father Sorge   I believe they are. There are many Christians who adhere, in varying degrees, to Marxism: 'Marxist Christians' who accept, as they claim, 'critically'—not dogmatically—all the main tenets of Marxism including atheism, which they see as 'a necessary, negative occasion for the recovery of faith in its totality'. Others, as for example the 'Christians for Socialism', embrace the Marxist method of economic and social analysis and the revolutionary practice which follows from it, without, however (or so at least they claim), identifying themselves with the underlying ideology. They reject any spiritual conception of their faith and stress its temporal aspect, especially as it expresses itself in politics. At the same time they expect Marxists to revise the theory of dialectical materialism—a somewhat far-fetched hope.

Urban   I find it a little difficult to understand in what sense Christians who reject the spiritual conception of their faith and embrace atheism can go on calling themselves Christians. These appear to me to be men and women who have lost their faith in

Christianity and are looking for a spiritually less exacting while psychologically equally satisfying substitute. Having dropped God, they may spontaneously converge with the Eurocommunists who have dropped Marx, but in the eyes of the Church surely the Christianity of such Christians would be open to question?

Father Sorge I would not disagree with you. Their error is manifest for the reasons I have just given.

Urban Why, then, is the Church so lacking in militancy in its encounter with these Christians?

I would have thought that the Church's main (and perhaps only remaining) justification is the uncompromising spirituality it embodies in the face of the omissions, evasions and compromises of the modern secular world. When everything else has fallen away, it is this stubborn espousal of the non-materialistic, non-practical, non-quantifiable aspirations of human nature that is the Church's saving rationale. Rendering unto Caesar was surely not meant to include the dilution of Christian spirituality?

Father Sorge It wasn't and isn't—and there lies the crux of our quarrel with Marxism. But we must widen the questioning: is our encounter with Marxism broad enough if we limit it to the question whether or not Marxism is acceptable to Christians? I believe it is not. Christians must confront Marxism with the positive challenge of their own vision. They must draw Marxists into the discussion of Christian concepts of man and his values. They must remember that Christianity does not call for passivity. The Christian hope is both Messianic and eschatological: if, on the one hand, the salvation promised by God transcends man's efforts and is God's gift to man, it is also true that man is already on his way to salvation through the death and resurrection of Jesus Christ. It is man's duty to further this work in the context of history. The knowledge that in us is vested the continuation of Christ's work, the building of His kingdom, is an irrepressible stimulus to action: 'For therefore we both labour and suffer reproach, because we trust in the living God' (I Timothy 4, 10).

Urban Can the Church broaden its encounter with Communists without a proper evaluation of the atheistic component of Marxism? I would have thought the Christian-Marxist dialogue might become a hopeful affair if atheism could be shown to be a subordinate issue in Marxist thinking. If, however, it turned out that, all tactical Marxist utterances notwithstanding, atheism and the attack on religion were inseparable parts of Communist ideology, then the chances of a Christian-Marxist dialogue would be gravely handicapped.

I am reluctant to press you on this point because the answer is obvious. Yet, if—as you have shown—there are Marxist Christians among Christians, there may well be Christian Marxists among the world's Marxists, in which case the atheism of Marxists may have to be looked at from a new point of view.

Father Sorge   Despite a few recent attempts to the contrary, no one can seriously deny that Marxism is an intrinsically atheistic ideology. Marx, Engels and Lenin regarded religion as a disease of the alienated mind which is destined to disappear as man's alienation is overcome in a classless society. Even Gramsci concurs with this diagnosis: 'Marxism rests on a philosophical structure', he wrote, 'which has "guillotined the idea of god"; to expect Marxism to accept the idea of religion is like saying: "turn a square into a triangle".' Wherever Marxism has come to power—whether in Russia or Yugoslavia or Vietnam—the Church has either been persecuted—its teaching functions abolished or severely curtailed and the monastic orders dissolved—or religion has been tolerated as a residual superstition which would gradually cease to appeal.

In recent years, however, a number of Western Marxist intellectuals have attempted to bring about a new cultural understanding of the Christian faith and Christian values. The efforts in this direction of Bloch in Germany, Garaudy in France and Machovec in Czechoslovakia are well known even if they have produced no tangible results. Institutional attempts in the same vein have been made by the Italian Communist Party. The first and most significant of these goes back to the 10th Party Congress in 1962: 'It is understood that not only can people of the Christian faith support a Socialist society but, faced with the dramatic problems of the modern world, their desire for a Socialist society may be stimulated by the sufferings of the religious conscience.' This thesis was reaffirmed by Togliatti in 1963, Longo in 1966 and has, since 1969, been a constant theme underlying negotiations about an 'historical compromise'. Indeed, in his reply to Bishop Bettazzi (21 October 1977), Berlinguer denied that the Communist Party professed an atheistic and materialistic philosophy. He described his Party as 'lay and democratic, and as such not theistic, atheistic or anti-theistic'.

What are we to think of all this? We are, of course, gratified to see that important sections of Western Marxism no longer consider religion to be the opium of the people—that, in fact, many feel that religion can release the springs of constructive energies for the creation of a just and more humane society.

But the basic question remains unanswered: do Marxists still consider religion as nothing but the result of man's alienation—as the 'superstructure' on an economic 'base'? If so, we must remain on our guard, for we know very well what happens to 'superstructures' in Socialist society, even if they were instrumental in getting Socialist society off the ground!

We are not asking Marxists to subscribe to religion. What we do ask is that religion be recognised as an essential element of the human personality and conscience, and be treated and respected accordingly.

Urban Is the doctrinal gulf between Church and Communism really as unbridgeable as you indicate? After all, side by side with the condemnation of Communism as a doctrine, the Church has, since Leo XIII, come out in support of many of the ideas Communists advocate.

The miserable condition of the working class was recognised in *Rerum novarum* in 1891; in *Quadragesimo anno* (1931) Pius XI perceived the importance of the class struggle and the need of trade unionism, and spoke of the wrong of concentrating great economic power in few and impersonal hands; in *Mater et magistra* (1961) John XXIII called for workers' participation, and in *Pacem in terris* (1963) he sought to establish the right to work as a human right.

Father Sorge Not only that; in a letter to the managers of Catholic enterprises, Pope Paul VI said: 'There must be something radically wrong with capitalism if it produces so many injustices'. In fact the Church has always condemned the mentality of capitalism as intrinsically wrong in the sense of the Gospel: 'For where your treasure is, there will your heart be also' (Matthew 6, 21).

Urban Seeing, then, that the Italian Communists are now ready to admit that religion has a part to play in the transformation of society, could one not envisage at least a minimalist cultural compromise? Can peace, real peace, prevail in society as long as the conflicting doctrines of Christianity and Communism are not reconciled but merely silenced or flattened into meaninglessness by sociological jargon?

Father Sorge The Church is neither for nor against any *political* system. It is willing to coexist with any provided that the system interferes neither with the spiritual freedom of its citizens nor with the right of the Church to fill that freedom with Christian meaning. But Marxism-Leninism is not just a political system. When it reduces man's spiritual needs to his economic condition, and when it perceives in religion a mere narcotic which man in his poverty-induced myopia cannot as yet do without but will cast away as soon as his bodily needs are fully met, and when attitudes of this kind continue to pervade the climate of thinking as well as the daily policies of most Communists, then we must recognise that we are faced with an ideology with which the

Church can have no *cultural* compromise. I do not regard this as a great tragedy—indeed, the success of our encounter with Marxists is predicated on the firmness of our own conception of man, his values and his spiritual universe. The tragedy would be if we thought that a compromise *could* be struck at this level of faith. But no one expects the Church to meet Communists half-way in their ideology—least of all the Communists themselves. And if a cultural *clarification* with the Communists also proves impossible, this will itself prove a clarification.

Remember: the Church has time—the Church does not weary. The Christian hope infuses the power of resurrection into history and the world: '. . . they that wait upon the Lord shall renew their strength; they shall mount up with wings as eagles; they shall run, and not be weary; and they shall walk, and not faint' (Isaiah 40, 31).

Urban In the Soviet Union and Eastern Europe the Church and Christians of all denominations have (as you observed) been very badly treated. It is only in recent years that certain East European régimes and individual Communist leaders appear to want to make their peace with the Church—on their terms. One marvels at the generosity with which they have been received by the Vatican.

I must digress here for a moment. I have just been through the harrowing experience of reading Milovan Djilas's *Wartime*—an autobiographical account of the Yugoslav Communist uprising and civil war. Among the many acts of awesome savagery committed by all sides one sticks in my mind as particularly instructive.

Djilas and Raja Nedeljkovic stumble on two unarmed German soldiers in uniform. They are asked for some information about the disposition of German troops which the prisoners readily give. Then:

> I unslung my rifle . . . I hit the German over the head. The rifle butt broke, and the German fell on his back. I pulled my knife and with one motion slit his throat. I then handed the knife to Raja Nedeljkovic, a political worker whom I had known since before the war, and whose village the Germans had massacred in 1941.. Nedeljkovic stabbed the second German, who writhed but soon was still. . . . Actually, like most prisoners, the Germans were as if paralysed, and didn't defend themselves or try to flee.

As night fell, something began to stir in Djilas's conscience.

Suddenly in my mind Christ appeared; the one from the frescoes and icons, with silky beard and a look of pity.... I found myself in some safe and glowing warmth. I tried to dispel that image, but in vain: it melted into a still sadder gentleness.... I began to speak to him: If you came into the world and suffered for goodness and truth, you must see that our cause is just and noble. We are, in fact, carrying on what you began. And you have not forgotten us, nor can you abandon us.... As I was saying this, I knew that I was not ceasing to be a Communist, and kept telling myself that this was in fact brought on by nervous tension and exhaustion.

For all we know, Djilas's vision may have been genuine. The murder he had committed that morning was reason enough for his sudden need of a gentle and forgiving Christ. Yet I find something deeply unconvincing about this unexpected upsurge of Christian sentiment in the breast of so hardened and cruel a partisan leader (this was not his first murder; nor was he unversed in ordering mass executions of prisoners and civilians). One suspects people who discover the 'safe and glowing warmth' of Christian love only *after* they have committed some unspeakable crime. If Djilas had found in himself the love of Christ a little earlier, he would probably not have murdered his unarmed prisoner. That, to my mind, would have been a more Christian thing to do than to indulge in self-justificatory reveries *after* the deed had been done.

I have recounted this episode only because I feel there may be a parallel between Djilas's 'kill first, pray later' type of attitude, and the Communist régimes' attitude to Christians and the Church in Eastern Europe over the past 30 years. Having persecuted the Church, dissolved the monastic orders, imprisoned, tortured and executed many bishops and priests, some East European Communist leaders are now anxious to make their peace with the Church to obtain that extra and most coveted element of legitimacy in the eyes of their own people which only Rome can confer. Why should Rome be so ready to confer and to forget?

Father Sorge Considerable progress has been made in the relations between the Church and the Communist régimes in Eastern Europe since the persecutions of the 1940s and 1950s. Please don't forget that the Church can only fulfil its essential pastoral duties if its organisational continuity is intact. If Church and State are in permanent conflict and the bishoprics cannot be filled, this also affects the Church's ability to administer the sacraments and thus to minister to the needs of the faithful. The same goes for the religious education of children and the recruitment and education of priests.

The Vatican's *Ost-Politik* has not been freely chosen. A painful but necessary decision had to be taken to safeguard the Church's evangelising mission. It is the personal policy of Paul VI, adopted in the interests of the good of the universal Church. Pope Paul VI embraced it fully conscious of the risk that many Catholics in Eastern Europe may not understand it. Certain hopes have already been disappointed, but some beneficial results are plainly forthcoming. The Church is sowing for the future. Above all, remember that the Church's prudence is not predominantly political but inspired by faith in the Word of God and His efficacy.

Of course, the peaceful coexistence of Church and régime in Eastern Europe does not, and cannot, mean any 'historical compromise' with Marxism as an anti-religious and atheistic ideology. It merely signifies a recognition that the pastoral care of souls is the Church's legitimate function with which the state does not interfere even though it did in the past. The Church, on its part, does not challenge the institutions of the secular order as long as that order is in accord with natural law. These delimitations are strictly functional and imply (to repeat) no concessions in matters of faith on our side, or in matters of ideology on the Communist side.

Urban   In other words, where fundamentals are concerned, no détente is possible—which is also the Communist position.

Father Sorge   That is so. Now, the long and patient work that has gone into the improvement of relations between Church and State in Eastern Europe is beginning to produce promising results. Some of these take us back to a problem you brought up at the beginning of this dialogue: the shared interest of Church and State in seeing that the moral fibre of society is protected and improved.

In Poland, for example, the Minister of Church Affairs (Kakol) has recently stated that there were no controversial problems between the Church and the régime, and in certain limited areas he envisaged close cooperation between them. These were: the moral education of the broad masses, the struggle against pornography and sexual licence, and the improvement of the morale and motivation of workers at their places of employment. The minister added that under certain circumstances coexistence between Church and State could become permanent. In Hungary, Church-State relations have made particularly good progress. At the time of Janos Kadar's recent visit to the Holy See, Pope Paul VI said that Kadar's call was uniquely important because it marked the road both sides had already succcessfully travelled. It was, he said, opening up a new phase 'in which an atmosphere of true religious peace would be created for the enhancement of the unity and loyal cooperation of all elements of social life'. Even in Czechoslovakia, where progress has been most restricted, President Husak's more accommodating attitude to Cardinal Tomasek, particularly since the recognition of his appointment as Archbishop of Prague in January 1978, may be a sign of relaxation.

When you consider that some of the most devout European Catholics live under Communist rule, and then cast your eyes back to the persecution they underwent 25 years ago, you must concede that these are no mean achievements. They involved great sacrifices which the Church would have much preferred not to have to make, such as the retirement of Cardinal Mindszenty as Archbishop of Esztergom and Primate of Hungary. But, on balance, the Church has done what it had to do so that Christ's work in Eastern Europe may continue.

Urban Isn't the Church a trifle too conscious of the importance of self-preservation? I know Christians in Eastern Europe who resent the emphasis the Church places on safeguarding its organisational structure to the detriment, as they see it, of its central function: the dissemination of the words of the Gospel and the salvation of souls. I know Poles and Hungarians whose respect for the Catholic clergy is only as old as the persecution of the Church in Poland and Hungary—who believe that Catholic priests should daily test their faith by *seeking* to be poor and harassed and falsely accused, and their only complaint is that the Church has probably not suffered *enough* to return it to its pristine inspiration.

From the Protestant side, too, evidence is reaching us that in the eyes of certain eminent pastors, especially in East Germany, Christians ought to welcome a determined ideological opponent as God's special blessing. Their argument is that in an increasingly permissive, hedonistic and chaotic world only the Communists take religion seriously enough to challenge and to persecute it. Whereas in bourgeois Western Europe Christianity is dying from indifference, in Eastern Europe (so it is argued) it thrives under oppression. 'It is our growing experience', writes the East Berlin pastor, Johannes Hamel, 'that God's work is like a hammer which smashes the greatest rocks. Who can but rejoice to be there when it works? A pastor in the West must long to come over to us, much as in the old days a young knight often longed for the day of his testing!'

Would you agree with any of this?

Father Sorge Personally, I have a good deal of sympathy with the views you have cited. At the same time one has to remember that the Church, enjoying as it does the trust and spiritual leadership of large numbers of Christians in Eastern Europe, is a secular as well as a religious factor in East European politics. It is, therefore, co-responsible, through the peace of the State and civil society, for the peace and spiritual welfare of all Christians. This is a heavy responsibility, for it does mean a fine interpretation of what exactly may be rendered unto the temporal authority without compromising the essence of Christian faith.

The fundamentalist attitudes you have quoted in criticising the Vatican's Eastern policies deserve respect. The Church is conscious of the possibility of being misunderstood—of being seen to be sacrificing too much for the orderly maintenance of its infrastructure. I do not think this is happening, but the charge has to be taken seriously. It is, alas, true that a man wrestling with his conscience in the privacy of the catacomb—real or symbolic—has a different range of spiritual and intellectual options from an established body representing 700 million Christians. The world has become immensely complex; its problems often defy not only resolution, but even definition, and whatever the Church does or refrains from doing has repercussions on a whole range of sometimes conflicting interests.

Remember also that in Poland, for example, the moderating guidance of the Church has had a restraining influence which Christians must welcome. Had it not been for this influence, the Polish people's resentment of the Communist régime might have erupted in civil war and quite possibly world war. You have mentioned the savageries committed in wartime Yugoslavia; let me remind you that the peace of the world is also a Christian objective—because once war has been let loose, conflicts of race, class and ideology will all be drawn into a single vortex. It is a combination we have reason to regard with the utmost horror.

Urban If the Vatican's policies were as successful in Eastern Europe as you have indicated, one need say no more. But there seems to be more than one opinion on this question within the Church itself. I notice that Cardinal König, Archbishop of Vienna, has recently (19 July 1977) expressed the view that, East European declarations to the contrary notwithstanding, the Communist régimes have in no way changed their attitude to religion. He quoted examples from the life of Christians in Czechoslovakia, Poland and Hungary to show that atheistic propaganda, the denial of the religious education of children, and a variety of other policies designed to stifle religious life continue. The Communist leaders' readiness to negotiate with the Vatican is an exercise in propaganda, König said. They are anxious to create the impression that between the Church and the Communist State there are no insurmountable difficulties. The reality, he added, is different. Asked what he thought of the Holy See's policies towards Eastern Europe, the Cardinal observed: it would be hard to imagine that the Vatican could envisage a solution permitting Christians and Communists to live together in a state of symbiosis.

As if this were not enough, within 24 hours of Cardinal König's statement, the Church's official policies received support from unexpected quarters. *L'Unità*, the Italian Communist Party's daily paper, expressed its disapproval of the Cardinal's views and offered its own interpretation of Vatican policy: 'At a time when Vatican diplomacy is busy improving and extending relations with the East European states, Cardinal König's polemical radio statement has created a certain surprise. The desire of the Vatican to conduct a dialogue with the Communists of countries in which Communists are in power must not be interpreted as meaning that the Holy See believes in the possibility of an alliance between Communism and Christianity.'

If we recall that, until very recently, Cardinal König was the Vatican's principal negotiator with Eastern Europe and an outspoken supporter of reconciliation with the Communist régimes, we are faced with the irony that the Church's own representative apparently no longer believes in Church policy, while the Italian Communist Party does.

Father Sorge Since the Vatican Council, discrepancies of this kind are not peculiar to the Church's East European policy. It is quite natural that Cardinal König should be disappointed at seeing how slowly attitudes change in Eastern Europe. But this should not be interpreted as meaning that there has been no change. The concessions have been piecemeal, uneven, utilitarian, grudgingly made and perhaps of uncertain duration—but progress there has been. Let me re-emphasise that we do not expect the Communist régimes to make doctrinal concessions to religion. We do not offer, nor would we accept, any 'historical compromise'. Any symbiosis between the Church and the régime can amount to no more than an agreement to disagree, and not allowing this disagreement to disturb the peace of the State or the integrity of the organisation of the Church.

Urban A non-aggression pact more than an alliance?

Father Sorge That is right. As to the Italian Communist Party's solicitude on behalf of Vatican policy: I find this encouraging, not because I believe that *L'Unità* really thinks that a philosophical bridge could ever be built between Christians and Marxists, but because it is a recognition of the abiding presence of

Christ and his Church in the hearts of millions of Italians whom the Italian Communists are anxious to win over or pacify. Similar considerations motivate the East European Communist leaders. It is not the kind of motivation one would ideally want, but it is an improvement on the past.

Urban At the beginning of this conversation we agreed, I think, that Christianity and Communism share a certain moral platform in that both are social stabilisers—upholders of the morality and social cohesion of the family and society. But one could also argue the contrary proposition, namely, that Christianity was as fierce a destabiliser in its early history as Marxism was in its. Marx and Engels were among the first to recognise this: 'The history of early Christianity', Engels wrote, 'has notable points of resemblance with the modern working-class movement. Like the latter, Christianity was originally a movement of oppressed people; it first appeared as the religion of slaves . . . of poor people deprived of all rights. . . . Both Christianity and the workers' socialism preach forthcoming salvation from bondage and misery. . . .' It is hard to fault Engels' thesis, for what could be more revolutionary or anarchic than the words of the Gospel: 'For I am come to set a man at variance against his father, and the daughter against her mother, and the daughter in law against the mother in law. And a man's foes shall be they of his own household' (Matthew 10, 35–36). (A cynic might argue that it was in a like spirit of blind devotion that Pavel Morozov, that celebrated child-hero of Stalinist Russia, denounced his father and caused him to be executed by the NKVD.) Wouldn't this cry for rebellion offer some basis ˜ for doctrinal reconciliation, even if the similarities between the two social programmes do not?

Father Sorge No, it would not. The analogy is purely formal. The whole content of the Christian revolution is the assertion of an uncompromisingly absolute moral standard in fulfilment of Christ's words: 'Love your enemies, bless them that curse you, do good to them that hate you, and pray for them which despitefully use you, and persecute you' (Matthew 5, 44). Marxism-Leninism glorifies and seeks to institutionalise the one truly backward-looking feature in human history: man's hatred for man and the concomitant relativisation of moral standards. 'We . . . reject every attempt to impose on us any moral dogma whatsoever as an eternal, ultimate, and forever immutable moral law . . .', Engels wrote in 1878. 'We maintain on the contrary, that all former moral theories are the product . . . of the economic stage which society reached at that particular epoch.' Here we come face to face with the root of all modern evil: if there are no absolute moral standards, everything is permissible—show trials are permissible, torture is permissible, genocide is permissible, the killing of hostages is permissible.

The demand Christianity makes on us with its breathtaking message, 'Love your enemies', is as shockingly new and revolutionary as the Marxist-Leninist message of hatred and moral relativity is old and deeply reactionary.

It is in this sense that we should read Pius XI's words in *Divini redemptoris*: 'There would be today neither Socialism nor Communism if the rulers of nations had not scorned the teachings and maternal warnings of the Church.'

Christians should take no pride in the contrast between their faith and the false messianic ideas of Marxism-Leninism. Rather should they seek to understand with all the humility they can muster why so much of the contemporary world's idealism has been given to Marxism-Leninism, and to turn that idealism to good account.

Notes on Contributors

Andrei Amalrik is one of the first and most outspoken Russian dissidents. He wrote *Will the USSR Survive until 1984?* and *Involuntary Journey to Siberia.*

Manuel Azcárate is a leading spokesman of the Spanish Communist Party. He is the International Secretary of the Party Central Committee and editor of the Party theoretical journal *Nuestra Bandera.*

Luigi Barzini is a former member of the Chamber of Deputies for the Italian Liberal Party and author of a number of books, including *The Italians* and *O, America!*

Jean Elleinstein is Deputy Director of the Marxist Research Centre of the French Communist Party and the author of *Histoire de l'URSS; Histoire du phénomène Stalinien* and *Le PC.* He is the leading spokesman of the Eurocommunist group in the French Party.

Renzo de Felice is Professor of History at the University of Rome and author of *Mussolini il revoluzionario; Mussolini il Duce;* and *Mussolini il fascista* (volumes I and II).

Fabio Mussi is Editor of the Cultural Department of the Italian Communist Party's weekly paper *Rinascita.*

Lucio Lombardo Radice is a leading member of the Central Committee of the Italian Communist Party, and Professor of Mathematics at the University of Rome. Among his many books is a life of Antonio Gramsci.

Rosario Romeo is Professor of Modern History and Director of the Institute of Modern History at the University of Rome. His recent publications include *Breve storia della grande industria in Italia; Momenti e problemi di storia contemporanea* and *Cavour e il suo tempo* (volumes I and II).

Domenico Settembrini is Professor of the History of the Labour Movement at the University of Pisa, and the author of *La Chiesa nella politica italiana; Due ipotesi per il socialismo in Marx ed Engels; Socialismo e rivoluzione dopo Marx* and *Il labirinto Marxista*.

Bartolomeo Sorge, S.J., is the Editor of the authoritative *La Civiltà Cattolica* and a close adviser of Pope Paul VI on Communist affairs. His publications include *Capitalismo—Scelta di classe— Socialismo* and *Evangelizzazione e promozione umana*.

Altiero Spinelli is a Member of the Italian Chamber of Deputies and a former Member of the Commission of the European Community (1970–77). He was in prison under the Fascist regime between 1927 and 1943.

G. R. Urban is a writer on contemporary history, a former Senior Research Associate of the University of Southern California and Research Fellow at Indiana University. He is editor and co-author of *Can We Survive our Future?*; *Toynbee on Toynbee*; *Détente*, and *Hazards of Learning*.

Index

'CP' stands for Communist Party.

Adenauer, Konrad, 194
Agnelli, Umberto, 180
Allende, Salvador, 45–6, 189–90
Althusser, Louis, 11
Amendola, Giorgio
    and European unification, 194–5
    on Fascism, 107, 125–8
    and Spinelli, 209–10
    mentioned, 33, 134, 188
Amendola, Giovanni, 63, 109
anarchists, 53–4
anarcho-syndicalism, 60, 103, 105
Annunzio, Gabriele d', 119
anti-Fascism, 116–17, 126–8, 130, 132–4
Antonioni, Michelangelo, 221
Aquarone, Alberto, 61, 104
Arendt, Hannah, 86
Aulard, Alphonse, 76
Azeglio, Massimo d', 214
Azevedo, Admiral, 232

Bad Godesberg programme, 199, 200
Balabanoff, Angelica, 152, 159, 162–3
Barca, Luciano, 174–5
Barzini, Luigi, 139, 141–2; see also Chapter 9
Benes, Eduard, 184

Bergson, Henri, 154
Berlinguer, Enrico
    on freedom, 64
    on Italy's crisis, 64, 66, 173–4
    and NATO, 51, 72, 197–8
    on the Soviet Union, 173
    mentioned, 34, 68, 200–1, 256, 268
Berlinguer, Giovanni, 145
Bernstein, Eduard, 158
Bettazzi, Monsignor, 260
Bierman, Wolf, 39
Boffa, Giuseppe, 144
Bombacci, Nicola, 100
Bordiga, Amadeo, 157–8
bourgeoisie/middle classes, and Fascism, 98, 119
Bulgakov, Sergei, 240

Cagliostro, as symbol of Italian character, 219–20, 223, 226
Campesino, El, 197–8
Cantimori, Delio, 161–2
Carrillo, Santiago, 193, 197, 208
Castro, Fidel, 264
Catholic Church
    and Communism, 219, 255–77; Italian CP, 182–3, 223, 234; Spanish CP, 30
    and Fascism, 103–4, 182–3
    and Italian nationalism, 214–15

Cavour, Count Camillo, 213
Céline, Louis-Ferdinand, 120
Chakovsky, Alexander, 40
Chamberlain, Austen, 119–20
Charter 77, 39,39–40, 67, 192
Chile, *see* Allende
China, 83, 244–5
Christian Democrats (in Italy), 64, 117, 130–1, 180, 184–5, 190
Christianity
  in Russia, 242–3
  see also Catholic Church
Christians for Socialism, 266–7
Churchill, Winston, 120
Ciano, Count Galeazzo, 102, 150, 162, 166
class war, Mazzini's view of, 212
coalitions, CPs and, 17; *see also under* Communist Party, Italian
Cocteau, Jean, 120
Comintern, 79
Communism (*see also* Eurocommunism; Leninism; Marxism; Stalinism)
  and Catholic Church, 255–77
  extremism of, inevitable, 9
  and Fascism, *see* Fascism, and Socialism/Communism
  models of/schism in, 82–3
  not monolithic, 73, 191, 192
  repression inevitable under, 227
Communist Manifesto, 8
Communist Party, French
  and dictatorship of proletariat, 8, 88, 89, 187–8
  and freedom, 81
  independent of Soviet Union, 18, 74, 81
  reform of, recent, 11, 88, 90–1
  Stalinist history of, 88
Communist Party, Italian, 216, 219
  and Catholic Church, 182–3, 223
  change/continuity in, 32–3, 50
  and coalition/Cooperation in government, 44–5, 65–6,

182–4, 190–1, 227, 228; *see also* 'historical compromise'
  and democracy, 56–7, 180, 185–6, 198–200
  and dictatorship of proletariat, 8, 50, 144, 187–8
  distrusted, 181
  and East-West confrontation, NATO, 11, 35–6, 41–2, 45, 51, 71–2, 196–7, 198, 202–6, 223, 231
  and Eastern Europe, 46–7, 68, 206–8
  and European unification, 179–80, 180, 193, 194–6, 210
  and Fascism, 34; *see also* Fascism, and Socialism/Communism
  and freedom, liberty, 36–7, 47–8, 68, 141–5, 226
  intellectuals etc., and, 220–1
  Marxism repudiated by, 188, 262
  as Social Democrats, 186, 200–1
  and Soviet Union, 71, 169–72, 181, 186, 187, 191–2, 201–2
Communist Party, Spanish
  and coalitions, 17
  and Marxism, 28, 30–1, 170–1
  and NATO, 11
  and religion, 30
  Stalinism rejected by, 29, 31, 197–8
  mentioned, 7, 208
conferences, Communist, 51–3, 73–4
corporative economy, 103
Corridoni, Filippo, 101
Croce, Benedetto, 62, 62–3, 107, 108–9, 127, 134–5, 234
culture, forces of, 20
Custine, Marquis de, 236–7, 238–9, 252
Czechoslovakia, 18, 46, 48, 49–50, 67, 91, 184

Index

283

Danilevsky, Nicolai, 241
Dante Alighieri, 213, 229, 235
Daudet, Léon, 120
democracy
  capitalism and, 24
  Eurocommunism and, 11, 14,
    19, 24; French CP, 76, 77,
    92; Italian CP, 56–7, 180,
    185–6, 198–200
détente, peaceful coexistence,
    East-West equilibrium
  Eurocommunism and, 28,
    95–6; French CP, 94;
    Italian CP, 71–2, 180
  see also East-West confronta-
    tion
Deutscher, Isaac, 80
dictatorship of the proletariat, 8,
  50, 88, 89, 144, 187–8
Dimitrov, Georgi, 33–4
Djilas, Milovan, 8, 246, 254,
  270–1
Dostoevsky, 241, 250–1, 252–3

East Berlin conference, 39, 51–2,
  73, 74
East-West confrontation
  Eurocommunist attitude to,
    11; French CP, 11, 93–6;
    Italian CP, 11, 35–6, 41–2,
    196–7, 198, 202–6, 223, 231
  war unlikely, 244
  see also détente; NATO
Eastern Europe
  Catholic Church in, 271–5
  Eurocommunist influence in,
    82, 175–8; French CP,
    83–4; Italian CP, 206–8
  Italian CP critique of, 46–7, 68,
    207
Elleinstein, Jean, 8; *see also* Chap-
    ter 4
emigrés, Russian, 248–50; *see also*
  Solzhenitsyn
Engels, Friedrich, 22, 148, 276
Eurocommunism (*see also* Com-
  munist Party, French; Italian;

Spanish; *also* Communism),
  7–31
  as Communist movement, 8
  as deception/manoeuvre, 12,
    14–15, 19, 71
  and democracy, 11, 14, 19, 24
  distrust of, 83, 85
  and European unification,
    25–6
  and freedom of opinion, 135
  independent of Soviet Union,
    11, 17–18, 22–3
  influence of, in Eastern
    Europe, 82, 175–8
  and NATO (*q.v.*), 11
  origins of, 15–18
  pluralism of, 19–20,
  and Social Democracy, 8–10,
    20, 177–8
  Soviet hostility to, 7, 10, 15,
    71, 224
  and Third World, 26–7
Europe, unification of, 25–6, 27,
  68–9, 179–80, 193, 194–6, 210

Farinacci, Roberto, 109 n.
Fascism (*see also* Mussolini; *also*
  National Socialists)
  and anti-British feeling, 101–2
  authoritarian character of, 102
  and the Church, 103–4, 182–3
  de Felice's definition of, 97
  freedom/repression under,
    107–8, 164–5
  and French revolution, 118
  as historical accident, 62
  history, in step with, 119
  imprisonment under, 208–9
  intellectuals etc. and, 119–21
  liberal support for, 34
  mass/working-class support
    for, 59, 118–19, 122–3, 125
  middle-class support for, 98,
    119
  as movement and as govern-
    ment, 102
  and nationalism, 54–5, 111–13
  Nazism different from, 98

origins of, 154–5
and ruling class, 104, 107
and Socialism/Communism, 60–3, 65, 99–100, 102–3, 104, 110–112, 146–70 *passim*, 182, 218
Soviet views of, 58
and technology, 105
totalitarianism of, 106–7, 158–9
Felice, Renzo de, 58, 60–2, 116–36 *passim*, 145, 167; *see also* Chapter 5
Ferrara, Giovanni, 134–5, 136
Finzi, Aldo, 159
first world war, 151–4, 232
Fischer, Ernst, 34–5
forced labour, in Soviet Union, 80
Franic, Archbishop, 256
freedom, liberty
disorder and, 228–9
Eurocommunism and, 135; French CP, 81; Italian CP, 36–7, 47–8, 68, 141–5, 226
Italian concept of, 216–7
personal, importance of, 225–6
Russian concept of, 237
French Revolution, Fascism and, 118
Freud, Sigmund, 121
Friedman, Milton, 139
Futurists, 60, 105, 106

Garibaldi, 213
Gasperi, Alcide de, 194
Genet, Jean, 247–8
Gentile, Giovanni, 119, 164
Gerö, Ernö, 184
Gide, André, 121
Giolitti, Giovanni, 191
Giraudoux, Jean, 120
Gorbatov, General, 87
Gorky, Maxim, 163–4, 245
Gottwald, Klement, 184
Gramsci, Antonio
on the Communist Party, 57
and democracy, 175
and first world war, 153–4

a great thinker, 218–19
and Lenin, Leninism, 50, 51, 70, 154, 263–4
and Mussolini, 61, 153–4, 156–7, 165, 170
mentioned, 16, 30, 59, 68–9, 129, 268
see also hegemony of the working classes; 'historical bloc'
Grandi, Dino, 126
Gregor, A. James, 164, 167–8
Guicciardini, as symbol of Italian character, 219, 220, 226
Guitry, Sacha, 120

Hamel, Johannes, 273
Hegel, 50, 129, 149
hegemony of the working class, 11, 50, 55–6
Herberstein, Baron von, 236, 238
Herzen, Alexander, 237, 243, 246
'historical bloc', 56
'historical compromise', 44–5, 179, 180, 188, 189, 199–200
Hitler, Adolf, 182; *see also* National Socialists
Howard, Roy, 174
human nature, proposals to change, 92–3, 159
Hungary, 48, 49, 133

Ibarruri, Dolores, 198
idealism, nineteenth-century, 149–50
Ingrao, Pietro, 144–5
Ionesco, Eugene, 221
Italian Social Movement (MSI), 97–8
Italy
freedom, Italian concept of, 216–17
industrialisation of, 215
language, Italian, 213–14
malaise of, 43–4, 114–15, 137–43; Berlinguer on, 64, 66, 173–4

national identity of, 211–15
nationalism in, 54–5, 111–13
people, Italian, 219–20

Jacoviello, Alberto, 207
Jaurès, Jean, 94, 152
Jews, Mussolini and, 159
John XXIII, Pope, 260, 261, 269
Jung, Guido, 159

Kennan, George, 168, 172, 206, 224, 239
Khrushchev, Nikita, 8, 17, 39, 253
Kissinger, Henry, 42, 203, 205, 206, 223, 232
Koestler, Arthur, 131
König, Cardinal, 274

labour theory of value, 265–6
Laiolo, David, 167
Lenin
  and barbaric methods, 12, 76
  and Constituent Assembly, 156
  and first world war, 151, 152–3,
  and idealism, 150
  and leadership for proletariat, 147, 147–8, 150–1
  liberty and democracy rejected by, 78
  on Mussolini, 61
  Mussolini compared with, 146–67 *passim*
  as revisionist of Marxism, 50, 147–8, 154, 158, 251–2
  on Russia's future 'backwardness', 10, 82
  and Social Democrats, 146
  totalitarianism of, 159
  mentioned, 93, 161, 190
Leninism (*see also* Marxism-Leninism)
  Eurocommunist departures from, 51, 64, 69–70, 75–6

Eurocommunist regard for, 30, 47, 64
mentioned, 43, 251–2
liberty, *see* freedom
Livorsi, Amadeo, 158
Lombardo Radice, Lucio, 68, 171–2, 172, 262; *see also* Chapter 2
Ludwig, Emil, 124, 150
Luxemburg, Rosa, 30, 152

Mafia, the, 217
Malaparte, Curzio, 105, 106, 119
Mann, Thomas, 247
Mao Tse-tung, 30
Maoists, 53–4
Marchais, Georges, 9, 73, 92
Marinetti, Filippo Tommaso, 60, 105, 106
Marshall Plan, 184
Marx, Karl, 8, 32, 148
Marxism (*see also* Communism), 256–9, 263–9
  Eurocommunists and, 8, 30, 188, 262–4
Marxism-Leninism (*see also* Leninism), 28–9
Maurras, Charles, 120
Mazzini, Giuseppe, 192, 211–12, 234
Medvedev, Roy, 36–7, 41
middle classes/bourgeoisie, and Fascism, 98, 119
Mindszenty, Cardinal, 49, 273
Mlynar, Zdenek, 37, 39
Mussolini (*see also* Fascism)
  and capitalism, 159–60
  and Catholic Church, 104, 182–3
  and first world war, 151–4, 232
  and Gramsci, 61, 153–4, 156–7, 165, 170
  and idealism, 149–50
  Italian people despised by, 124
  and Marxism, 148
  and nationalism, 54–5, 111–13
  and origins of Fascism, 154–5
  personality of, 99, 124, 166

proletariat despised by, 149–50
and race, Jews, 159
and second world war, 98–9
and Socialism/Communism, 61, 65, 99–100, 104, 104–5, 110, 146–70 *passim*
mentioned, 109–10
Mussolini-Ciano, Edda, 137, 162–3

Napolitano, Giorgio, 174–5, 227
National Socialists, Nazism, 103, 182
and capitalism, 85–6
Fascism different from, 98
Socialism different from, 86–7
nationalism, in Italy
Fascism and, 54–5, 111–13
Italian CP and, 55
NATO, Eurocommunists and, 11; French CP, 94; Italian CP, 35–6, 42, 45, 51, 71–2, 196–7, 198, 202–6, 223; Spanish CP, 11; *see also* East-West confrontation
Nenni, Pietro, 194
Nolte, Ernst, 147

Old Believers, 38
Owen, Dr David, 9–10, 14

Pajetta, Giancarlo, 171
Palme, Olaf, 224
Pan-Turkic movement, 240–1
Papini, Giovanni, 101, 119
Pareto, Vilfredo, 124
Paris, May 1968 riots in, 18
Pascal, Blaise, 93
Paul VI, Pope, 262, 269, 272
peaceful coexistence, *see* détente
Peron, Juan Domingo, 97
Petrarch, 40
Pinochet, Augusto, 111
Pirandello, Luigi, 119
Pius IX, Pope, 259

Pius XI, Pope, 259, 269, 277
Pius XII, Pope, 260
Plekhanov, G. B., 152
polycentrism, 68–9, 191
Popular Fronts, 16–17, 33–4
private enterprise, Eurocommunism and, 21
proletarian internationalism/solidarity, 74–5
proletariat, *see* working class

race, Mussolini and, 159
Red Week, 101
Risorgimento, 193, 211
Robespierre, 149
Romains, Jules, 120

Salò, Republic of, 99–100, 164, 166–7, 167–9
Sarfatti, Margherita, 124, 159
Sartre, Jean-Paul, 120–1
Schapiro, Leonard, 148
Schubart, Walter, 242
Schumann, Robert, 194
scientific-technical revolution, 18, 20, 24, 105
Sedov, Yuri, 75
Selye, Hans, 137
Sforza, Carlo, 108
Simonet, Henri, 205
Smith, Denis Mack, 129
Smith, Hedrick, 78
Social Democracy
Eurocommunism and, 8–10, 20, 177–8, 200–1
Socialism distinguished from, 90
Soffici, Ardengo, 99–100, 100
Solzhenitsyn, Alexander, 36, 38, 39, 49, 248–9
Sorel, Georges, 154
Soviet Union
communists' need to support, 34–5, 41, 79
dissidence/progressive forces in, 36–8, 40–1, 67, 236, 238
and Eurocommunism, *see*

under Eurocommunism *and under* Communist Party, French; Italian
as Holy Russia, 38
messianic trait in Russian character, 239–44
and the West, *see* East-West confrontation
Spinelli, Altiero, 165; *see also* Chapter 8
Spirito, Ugo, 103, 111–12, 164, 166
Stalin
  admired as strong leader, 78
  and Popular Fronts, 33–4
  on world revolution, 174
  mentioned, 79, 253
Stalinism
  Eurocommunist rejection of, 8, 29, 78–80
  intellectual roots of, in Marx, 8, 252
  Marxism-Leninism-Stalinism, 28–9
  Nazism contrasted with, 86–7
  Socialism distinguished from, 80–1, 85–6
  and State power, 23
  mentioned, 16, 93
suffering, hardship, value of, 245–7
systematisation, Italian flair for, 229–30

Terracini, Umberto, 182, 210
terrorism
  in Italy, 138
  in West Germany, 247–8
Third World, 26–7
Thorez, Maurice, 90, 187
Togliatti, Palmiro
  and democracy, 182
  on Fascism, 59, 98, 103, 104, 123, 160, 161, 167

on Gramsci, 165
and Leninism, 51
on Marxism, 188
on Mussolini, 61
and Popular Front, 33–4
and Stalin, Stalinism, 90, 181, 184
mentioned, 69, 171, 191
Tomasek, Cardinal, 273
Toscanini, Arturo, 119
Toynbee, Arnold, 60, 145
Trotsky, Leon, 61, 77, 169–70

United States
  and Europe, 13, 45, 203–4, 232–3
  and Italian CP, 42–6, 232–3
  see also NATO
universities, Italian, threats to, 138–9

Valiani, Leo, 121–2, 133
Volpe, Gioacchino, 129
Voltaire, 79

Warsaw Pact, 203
Weber, Max, 215
Witte, Count S.Iu., 238
women's liberation, 21–2
working class, proletariat
  dictatorship of, 8, 50, 88, 89, 144, 187–8
  and Fascism, 59, 118–19, 122–3, 125
  and foreigners, 195–6
  hegemony of, 11, 50, 55–6

Yugoslavia, 184, 197, 224

Zangrandi, Ruggero, 162